'The Effective Provision of Pre-school, Primary
research programme was probably the most c
pre-school, primary, and secondary schooling
UK, and the reports from the project over the
produced unrivalled insights into the long-term effects of effective
primary schools, and what it is that these schools do differently. Now,
for the first time, the key findings from this massive research programme
are available in one accessible book. Perhaps the most remarkable
feature of the EPPSE programme is the way that multiple sources of
data – including sophisticated statistical techniques, data obtained from
validated classroom observation procedures, and rich field notes from
trained observers – are integrated to produce findings about the factors
most closely associated with effective teaching in primary schools that are
at the same time both rigorous and rich in detail. Anyone interested in
improving primary education – whether in a single classroom, a school,
or across an entire system – would benefit greatly from reading it.'

**Dylan Wiliam, Emeritus Professor of Educational Assessment,
UCL Institute of Education**

'Steers an accessible path through high-quality research and
articulates clearly the classroom practice and behaviours that
have the greatest impact. The depth, breadth and quality of the
research is impressive. A fascinating analysis of classroom practice
and behaviour that will inform and inspire those who genuinely
want to make a difference and secure the best possible educational
outcomes for all children. Teachers, School Leaders, Providers
of Initial Teacher Training and ongoing CPD ... take note!'

Judy Shaw, Headteacher and NAHT National President 2019-2020

Teaching in Effective Primary Schools

*This book is dedicated to the EPPSE children and their families who,
through their generosity, were part of our lives for so long.
We wish them well for the future.*

Teaching in Effective Primary Schools
Research into pedagogy and children's learning

Iram Siraj, Brenda Taggart, Pam Sammons, Edward Melhuish, Kathy Sylva and Donna-Lynn Shepherd

is an imprint of

First published in 2019 by the UCL Institute of Education Press, 20 Bedford Way, London WC1H 0AL

www.ucl-ioe-press.com

British Library Cataloguing in Publication Data:
A catalogue record for this publication is available from the British Library

ISBNs
978-1-85856-506-4 (paperback)
978-1-85856-906-2 (PDF eBook)
978-1-85856-907-9 (ePub eBook)
978-1-85856-908-6 (Kindle eBook)

Typeset by Quadrant Infotech (India) Pvt Ltd
Printed by CPI Group (UK) Ltd, Croydon, CR0 4YY

Cover image © s_maria/Shutterstock.com

Contents

Acknowledgements

The authors would like to thank all of the children, families, and pre-school, primary and secondary-school staff who have supported the Effective Pre-school, Primary and Secondary Education (EPPSE) project since its inception in 1996. In addition, this book would not have been possible without the help and support of our team of field and analytical researchers and support staff who have been an essential part of the project, particularly Dr Sofka Barreau, who conducted the quantitative analyses of the observational data, and Wesley Welcomme. We are also grateful to our colleagues in the Department for Education and those who sat on our steering and consultative groups.

Foreword

Start from what we know. This shouldn't be a radical or challenging idea but, in the world of education policy, all too often it is. The history of education is littered with ideology, headline-grabbing here today, gone tomorrow policies and the hyped ideas of education gurus. Cutting through the fads and fashions, this book, by some of the UK's most eminent education academics, gives us firm foundations for effective primary education.

Evidence, moreover evidence over time – that rare beast, a longitudinal study – provides the raw material that anchors the work. Notably, the UK's 17-year Effective Provision of Pre-school, Primary and Secondary Education research study (EPPSE, 1997–2014) is the core source for findings. Picking up the baton from education effectiveness research, which was world leading throughout the 1980s and the early part of the 2000s, the EPPSE team were allocated long-term government funding to study a cohort of 3,000 children longitudinally, and these children attended more than 850 primary schools.

Their initial work focused on the challenge of tackling economic inequality and the importance of early learning in, and out of, formal education. Conscious of the prevailing research landscape and tradition, the design wisely followed the lead set by the seminal Oracle investigation (Galton *et al.*, 1980) and School Matters study (Mortimore *et al.*, 1988). The researchers recognized the importance of the classroom as a unit of analysis with a focus on children's outcomes rather than on only observing teachers' practice. The fact that this type of research design is a given in 2019 speaks to the growing influence of the EPPSE study and the need for such educational research. At the time it was a brave and unusual design. Through its mixed-method approach the study focused as much on the big how questions as on the what and why questions, which is reflected in this book.

The focus on impact alongside the identification of effective practice ensured that the early results informed policy and influenced the development of the Sure Start programme. Employing quantitative methods to measure impact, alongside sophisticated tools to support the careful examination of teachers' beliefs and behaviours, the EPPSE team spoke across the aisle, engaging both politicians and educators. The success of the initial work led to continued support and the opportunity to follow in depth a subsample of the EPPSE children as they moved from the early years through to Year 5 in 125 different, focus primary schools.

Deploying a range of observation tools, assessment approaches and questionnaires, the team has examined and categorized the practice of Year 5 teachers, looking for relationships between excellent, good and poor classroom pedagogy and pupil outcomes. The purpose of this is to highlight the practices that differentiate more and less effective schools.

This study has revealed significant variation in teacher practice and effectiveness. Variation within and between schools is at the heart of the school-improvement challenge. The reference points demonstrating what can be achieved are found in classrooms and schools of every type serving the full range of communities across the UK. As with the classrooms and schools in the EPPSE study, we struggle to provide reliable and consistent provision.

Highlighting the features of teaching in effective schools provides a useful guide and should reassure teachers that what they do matters. This work reminds us that what seems to separate effective schools from less successful ones aren't huge matters that require legislative change or structural overhaul. Instead they are matters that can be shaped by and determined inside individual classrooms and largely by individual teachers' day-to-day practices.

These findings are consistent with many meta-studies and the overall findings are captured in synthesis and reviews, including the work of John Hattie (2008) and the Education Endowment Foundation's *Teaching and Learning Toolkit* (EEF and Sutton Trust, 2011), which guides and informs much of my work. For me, the absence of novelty or radical new approaches is reassuring and comforting. We need to be constantly reminded that the organization, culture and routines of classrooms matter. Sharing learning objectives and taking the time to review and assess so that children can reflect on, consolidate and deepen their learning appear to support better progress. Employing dialogic teaching to promote effective feedback is highlighted as particularly important in maths. EPPSE confirms with authority and examples from practice what matters. The challenge is to bring what we know to life.

The correlational findings examined in this book should act as a wake-up call for those looking for short cuts or backing narrow managerial solutions to improve outcomes. EPPSE represents a step forward for education effectiveness research (EER). It demands that we go to the next level, move from correlation studies and use the hypotheses to test the value and impact of deliberate and planned interventions. When we shift from observing what appears to be different in classrooms that are effective to knowing more about what works when a teacher is supported to adopt these behaviours, we can use the EPPSE study findings to support all teachers to improve, and hence all children to receive the education they deserve.

Sir Kevan Collins, Chief Executive Education Endowment Foundation

Glossary of terms

Child background factors Characteristics such as age, gender and ethnicity.

Classroom Observation System for 5th Grade (COS-5) A systematic classroom observational rating scale measuring, using numerical values, the quality of pedagogy in our Year 5 classrooms (NICHD, 2001; Pianta *et al.*, 2008b).

Controlling for Several variables may influence an outcome, and these may themselves be associated. Multilevel statistical analyses can calculate the influence of one variable on an outcome, simultaneously controlling for the effects of other variables. When this is done the 'net effect' of a variable on an outcome controlling for the influence of other variables can be established.

Correlation A measure of the strength of any statistical association that ranges from 1 to −1.

Early Childhood Environment Rating Scale (ECER) The US ECERS (ECERS-R: Revised) (Harms *et al.*, 1998) is based on child-centred pedagogy and also assesses resources for indoor and outdoor play. The English scale (ECERS-E: Extension) (Sylva *et al.*, 2003) was intended as a supplement to the ECERS-R and was developed specially for the EPPE study to reflect the Desirable Learning Outcomes (since replaced by the Early Learning Goals), and more importantly the Curriculum Guidance for the Foundation Stage, which at the time was at the trial stage. ECERS scores were used to provide indicators of the **quality of pre-schools** in the main EPPE study.

Educational effectiveness Research design that seeks to explore the effectiveness of educational institutions in promoting a range of child/ student outcomes (often academic measures) while controlling for the influence of intake differences in child/student characteristics.

Effect size (ES) This is a statistical measure of the strength of the relationship between different predictors and the children's outcomes under study. An ES of 0.1 would be a weak effect, 0.3 a medium effect and 0.5+ a strong effect. It is generally recognized that, in educational research, ESs are typically small to moderate. This does not mean that they are unimportant. It is also recognized that the magnitude of ES depends on the context and the models used (see Schagen and Elliot 2004; Bloom *et al.*, 2008).

Family factors Examples include mother's qualifications, father's employment, family socio-economic status (SES) and eligibility for free school meals (FSMs).

General Certificate of Secondary Education (GCSE) is a set of exams taken in England, Wales, Northern Ireland and other UK territories. They are usually taken by most students aged 15–16 after two years of study. Most students taking their GCSEs study between 5 and 10 subjects. The percentage of those obtaining five GCSEs at grades A*–C, including English and maths, was recognized as a measure of good achievement by the Department for Education and Employment (DfEE), the Department for Children, Schools and Families (DCSF) and the Department for Education (DfE). At the time this research was carried out, this was the final public exam taken by students at age 16 at the end of compulsory schooling, which in part determined their post-16 destination (higher academic, vocational, employment route). Since then there has been legislation to increase the age at which young people must remain in education.

Home-learning environment (HLE) in the early years Measures derived from reports from parents (at interview) about activities children engaged in at home in the early years, such as playing with numbers and letters, singing songs and nursery rhymes (for further details, see Sylva et al., 2010).

Instructional Environment Observation (IEO) A systematic rating scale ascribing numerical values at the classroom level to measure the quality of different features of pupil learning experience and teacher pedagogical practice (Stipek, 1999).

Key stages These are distinct phases of education as follows: reception and foundation (up to age 5), Key Stage 1 (5–7), Key Stage 2 (7–11), Key Stage 3 (11–14), Key Stage 4 (14–16).

Multilevel modelling A statistical technique that allows data to be examined simultaneously at different levels within a system (for example, young children, pre-school centres, local authorities [LAs]). It is essentially a generalization of multiple regression. It was used in this research to develop models that predict children's attainment and social behavioural development, and to control for the effects of relevant background influences.

Multiple regression A method of predicting outcome scores on the basis of the statistical relationship between observed outcome scores and one or more predictor variables. In the EPPE study, children's attainment and social behaviour scores were treated as outcomes.

Net effect The unique contribution of a particular variable (predictor) to an outcome measure (dependent variable) while the influence of other variables (predictors) in a statistical model are controlled.

Office for Standards in Education (Ofsted) The national inspection agency for maintained schools in England, established in 1993. Schools are inspected on a regular basis and reports are published. A range of measures of primary-school quality were obtained from schools' inspection reports to provide independent external (from the EPPE study) measures of the quality of schools attended by the EPPSE children in this study.

Prior attainment Measures that describe pupils' achievement at the beginning of the phase or period under investigation (that is, taken on entry to primary or secondary school or on entry to the EPPE study). In the study of children's progress featured in this book, children's attainment in National Foundation for Educational Research (NFER) tests of reading and maths in Year 1 was treated as prior attainment measures to control in predicting the children's attainment in Year 5.

Quality of pre-schools Measures of pre-school centre quality collected through observational assessments (Early Childhood Environment Rating Scale-Revised [ECERS-R], Early Childhood Environment Rating Scale-Extension [ECERS-E] and Caregiver Interaction Scale) made by trained researchers.

Socio-behavioural development A child's ability to socialize with adults and other children and their general behaviour with others. Details of measures used in the pre-school and primary period are shown by Sylva *et al.* (2010).

Socio-economic status (SES) Occupational information about the mother's and father's employment was collected by means of a parental interview when children were recruited to the study. The Office of Population Census and Surveys (OPCS, 1995) Classification of Occupations was used to classify the mother's and father's current employment into one of eight groups: professional I, other professional non-manual II, skilled non-manual III, skilled manual III, semi-skilled manual IV, unskilled manual V, never worked and no response. Family SES was obtained by assigning the SES classification based on the parent with the highest occupational status.

Standard deviation (SD) A measure of the spread around the mean in a distribution of numerical scores. In a normal distribution, 68 per cent of cases fall within 1 SD of the mean and 95 per cent of cases fall within 2 SD.

Teaching assistant An adult who does not have qualified teacher status who works alongside a teacher. They may have specific responsibilities to support children who have special educational needs (SEN) or they may help out generally with classroom activities, as directed by the teacher.

Value-added models Longitudinal multilevel models exploring children's cognitive progress over time, controlling for prior attainment and in contextualized value-added models also controlling for significant child, parent and home-learning environment (HLE) characteristics. In this study of primary-school teaching, progress was studied from Year 1 to Year 5. See also **multilevel modelling**.

Value-added residuals Differences between predicted and actual results for primary schools (where predicted results are calculated using contextual value-added multilevel models), providing indicators of the academic effectiveness of primary schools (Melhuish *et al.*, 2006).

List of figures

List of tables

List of boxes

List of abbreviations

BERA	British Educational Research Association
CLASS	Classroom Assessment Scoring System
COS-5	Classroom Observation System for 5th Grade
CPD	continuous professional development
CPR	Cambridge Primary Review of the Curriculum
CVA	contextualized value added
DCSF	Department for Children, Schools and Families
DfEE	Department for Education and Employment
DfES	Department for Education and Skills
EAL	English as an additional language
ECERS	Early Childhood Environment Rating Scale
ECERS-E	Early Childhood Environment Rating Scale-Extension
ECERS-R	Early Childhood Environment Rating Scale-Revised
ECP	Effective Classroom Practice
EEF	Education Endowment Foundation
EER	educational effectiveness research
EIU	Economist Intelligence Unit
EPPE	Effective Provision of Pre-School Education
EPPSE	Effective Pre-School, Primary and Secondary Education
EPPSEM	Effective Primary Pedagogical Strategies in English and Mathematics
ES	effect size
FSM	free school meals
GCSE	General Certificate of Secondary Education
HLE (early)	home-learning environment
IEA	International Association for the Evaluation of Educational Achievement
IEO	Instructional Environment Observation
LA	local authority
n/a	not applicable
NFER	National Foundation for Educational Research
NICHD	National Institute of Child Health and Human Development
NPD	National Pupil Database
ns	not significant

List of abbreviations

OECD	Organisation for Economic Co-operation and Development
Ofsted	Office for Standards in Education
PIRLS	Progress in International Reading Literacy Study
PISA	Programme for International Student Assessment
PLASC	Pupil Level Annual Schools Census
QCA	Qualifications and Curriculum Authority
RS	residual score
SD	standard deviation
SEN	special educational needs
SER	school-effectiveness research
SES	socio-economic status
SESI	School Effectiveness and School Improvement
TC	target child
TIMSS	Trends in International Mathematics and Science Study

About the authors

Iram Siraj is Professor of Child Development and Education in the Department of Education at the University of Oxford and has worked as a primary school and advisory teacher. For the last 30 years she has been a researcher and academic working on the impact of disadvantage on children's lives and how we can help them 'to succeed against the odds' in education. Among her many published works are award-winning books, including *Social Class and Educational Inequality: The impact of parents and schools* (2015) with Aziza Mayo and *Effective and Caring Leadership in the Early Years* (2014) with Elaine Hallet.

Edward Melhuish is Professor of Human Development in the Department of Education at the University of Oxford. He contributed to policy in the UK for families, early-years services and education. His research influenced the 1989 Children Act, the 2005 Children Act, the 2006 Childcare Bill and policy on childcare, early education, child poverty and parental support in the UK and abroad (for example, Australia, Sri Lanka and Canada). He advises children's organizations (for example, UNESCO), government departments (for example, the Department for Education, the Treasury), media companies, House of Commons select committees, international research organizations and governments, the European Commission, the Organisation for Economic Co-operation and Development and the World Health Organization. He chairs the Foundation Years Trust and advises charities.

Pamela Sammons BSocSci PhD HEA FRSA is Professor of Education in the Department of Education at the University of Oxford, and emeritus fellow at Jesus College, Oxford. Previously she was a professor at the University of Nottingham and the Institute of Education – University of London, directing its International School of Effectiveness & Improvement Centre. Her research focuses on school effectiveness and improvement, leadership, teaching, and equity in education. She was a principal investigator for the EPPSE 3–16+ study. She has provided research advice to inspection and government agencies in various countries and for many committees and inquiries. She has been a primary and a secondary school governor.

Donna-Lynn Shepherd divides her time between the classroom and academia. She is Head of Maths and Progress Lead at Arc School Ansley, lectures at Coventry University and spends her holidays teaching in nursery schools. Her research interests include maths education, autism and effective teaching in challenging environments. She has been a researcher in the Institute of Education at University College London and at Coventry University, and she has worked in primary and secondary schools in England, Canada, Zambia and Zimbabwe.

Kathy Sylva is Professor of Educational Psychology in the Department of Education at the University of Oxford. She has conducted large-scale studies on the effects of early education/care on children's development. She has been a lead researcher on the Effective Pre-school, Primary and Secondary Education study and the national Evaluation of Children's Centres. She led three randomized controlled trials to evaluate parenting interventions. She was specialist adviser to parliamentary select committees and currently advises the Office for Standards in Education, the Early Intervention Foundation and the Education Endowment Foundation. She has published seven books and 230 papers on early childhood, literacy, and supporting families. She received an OBE and the British Educational Research Association's Nisbet Award for outstanding contribution to research, both in 2014.

Brenda Taggart has been a teacher, trainer, lecturer and researcher, and she was one of the principal investigators and the research coordinator of the Effective Pre-school, Primary and Secondary Education project (EPPSE, 1997–2014), a longitudinal study funded by the UK Government. She has developed, published and administered research instruments, as well as worked on both quantitative and qualitative data to code, analyse and interpret findings. She has advised governments on early years policies, and worked with practitioners on issues of quality and pedagogy. She is known for making complex research findings accessible to a range of audiences.

Introduction: The flame of inspiration

Around the turn of the millennium, the UK Government launched one of its regular campaigns to recruit additional teachers for its state-controlled primary schools. One image dominated this particular campaign: the compelling picture of a young boy.

A photographer had captured a look in the boy's eyes that suggested that 'a penny had just dropped' in his mind. The government used this representation of 'a flash of inspiration' to try to attract new entrants into the teaching profession, with the promise of an exciting and rewarding career spent inspiring young people like the boy in the photograph. It was a striking image that expressed the reason for many in becoming a teacher.

Over time, however, most teachers learn that keeping the flame of inspiration alight is harder than igniting it in the first place (Sammons *et al.*, 2014a,b, 2016; Bryson and Hand 2007; McGuey and Moore 2007). The ability to remain inspiring sets effective teachers apart from the rest of their profession. Effective teachers keep on inspiring and enabling their pupils to turn their penny-dropping moments into a strong and lasting foundation, which supports lifelong learning.

In recent years, there has been a helpful move away from examining what education systems do to enquiring how they do it. It is this shift that has prompted many to try to identify the precise educational processes that create better child outcomes, and to understand exactly how effective teachers promote sustained and successful learning (Siraj and Taggart, 2014).

The big questions

For many years, governments, universities, local authorities (LAs), school governors, academies, teachers and so on have all been asking the same questions. How can we facilitate, establish and sustain effective teaching in our schools? How can we create the ideal framework, the best set of circumstances, for effective teachers, leading to sustained inspiration, to better child outcomes, to a love of long-lasting learning, to deep understanding and to high achievement? Put simply, how can we keep the flame of inspiration burning at all times?

This book seeks to contribute to, and inform, the ongoing search for answers to these important questions. It does this by introducing some key research into pedagogy, children's learning and the promotion of effective teaching in primary schools. The findings are summarized especially with school practitioners in mind.

In particular, the book presents some of the processes and results from the UK's 17-year Effective Provision of Pre-school, Primary and Secondary Education research project (EPPSE, 1997–2014). This was a large-scale, longitudinal, mixed-method study following the progress of more than 3,000 children from their early years to past their 16th birthdays, and it provides important insights into the nature of teaching in effective schools.

The final reports of the EPPSE research were published in the autumn of 2014 with a summary report published by Taggart *et al.* (2015). A further study, funded by the Sutton Trust, reported on students' outcomes at ages 17 and 18 (Sammons et al., 2015a,b,c, 2018). Appendix 1 contains further information about the EPPSE reports. The whole programme of EPPSE research and its many findings will doubtless influence scholars and governments around the world for many years to come. The leaders of the project, all of whom have held senior education posts in UK universities, have provided this summary of their findings about teaching in effective English primary schools to make this aspect of their work more accessible to a wider audience.

This book begins by outlining the historical background to the EPPSE study of teaching in effective schools. It shows how, over many years, the scholarly focus had shifted slowly from what is taught to how it is taught. It introduces the EPPSE research and describes many of the pedagogical ideas and technical terms used in the rest of the book.

Chapter 2 summarizes the methodologies, approaches and sampling strategies that enabled the EPPSE research team to identify the distinctive features of those teaching in effective schools. Chapters 3–6 summarize the results of the research. They are practical in nature and outline the most significant findings for head teachers, practitioners and policymakers. Chapters 7 and 8 are more technical and set out the quantitative analyses and findings in more detail. They describe the variations in teaching practice (Chapter 7) and the associations between teaching quality and pupil outcomes (Chapter 8). Chapter 9 returns to the key findings and the implications of the research.

Chapter 1

The research landscape and the Effective Primary Pedagogical Strategies in English and Mathematics study

Back in 1997, the newly elected Labour Government in the UK funded a study that came to be known as the Effective Provision of Pre-school, Primary and Secondary Education research project' (EPPSE, 1997–2014). Although the study had originally been tendered by the previous Conservative Government, it was expanded by New Labour as one manifestation of its much vaunted policy priority: education, education, education. The project focused on children in pre-school in England because Scotland, Northern Ireland and Wales have different education systems. The period called pre-school in England is the time before children enter compulsory schooling at age 5. The focus of the original research was on the experiences of children between 3 and 5 years old.

The project was prompted, shaped and informed by the great mass of academic literature that preceded and surrounded it, and it was designed as a large-scale, longitudinal, mixed-method study. It was funded originally to examine the impact of pre-school. Later phases examined the influence of primary (ages 5–11, see Sylva *et al.*, 2010) and secondary education (ages 11–16), but its early findings led to additional government investment in early years education and care, and a wider research brief, such as studying the impact of family characteristics on children's outcomes.

The project eventually lasted more than 17 years and studied the progress and development of more than 2,800 children in England from their third to beyond their 16th birthdays. An additional subsample of just over 300 'home' children (those who had not attended pre-school) were recruited at school entry for comparison and they were followed from ages 5 to 16+, making a total sample of 3,000+ children (Sammons *et al.*, 2005; Siraj-Blatchford *et al.*, 2006; Sylva *et al.*, 2010).

To grasp the strength and significance of the EPPSE findings about teaching in effective primary schools, it is important to appreciate something of the research landscape in which the study was set.

Two key predecessors

During the 1970s and 1980s, two seminal UK studies investigated the relationship between primary-school practice and pupil outcomes. They sought to establish whether some schools and classrooms were more effective than others, and the extent to which attending a particular school/class made a difference to a child's outcomes.

The projects were driven by the need to investigate the role that schools and classrooms played in enhancing child outcomes, particularly in the light of emerging knowledge about the impact of family and child background factors on a pupil's development (Coleman *et al.*, 1966; Jencks *et al.*, 1972). There was also academic interest in exploring the extent to which research already undertaken in secondary schooling (Rutter *et al.*, 1979) could be applied to primary education.

The two studies were the Oracle investigation (Galton *et al.*, 1980; Galton and Simon, 1980; Galton *et al.*, 1987) and School Matters (Mortimore *et al.*, 1988). Like the EPPSE project, they both recognized the importance of the classroom as a unit of analysis, and their starting points were the assessment of children's outcomes rather than just a focus on observing teachers' practice. The School Matters research explored school effects as well as those related to teachers, recognizing that school and teacher effects may be linked. It should be noted that since this pioneering research, through advances in statistical techniques, the EPPSE research has benefitted from more detailed pupil- and school-level data, allowing for more robust value-added school effectiveness analyses.

The results of these two pioneering studies influenced the emerging research discipline of School Effectiveness and School Improvement (SESI), and highlighted the need to study in more detail the various ways children's backgrounds, their teachers and their schools shaped differences in pupils' outcomes. The SESI and associated teacher effectiveness research fields have grown in international importance over the last three decades and have proved influential in informing both practice and policy in many countries (Sammons, 2007; Kington *et al.*, 2014; Muijs *et al.*, 2014; Reynolds *et al.*, 2014; Chapman *et al.*, 2016).

Interest in the potential influence of classroom teachers and schools laid the foundation for other studies (Reynolds and Muijs, 1999; Muijs and Reynolds, 2000; Askew *et al.*, 1997) that drew on a broader framework for observations and analyses. The key factor behind the rapid development of the school-effectiveness research (SER) movement, around the turn of the millennium, was simply the extent to which researchers could, by then, draw on a wealth of data at national and school level to make comparisons and contextualize findings.

The EPPSE project was the first European pre-school longitudinal study to follow children both during and beyond their pre-school years into further phases of schooling. It used standardized assessments of children's attainment (for example, Elliot *et al.*, 1996) and progress as well as measures of children's socio-emotional development (for example, Goodman, 1997). It built on the work of earlier studies, such as the Oracle research and School Matters, but went further by incorporating into the methodology and analyses the ability to track children across different phases of education and so explore influences from pre-school, the home-learning environment (HLE) and school simultaneously.

In addition, the EPPSE study was able to:

- include national assessment data on each pupil's academic attainments at specific ages (7, 11, 14 and 16) as well as the results of standardized tests administered at ages 3, 5, 6 and 10
- incorporate school performance ratings produced from school inspections by the Office for Standards in Education (Ofsted) within a national context
- achieve a deeper understanding of practices evident in a range of settings by combining qualitative and quantitative methods in case studies of children and families, pre-schools, and selected classes and teachers.

SER

Over many years, there have been frequent attempts to identify the particular national variations in educational structures and regulatory frameworks that account for the differences in pupil outcomes between countries (Döbert *et al.*, 2004; OECD, 1994, 2005).

However, structures and regulations provide only a limited insight into either schools or children's performance. In the 1980s and 1990s, the SER movement had started to provide a wider perspective on what really matters for pupil outcomes. It was pioneered in the UK by Mortimore, Sammons and Reynolds, in mainland Europe by Creemers and Bosker, in the USA by Stringfield and Teddlie, and in Australia by Rowe.

These researchers gathered a large body of evidence, which, together with studies by many others (for example, Sammons, 1999; Reynolds *et al.*, 2002; Creemers *et al.*, 2010; Townsend, 2007; Chapman *et al.*, 2016; Muijs *et al.*, 2014), points to the importance of considering children's characteristics (for example, gender), their social demographics (for example, parental socio-economic status [SES]) and school-level variables (for example, leadership, ethos) when accounting for the differences in their performance.

In exploring the idea of an effective school and effective classroom practices, the SER movement started the process of shifting the spotlight away from regulatory frameworks towards what actually happens in the classroom between teachers and children. Over the years, SER has become broader and it is now commonly termed educational effectiveness research (EER), recognizing the way schools, classes, teachers and pupils are interlinked in real-life educational settings.

When measuring variations between different schools and their impact on their pupils' educational outcomes, educational effectiveness researchers took into account the differences between pupils' prior attainments, as well as other characteristics of the cohorts of pupils that enter the school. In the EER literature, the characteristics of pupils in any one year group are often referred to as the characteristics of the school's intake (Sammons, 1996; Scheerens and Bosker, 1997), a term that is used throughout this book. This means, therefore, that EER indicates the size and significance of a school's impact on children's academic and socio-behavioural outcomes by using a contextualized value-added (CVA) approach to measuring pupil progress (Teddlie and Reynolds, 2000; Creemers *et al.*, 2010).

This value-added approach explores the extent to which, given a defined starting point, children's progress in schools exceeds that predicted by their starting points, such as their family background characteristics. EER analyses the added value or extra boost that schools and teachers give to their pupils' academic and socio-behavioural progress above and beyond the non-school influences on the pupils (for example, their background characteristics).

These CVA studies describe and evaluate the strength of other individual, family and neighbourhood characteristics expressed as effect size (ES, Schagen and Elliot, 2004), so that their impact on the children's learning and development can be compared. The EPPSE project made considerable use of value-added measures and it often refers to this as CVA analysis because it **controlled for** a range of contextual influences related to child, family and neighbourhood characteristics.

International comparative research

While it has always been possible for academic educationalists to compare the structural aspects of schooling internationally (for example, age at start of school, adult:child ratios), they have only recently developed systems that enable them to make international comparisons of the outcomes and processes of education. These new systems of analysis have facilitated a much wider and better-informed global debate about what makes the difference in educating a country's children (Siraj and Taggart, 2014).

In 1995 the International Association for the Evaluation of Educational Achievement (IEA) was working on an ambitious international assessment of pupil outcomes: the Trends in International Mathematics and Science Study (TIMSS, Gonzalez and Smith, 1997). This research programme initially tested and compared the academic performance of children aged 9/10 and 13/14 with a common set of assessments and made comparisons between 45 countries.

This was the culmination of work, begun in 1961, that focused in the first instance on maths (First International Mathematics Study) and then on science (First International Science Study). The assessments, and their names, were refined over 30 years, resulting in the TIMSS programme.

Since 1995, at four-yearly intervals, TIMSS has collected both pupils' test scores and information about their background demographics, attitudes and school experiences. Following the success of TIMSS, the IEA introduced the Progress in International Reading Literacy Study (PIRLS, see Mullis *et al.*, 2001) in 2001. This research programme monitored the reading achievements and behaviours of children aged 9/10 in 36 countries, with follow-up studies being conducted every five years.

In 1997, the Organisation for Economic Co-operation and Development (OECD) developed the Programme for International Student Assessment (PISA, OECD, 2000), which is now the best-known international educational outcome study. Every three years, PISA produces international comparisons of education systems in OECD countries (mostly higher-income countries) worldwide by investigating pupils' academic performance at age 15 in maths, science and reading. By 2009, approximately 470,000 teenagers in 65 nations had participated in PISA.

These three means of tracking educational outcomes internationally are now firmly established. Many countries have used the results both to compare international systems and to inform the development of their internal education policies (EIU, 2012, 2014).

Early results, which placed many Pacific Rim countries at the top of the resulting league tables, and some Western European countries farther down, were instrumental in igniting debates about how education works at both macro- (national policies and regulation) and micro- (school and classroom) levels, and about how these compare across countries. Indeed, the comprehensive data produced by PISA, PIRLS and TIMSS underline the importance of measurable pupil outcomes (Reynolds, 2006; Reynolds *et al.*, 2002) set within the context of different educational systems.

The search for key factors

The work of EER academics has provided many insights into the factors that help to make schools effective places of learning (James *et al.*, 2006; Sammons., 2007a; Sammons *et al.*, 2007a) and has prompted numerous lists of key characteristics of effective schools.

For example, Rutter *et al.* (1979) identified eight characteristics of an effective secondary school based on a study of 12 London schools: positive school ethos, effective classroom management, high teacher expectations, teachers as positive role models, positive feedback and treatment of students, good working conditions for staff and students, students given responsibilities and shared staff-student activities.

The much larger School Matters research based on 50 London primary schools (Mortimore *et al.*, 1988) revealed 12 factors: purposeful leadership, deputy head involvement, teacher involvement, consistency among teachers, structured sessions, intellectually challenging teaching, work-centred environment, limited focus within sessions, maximum communication between teachers and pupils, record-keeping, parental involvement and positive climate.

However, Brighouse and Tomlinson (1991) summarized different studies and drew attention to seven broader factors: leadership at all levels, good management and organization, collective self-review, regular staff development, uplifting environment/buildings/ethos, focused teaching and learning, and parental involvement.

In a major international review, Teddlie and Reynolds (2000) argued for nine criteria: effective leadership, effective teaching, developing and maintaining a pervasive focus on learning, positive school culture, high and appropriate expectations of all, emphasis on student responsibilities and rights, monitoring progress at all levels, developing staff skills at the school site, and involving parents in productive and appropriate ways.

While these lists identify some similar concepts, there are some differences between them. This suggests that there is no single universal list of school factors that make a school effective, although there is quite a lot of evidence to support there being factors that are of particular importance. A review by Reynolds *et al.* (2014) showed that the quality of teaching is generally found to be a key feature, and this has been echoed in many other studies (Ko *et al.*, 2013; Muijs *et al.*, 2014; Devine *et al.*, 2013; Coe *et al.*, 2014; Kington *et al.*, 2014).

SER, however, is not confined to the study of school-level variables. Research on the relationship between School Effectiveness and School Improvement (SESI) indicates that schools are better studied as organizations with nested layers (for example, pupils in classrooms, departments in schools). A widely accepted view of cross-level influences in nested models of school effectiveness is that higher-level conditions (for example, school leadership, policy and organization) facilitate lower-level conditions (for example, teaching and learning in classrooms), which, in turn, impact directly on children's academic outcomes (Goldstein, 1997; Hill and Rowe, 1996, 1998).

Henchey (2001) and Raham (2002) both drew attention to the characteristics of high-performance, low-SES schools in Canada, while Hopkins (2001) identified similar school improvement strategies for schools in challenging circumstances. Their results confirmed and extended earlier research that had shown the importance of leadership and school culture, and how this in turn influenced classroom culture. This view was confirmed by a review of research on effective schools in challenging circumstances (Muijs *et al.*, 2004) and by an investigation into the impact of improvement programmes associated with high-reliability organizations (Reynolds, 2004).

An important report that focuses on the what of teaching (Harris and Ratcliffe, 2005) emphasized that the way schools and teachers understand and respond to lists of school effectiveness characteristics is key to linking effectiveness and improvement at the school and the teacher levels. This insight linked the fields of improvement and effectiveness built on earlier SER, and it helped to shift the spotlight away from what happens at the wider school level and towards what happens at the classroom level – away from what is taught (the content/curriculum) and onto how it is taught (classroom pedagogy, Sammons *et al.*, 2014a,b, 2016; Van der Lans, 2016; Day, 2004).

Further important insights are revealed in the Dynamic Model of Educational Improvement, which makes explicit connections between the school and classroom levels and highlights features of teachers' practice. It moves away from a static notion of effectiveness to the dynamic notion that recognizes that school and classroom change lies at the heart of all efforts to improve practice and outcomes for pupils (Creemers and Kyriakides, 2008, 2010, 2012).

Content and curricula

What is taught will, of course, always be important and contentious. International reviews (Sargent *et al.*, 2013) demonstrate the wide variation in international approaches to curriculum and pedagogy. France has a prescribed framework that requires fidelity across all schools. England has the National Curriculum but exempts certain categories of school, such as free schools and academies. While some may argue that 'National Curriculum' is something of a misnomer, given the number of those who may opt out, in reality the vast majority of schools in England follow national frameworks. A number of countries, such as Hungary, Ireland, Japan, Korea, the Netherlands, New Zealand, Norway, Portugal, Singapore and Spain, have prescribed curricula, but there are many variations on this theme. Italy has a national curriculum defined through national guidelines. Germany and Switzerland have federal/state variations with no national framework. Canada has provincial variations based on levels of achievement. Finland simply has guidelines. The USA has state variation but, in recent years, many states have introduced common core guidelines for the teaching of English and maths.

Not only is there wide international variation in what is taught but also the content of the curriculum has changed over time in most countries. The English National Curriculum, for example, was introduced in 1988. Its numerous reviews and revisions, under different political administrations, are testament to the contentious nature of content. The battle in the UK over, for instance, which topics should be included in a history curriculum has raged for decades, with different positions influenced by contrasting ideologies, values, lobby groups, academics and politicians (Alexander, 2006, 2008).

International comparisons of educational outcomes have a distinct approach to the question of what should be taught. The PISA, TIMSS and PIRLS assessments were developed only after extensive collaboration with experts in education across the participating countries, which drew on their knowledge of assessment frameworks, research instruments and other factors that influence learning opportunities. These comparative assessments are not predicated on one specific curriculum. Rather, they are based on the common content in curricula systems around the world. Their tests assess the extent to which pupils can apply their knowledge to real-life situations in order to equip them for later life, employment and social participation.

TIMSS is clear about its approach to the curriculum. It sets out to investigate it at three levels:

- intended curriculum: what societies intend for their children to learn and how their education systems are organized to meet these demands
- implemented curriculum: what is actually taught in classrooms, who teaches it and how it is taught
- achieved curriculum: what pupils actually learn.

Academics who study the relationship between school effectiveness and school improvement (SESI) are interested in the intended and the achieved aspects of the curriculum because these provide important contexts and outcomes for learning. Over the years, however, these scholars have emphasized more the implemented aspect. They argue that the fundamental question of education is: How can teachers engage their pupils most effectively in learning? They also argue that a range of child outcomes should be studied to provide a rounded picture of effectiveness.

Policy changes

How teachers teach, just like what they teach, is important and yet contentious, and thus has serious implications for national policy. Following national concerns about standards in education and analyses of national assessment data that revealed wide variations between schools, plus some early results from international comparison data on maths concerning a long tail of underachievement, the UK's New Labour Government introduced the National Literacy and Numeracy Strategies for primary schools from 1998, and this context was relevant to practice in schools attended by children in the Effective Provision of Pre-school Education (EPPE) sample. There was a strong emphasis on raising standards, enhancing equity in outcomes and school improvement, with targets being set for the achievement of all children. New Labour was determined to make radical changes to the national education policy and practice (West and Pennell, 2002; Sammons, 2008) that it had inherited. It set up a Standards and Effectiveness Unit in the Department of Education in order to bring in wide-ranging changes to teaching and learning with an emphasis on raising standards. These combined extra resources, professional development and a zero tolerance of failure, noted as a policy of pressure and support. The unit was particularly interested in learning from abroad and comparing typical practices in England with those evident in well-performing countries. For an account of political changes undertaken at this time, see Barber (2007) and Sammons (2008).

The emphasis in high-scoring Pacific Rim countries on interactive, whole-class teaching, focused group work and clearly defined learning objectives (Barber, 1996; DfEE, 1999, 2000a) led to the UK's first nationwide prescriptive programme for teaching literacy. The Primary Literacy Strategy (DfEE, 2000b) from the newly named Department for Education and Employment (DfEE) was heavily influenced by the findings from overseas programmes. The DfEE invested £12.5 million (Machin and McNally, 2004a,b) in transforming the teaching of reading in UK schools through regulation, extensive support materials (DfES, 2001a,b) and, most importantly, a comprehensive in-service training programme for practitioners. It should be noted that the government department with responsibility for education has undergone several name changes under successive governments since its inception in 1839. For a chronology, see Appendix 2.

Alongside this, the then government introduced a similar radical strategy for teaching maths (DfEE, 1998a). These two approaches were eventually reviewed and combined into the Primary National Strategies Framework (DfES, 2007).

These national strategies, while not completely content free and still championing whole-school approaches to the curriculum, stressed the importance of how children are taught. They reinforced the message from SESI researchers (Stoll and Fink, 1996) that what happens inside the classroom, and the interactions between pupils and teacher, are fundamentally important to a range of academic, social and attitudinal outcomes (Andrews, 2011). The slow shift in emphasis over the years had finally led to binding national strategies that focused on pedagogy (the how of teaching).

SESI researchers continue to draw attention to the centrality of teaching, learning and classroom processes in determining schools' academic effectiveness (Creemers, 1994; Scheerens and Bosker, 1997; Hill and Rowe, 1998; Teddlie and Reynolds, 2000; Muijs *et al.*, 2014). They argue that theories of learning and instruction are at the core of educational effectiveness, with wider school factors merely facilitating the conditions for the classroom factors (Creemers 1994; Scheerens 1992).

The report *Research into Teacher Effectiveness* developed a model of teacher effectiveness that links pupil progress to professional characteristics, teaching skills and classroom climate (Hay McBer, 2000). It suggests that more than 30 per cent of the variance in pupil progress can be predicted by these three factors alone and it stresses the importance of the teacher's role in creating an excellent classroom climate.

Finally, the spotlight moved away from the wider school and the national curriculum, instead shining sharply, brightly and directly on the child's classroom and their teacher's observed pedagogy.

Pedagogy

With the spotlight on the how rather than the what of teaching, it is important to grapple with the word 'pedagogy'. This is used by educational academics as shorthand for some complex ideas, and it is this complexity that continues to make pedagogy both misunderstood and controversial (Alexander, 2008).

The lay understanding of pedagogy usually focuses on the work of a teacher in the classroom: on what teachers do and how they do it. Wikipedia, for example, states that pedagogy 'is the study of how knowledge and skills are exchanged in an educational context, and it considers the interactions that take place during learning'.

There have been numerous definitions of pedagogy, and much time and expense has been devoted to debating their subtleties (Ko *et al.*, 2013). Furthermore, academic ideas have changed over the years (Vygotsky, 1963; Bruner, 2006) by context (Leach and Moon, 2008), by culture (Alexander, 2000; Durden, 2008) and across nations (Alexander, 2001; Reynolds and Farrell, 1996; Watkins and Mortimore, 1999; Simon, 1999; Alexander, 2000).

Academic definitions are inevitably more complex and include elements such as teachers' knowledge, beliefs and attitudes. For example, Williams (2008) describes pedagogy as 'generally used by researchers and teacher educators to encompass both classroom practice and the teacher's knowledge and beliefs about the subject and the learning and teaching that underpin it' (p. 63), while Alexander (2010) defines it as 'the act of teaching together with its attendant discourse of educational theories, values, evidence and justifications. It is what one needs to know, and the skills one needs to command, in order to make and justify the many different kinds of decision of which teaching is constituted' (p. 280).

In the 1980s, Gage (1985) described pedagogy as 'the science of the art of teaching', as a science that is continually developed by innovative teachers and the academic researchers who study their practice. More than a decade later, Watkins and Mortimore (1999) defined it as 'any conscious activity by one person designed to enhance the learning of another'.

However, Alexander argued that pedagogy was understood too narrowly, and he criticized definitions limited to the actions of teachers. He distinguished pedagogy from teaching, suggesting that 'teaching is an act while pedagogy is both act and discourse. Pedagogy encompasses the performance of teaching together with the theories, beliefs, policies and controversies that inform and shape it' (Alexander, 2000: 540).

Gage's definition of pedagogy as 'the science of the art of teaching' remains one of the most appealing because it encompasses not only the more technical aspects of pedagogy (the science) but also the creativity evident in the classrooms of effective teachers (the art), while remaining open to individual interpretation.

This view proposes that pedagogy is a science that is continually being developed by innovative teachers, by academics who study their practice and by dialogue between the two. It is this dynamic interaction that led to assessments and feedback based less on summative test results and more on formative assessments and dialogue. This resulted in pedagogical practices that are explored in 'Assessment and classroom learning' (Black and Wiliam, 1998a,b) and *Dialogic Inquiry* (Wells, 1999) becoming widely accepted by many in the teaching profession.

Gage's view can also be interpreted as suggesting that effective teachers are both trained scientists (who are aware of a scientific pool of knowledge, such as developmental theories) and practising artists (who select the most appropriate tool to use in any given learning context). Every day, effective teachers provide their pupils with the most effective, engaging, memorable and rewarding learning experiences by drawing creatively from their scientific knowledge of the interests and capabilities of the children in their care and an artistic range of material, cultural and intellectual resources to make the curriculum and teaching accessible to children.

Pedagogy, then, can be considered to be the combination of beliefs, attitudes and a solid body of knowledge, plus the relevant skills that allow teachers to make appropriate, well-informed choices for their pupils.

This book, like the EPPSE project, adopts the perspective of Siraj-Blatchford *et al.* (2002) that pedagogy is:

> the instructional techniques and strategies that enable learning to take place. It refers to the interactive process between teacher and learner, and it is also applied to include the provision of aspects of the learning environment, including the concrete learning environment and home and community. (p. 10)

Effectiveness

SESI research made the early links between classroom/school pedagogy and pupil outcomes, leading to the idea of effective teachers. Effectiveness, however, whether at school, classroom or teacher level, is a controversial concept. It is a politically contested idea that evokes strong emotions: some people associate it with notions of professional competency and high-stakes accountability; others think that it challenges teachers' professional autonomy; and a few use their ideas about the constitution of high-quality teaching, and the proposition that teaching is more art than science, to question the validity of effectiveness.

Ko and Sammons (2008), for example, produced an analysis of observational data from the mixed-methods Effective Classroom Practice (ECP) research project (Day *et al.*, 2007, 2008). They noted that some theories of teacher effectiveness stress a differentiated model (suggesting that teacher practice and effectiveness vary with time and context), while others emphasize a generic model (suggesting that effective teachers can be distinguished from less effective teachers).

The ECP project investigated the practice of teachers and concluded:

> Although many aspects of effective classroom practice were utilised by both effective and more effective teachers, the more effective teachers seemed to possess and combine a greater range of teaching and learning strategies ... in consistently positive and more reflective, complex and contextually responsive ways. (Day *et al.*, 2008)

Given that pedagogy is fundamentally important to learning, it is natural to wonder what it is that teachers actually do in their classrooms that leads to poor, good or excellent progress for their students. The EPPSE project was able to study children's progress and from this distinguish the schools in which they had been most successful. The EPPSE team sought to answer this vital question first by analysing their quantitative data to identify schools where children made better progress than would be expected given their background characteristics (for example, social class, gender).

In the quantitative analyses the EPPSE project used a value-added measure of academic effectiveness for primary schools that indicates whether pupils were performing at, below or above their expected level of academic achievement based on pupils' initial attainment and background characteristics using national data (Melhuish *et al.*, 2006).

The researchers considered this the most useful approach because it facilitated comparisons between different groups of schools: those more effective, those of average effectiveness and those that were less effective in terms of pupil value-added scores. Melhuish *et al.* (2006) explained:

primary schools where children make significantly greater progress than predicted, on the basis of prior attainment and intake characteristics, can be viewed as 'more effective' (positive outliers in value-added terms). Primary schools where children make less progress than predicted can be viewed as 'less effective' (negative outliers in value-added terms) and this is the approach we have adopted. (p. 4)

Having conducted these analyses, the EPPSE study could then allocate schools to three distinctive groups: more effective, average effective and less effective (with the distribution into the three groups being based on the numerical spread of the data). As a mixed-methods research study (Siraj-Blatchford *et al.*, 2006; Sammons *et al.*, 2005) that combines quantitative and qualitative methods (Sammons and Davis, 2017; Teddlie and Sammons, 2010; Lindorff and Sammons, 2018), the EPPSE project was well placed to engage in a study of what happens in the classrooms of schools with different levels of effectiveness. This research is important because the findings reveal practices that are useful for both policymakers and practitioners. The EPPSE project results, summarized in later chapters, point to the significance and importance of what happens inside classrooms. Like the work of other academics, such as Hattie (2012), who have collated the findings of dozens of studies of classroom practices, the EPPSE project results seek to make learning visible to the people who matter the most: to the primary-school teachers.

Pedagogy and effectiveness

The relationship between academic effectiveness and quality of pedagogy is considered in a range of scholarly literature. For example, major reviews of the field include those by Muijs *et al.* (2014) and Ko and Sammons (2013). Despite differing emphases, the literature contains many common themes. These are introduced briefly below as part of the research backdrop to the EPPSE project, but they are developed more fully in later chapters, where they are rooted in the findings of the EPPSE research on teaching in effective schools.

Organization

Scholars accept, almost universally, that the organization of classroom routines and the structure of individual lessons form an important element of effective pedagogy.

The Cambridge Primary Review of the Curriculum (CPR) states that good teaching 'is well-organised and planned' (Alexander, 2010: 281).

The *Independent Review of the Teaching of Early Reading* (Rose, 2006) reveals that difficulties in learning to read can be caused by poor classroom organization, and that efficient classroom organization and management, as well as clear lesson objectives, are characteristics of good and outstanding teaching.

Early EPPSE research (Sammons *et al.*, 2008c) reported that children in disorganized Year 5 (age 10) classrooms make less progress in reading and maths than their peers in better-organized classrooms, and that levels of pupil hyperactivity are higher in these classrooms. The team rated observed practice more favourably in Year 5 classes where plenary sessions (an essential part of each lesson according to the UK national strategies) took place (Sammons *et al.*, 2006).

Scholars also generally agree that the pace of lessons is a good measure of organized lesson-planning, and it is included in the list of effective classroom interventions that help to 'close attainment gaps for children living in poverty' (Sharples *et al.*, 2011: 14). Most research indicates that effective organization is a powerful strategy for effectiveness. Williams (2008), for example, highlights: 'the need for careful and flexible planning as an effective pedagogical strategy for teaching maths, particularly as a way of adapting lessons to the sometimes unpredictable needs of pupils.

Lesson structure and the plenary

The UK national strategies stressed the importance of good lesson structure (DfEE 1999; DfES 2001a) and divided numeracy lessons into three parts: whole-class starter (10–15 min), main lesson (30–40 min, beginning with whole-class instruction and followed by individual or group work) and whole-class structured plenary session (10–15 min).

A plenary session is intended to play an important role, so that time for consolidation, dialogue, reflection and extension are built into the end of every lesson. It provides an opportunity for the teacher to gauge whether or not the objective of the lesson was met, what has been learnt and what needs to be planned for the next stage of learning. It gives children a chance to demonstrate and consolidate their learning from that particular lesson. It is an important component of the three-part lesson format that was originally suggested by the UK national strategies because of its important place in children's learning.

The strategies prescribed an even tighter structure for literacy lessons, dividing them into four parts: text-level work (15 min), sentence- or word-level work (15 min), group work (20 min) and whole-class plenary (10 min). This emphasis on defining the structure of lessons was based on the widespread scholarly view that lesson structure is a prerequisite for effective teaching (Muijs and Reynolds, 2011).

Despite this clear guidance, EPPSE researchers reported that plenaries took place in only about half of the lessons they observed (Sammons *et al.*, 2006). The team found that both the quality of teaching and the pupil responses were consistently better in classes where a plenary session was used in both literacy and numeracy lessons, and consistently poorer in classes where a plenary was not used in either subject.

Shared objectives

The importance of sharing learning objectives and goals with students is another common feature from the literature. The CPR states: 'learning is primarily a social activity which requires common goals and shared activities. This should be the teacher's starting point' (Alexander, 2010: 289).

It is becoming more widely accepted that it is helpful for children to understand lesson objectives and goals for their learning, and teachers often seek to make these explicit at the start of the lesson. The importance of sharing learning objectives and goals with students is another common feature from the literature (Clarke, 2001, 2014). The CPR states: 'learning is primarily a social activity which requires common goals and shared activities. This should be the teacher's starting point' (Alexander, 2010: 289). This implies that making sure that every pupil understands the learning goals, and is working towards them, is an important component of effective teaching.

Homework

Homework (schoolwork set for children to complete outside school hours) has been used to supplement the curriculum since the mid-nineteenth century. Views about whether or not setting homework is an effective pedagogical strategy, however, have changed, 'depending on political, economic, social and educational factors' (Hallam, 2004: 1; Hallam and Rogers, 2018). Many still believe that homework is an essential part of a child's education, while some now think that it infringes on children's freedom and play/leisure time.

Homework is used for many purposes: consolidating and extending learning that has taken place in the classroom, practising basic skills (for example, times tables, spelling), assessment (of both the child and the teaching), developing independent study skills, time management (work completed at home can free space on the timetable for other activities), building home-school links, and meeting the requirements of the school, parents, statutory policy and external inspectors (Hallam, 2004; Ofsted, 1995; Cooper, 2006).

The Ofsted report *Homework in Primary and Secondary Schools* found, 'in general, teachers and parents believed that homework played a valuable part in pupils' education' (Ofsted, 1995: 4. Most English schools today still consider homework to be an integral part of education. The DfEE (1998b) recommended 30 min of homework per day for children in Years 5 and 6 (ages 10 and 11), and many schools have homework policies and timetables that prescribe the days when homework should be set, as well as the amount of time children should spend on each subject.

The CPR, however, raised the concern that homework might increase the gap between more and less advantaged pupils. Unlike children from more affluent families, those from more impoverished homes are less likely to have parents who are able to support them in their homework, to have an appropriate space in which to work and to have access to extra resources (for example, computers, internet, books, library resources outside the school).

They suggested that, taken together, these factors could mean that children from affluent families can make greater gains from the additional learning opportunities provided by homework. However, the CPR concluded that, on balance, the evidence of homework's influence on achievement was tenuous, and that homework was unlikely to exacerbate the differences between the more and less advantaged.

However, the EPPSE team's research demonstrated that their cohort of 3,000+ children made significantly more progress between Year 1 and Year 5 (ages 6–10) in schools where teachers reported that they emphasized homework (Sammons *et al.*, 2008c). The EPPSE research found further strong evidence of the benefits of spending time on homework in lower secondary school (Key Stage 3, age 14, Sammons *et al.*, 2011), after controlling for the influence of the HLE, parents' educational level, SES and family income. Girls tended to report that they spent more time on homework, which may in part explain their better academic results at age 16 in their General Certificate of Secondary Education (GCSE) exams.

Classroom environment and relationships

Almost all scholars agree that the classroom environment contributes to children's learning. The early EPPSE results reported generally positive classroom climates and low levels of teacher detachment, but with considerable variation (Sammons *et al.*, 2006). This means that some of the 3,000+ children that the EPPSE study followed were learning in less favourable environments than others. Keiser and Schulte (2009) recommended that school and classroom climate should be assessed objectively because it can influence pupil outcomes.

The relationship between teachers and pupils is a key contributor to classroom climate. Whitebook *et al.* (2009) considered the research evidence and concluded that 'certain types of teacher–child relationships are associated with better developmental outcomes for children' (p. 10).

When considering the impact of child–teacher relationships on gifted pupils, Kesner (2005) used Pianta's (2000) Student–Teacher Relationship Scale and found: 'a highly successful teacher of the gifted is able to inspire and motivate students, reduce tension and anxiety for gifted students, and appreciate their high levels of sensitivity' (p. 222). A teacher must have a positive interpersonal relationship with his/her gifted students to accomplish these things. The results from this study indicate that this type of relationship must be possible. These positive relationships with gifted students suggest that teachers were able to meet the affective needs of the gifted students in their classrooms. This kind of relational pedagogy is important for all classrooms and effective learning.

Providing a safe, supportive environment for children is another important aspect of classroom climate (Creemers and Reezigt, 1999). In their study of 300 Grade 9–12 secondary-school pupils (age 14+), Murphy and Milner (2009) noted:

> All four teachers worked to craft a safe and comfortable learning environment. This appeared to factor into student engagement in class. Teachers encouraged students to be supportive of one another and did not tolerate negative remarks directed from student to student. This would seem to also increase student confidence as well as the frequency of student comments and questions. Children need an environment that encourages them to safely explore and try new things, without fear of ridicule or unwarranted reprimand. (p. 90)

Managing behaviour

The CPR states that good teaching 'depends on effective classroom management of behaviour' (Alexander, 2010: 281). Children cannot learn effectively in an environment where other pupils persistently misbehave and disrupt lessons. Although early results from the EPPSE project found that 'observed off-task behaviour is lower than that found in studies in the 1970s and 1980s' (Sammons *et al.*, 2006), there was enough variation to suggest that the behavioural climate remained a significant problem in some schools and that it has a negative impact on the educational experiences of the children in those classrooms.

Sharples *et al.*'s (2011) review of evidence from international experimental research found: 'Classroom interventions that close attainment gaps for children living in poverty adopt proven classroom management strategies e.g. rapid pace of instruction, using all-pupil responses, developing a common language around discipline' (p. 14).

When the review considered UK evidence of what works for schools in high-poverty areas, it found that managing behaviour was important for every school, not just for those in areas of greater deprivation. It reported that three factors contributed to improving children's outcomes:

- cultivating values of respect, good behaviour and caring, supported by a clear approach to discipline
- understanding and developing staff and pupils with personal and professional support
- having clear lines of authority, responsibility, accountability and autonomy (ibid.: 21).

The early EPPSE research found that children spent very little time working in truly collaborative settings. Although the team observed that pupils were generally seated in groups in primary schools, they found that they spent most of their time working in whole-class settings, with around a third of their time working individually. Once again, however, there was considerable variation between classrooms, with some children spending much more time working collaboratively in small and large groups than others (Rojas-Drummond and Mercer, 2003). Research reviews have found interactive whole-class teaching to be particularly beneficial (see Muijs *et al.*, 2014).

Sharples *et al.*'s (2011) review showed that cooperative learning significantly raised outcomes, especially for children living in poverty, and it described several US programmes using cooperative learning, including one for teaching phonics, that were particularly effective. It should be noted that the 'cooperative learning' referred to in the report is more akin to structured cooperative learning (for example, group goals, individual accountability) and is different from the use of the term 'collaborative learning' as used, for instance, in the results of Ofsted surveys.

Personalized learning

The CPR (Alexander, 2010) discusses the importance of personalized learning and states that teaching needs to be adapted to the specific needs of the learner. It stresses that teachers need to understand their children's developmental needs so that their teaching can be personalized by building on their prior pupil knowledge, by looking forward to the next steps and by stimulating their children's creativity and imagination.

Classroom talk and language

Scholars also generally agree that talk in the classroom is vital. Dialogic teaching and learning (teaching through discussion and dialogue) make vital contributions to children's learning. Wells (1999) highlighted the importance of language and meaningful interactive discussion. He wrote: 'education should be conducted as a dialogue about matters that are of interest and concern to the participants'.

The contribution of language to children's learning extends beyond literacy and English to every area of the curriculum, including maths. Research that investigates the link between language and maths shows that children with language difficulties also demonstrate challenges in maths that cannot be accounted for by other factors, such as memory or processing speed (Cowan *et al.*, 2005; Donlan *et al.*, 2007). Language, shared discussions and one person's input informing another's all contribute significantly to children's education.

Every academic review of pedagogical strategies presents spoken language as an important element of effective pedagogy and this is the only recommendation that the CPR (Alexander, 2010) makes about pedagogy. It argues throughout that teachers should make their own decisions about how to teach, yet then states in Recommendation 61:

> We do not nominate any best buys from recent pedagogical fads and fashions. At the same time, we note the extent to which research from many different sources converges on language, and especially spoken language, as one of the keys to cognitive development, learning and successful teaching, and indeed to the learner's later employment and democratic engagement. In many classrooms ... talk remains far from achieving its true potential. We urge all concerned, especially teachers and researchers, to act together to effect the pedagogical transformation which is needed, and which in some schools and local authorities has already begun. (p. 496)

Assessment

Assessment for learning is 'usually informal, rooted in teaching and learning, and can occur many times in every lesson' (Black *et al.*, 2003).

As Black *et al.* (ibid.) argue, it refers to all of the activities undertaken by teachers and their students that provide feedback that shapes and develops the teaching and learning activities engaged in by the class. This becomes formative assessment when the evidence is used to adapt the teaching work to meet the students' learning needs.

During a study of the test results of students in 25 secondary-school classes, Black *et al.* (ibid.) found that classes with teachers who used assessment for learning practices produced results that showed substantial gains in learning. The CPR supports the view that 'assessment for learning helps teachers promote learning how to learn' (Alexander 2010: 290).

The EPPSE project and the Effective Primary Pedagogical Strategies in English and Mathematics (EPPSEM) research

The core initial question for the EPPSE project, set by the UK Government, was whether pre-schools, primary schools and children's HLE could reduce inequality. Early results from the first stage of the study soon established that child outcomes are significantly related to both their background characteristics (for example, parents' SES and qualifications) and the quality of their early HLE (Melhuish *et al.*, 2001, 2008; Sammons *et al.*, 2002, 2003, 2004).

More importantly, the early results showed that educational influences (pre-school and primary-school quality and academic effectiveness) shape children's educational and socio-behavioural outcomes (Sammons *et al.*, 2008a,b; Melhuish *et al.*, 2006).

Given the success of the EPPSE research on policy (Taggart *et al.*, 2008), and the pedagogical strategies evident in effective pre-school (Siraj-Blatchford *et al.*, 2008) that were related to child outcomes (Siraj-Blatchford *et al.*, 2003), the Department for Children, Schools and Families (DCSF, 2010) commissioned the EPPSE researchers to undertake a similar study of pedagogy for children in effective primary schools. The team set a number of research questions, as follows:

- In what areas do teachers vary in their classroom practices?
- Are there relationships between classroom pedagogy and pupil outcomes?
- What are the practices evident in more and less effective schools?

To investigate how classroom practice influences children's academic and socio-behavioural outcomes, and to answer the above research questions, the EPPSE team had to complete a number of research stages. This approach was essential because the work involved an iterative mixed-method approach (Siraj-Blatchford *et al.*, 2006; Sammons *et al.*, 2005) where the results from one stage of the project informed the methodology and development of the next.

While all the EPPSE children were attending primary school, the team completed these stages and the findings were published in a number of reports, as follows:

- The first research question concerning the variation in teachers' classroom practice was answered in the report *Effective Pre-School and Primary Education 3–11 Project (EPPE 3–11): Summary report: Variations in teacher and pupil behaviours in Year 5 classes* (Sammons *et al.*, 2006). The findings are discussed in more detail in Chapter 7.
- The second research question concerning the relationships between classroom pedagogy and outcomes was answered in the report *Effective Pre-School and Primary Education 3–11 Project (EPPE 3–11): The influence of school and teaching quality on children's progress in primary school* (Sammons *et al.*, 2008c). The findings are discussed in more detail in Chapter 8.
- A composite report summarized the findings from the classroom study as well as results from the full EPPSE sample in terms of the pupils' academic and socio-behavioural development: *Effective Pre-School and Primary Education 3–11 Project (EPPE 3–11): Final report from the primary phase: Pre-school, school and family influences on children's development during Key Stage 2 (age 7–11)* (Sylva *et al.*, 2008).
- The third question was explored in a substantial substudy called *Effective Primary Pedagogical Strategies in English and Mathematics (EPPSEM) in Key Stage 2: A study of Year 5 classroom practice from the EPPSE 3–16 longitudinal study* (Siraj-Blatchford *et al.*, 2011).

These are the key technical reports whose findings about the nature and impact of teaching in effective primary schools form the core of this book.

Finding effective primary schools

To investigate what happens in effective schools, it is essential to identify which schools are more or less effective, and this posed the first research challenge. To identify schools, researchers conducted statistical, CVA analyses of pupil progress based on the 2002–4 national assessment results for Key Stages 1 (age 7) and 2 (age 11) in all of England's primary schools (Melhuish *et al.*, 2006). These involved **multilevel modelling** that analysed children's progress and attainment, having controlled for prior attainment, gender, age, ethnic background, level of disadvantage, special educational needs (SEN) and English as an additional language (EAL).

While it was clear that many of the background factors influenced children's progress and attainment, the results showed that a child's prior attainment was the greatest contributor to their Key Stage 2 assessment results at age 11. Even so, there were significant differences in children's progress that were associated with the particular primary school that they attended. This suggests that a school's overall academic effectiveness might be linked to the schools' strategy for helping lower-achieving children to make good progress. Having conducted these analyses of all primary schools in England, the researchers could look more closely at the results for those schools attended by the EPPSE children.

Selecting schools

The researchers chose a sample of 125 primary schools for closer inspection. These are referred to in later chapters as the focal schools. The team chose from the 850 attended by the 3,000+ EPPSE children, and the 125 included schools with high, medium and low academic-effectiveness scores (as determined by CVA analyses). The focal schools had the largest number of EPPSE children and included a range of contexts (for example, inner city, suburban, rural), and all 125 had at least four EPPSE children on the roll. There was a good selection across the range of schools with more and less advantaged pupil intakes, as measured by the percentage of pupils eligible for free school meals (FSM, an indicator of poverty). Having selected these schools with a range of academic-effectiveness scores, the researchers approached them and gained their consent to undertake observations in their Year 5 classrooms. This age group (10) was chosen because their classroom practices were less likely to be influenced by the national assessment focus of Year 6 (age 11).

Measuring outcomes

All EPPSE children were assessed using independent, standardized tests to measure their academic attainment in reading and maths in Year 1 and again in Year 5. In addition, the teachers completed profiles of their pupils' socio-behavioural development. These data were available for the EPPSE sample in all 125 focal schools. In these schools' Year 5 classrooms, researchers observed lessons and collected information about classroom practices that was used to investigate variations in practice. Chapter 2 describes this in more detail, and later chapters summarize important findings about teaching in effective schools.

As well as exploring variation in practices, the research linked observational data to other available independent information to explore the relationships between pupil progress and classroom/school factors. It explored the associations between children's outcomes and the measures of school attributes (for example, overall school effectiveness, improvement, and features of learning and teaching) reported by inspectors from Ofsted. The analyses and results are described in later chapters.

The analytical strategy

The EPPSE project's analytical strategy was predicated on quantitative and qualitative measures of teaching, pedagogy and behaviours, which were collected using two international systematic rating scales: the Classroom Observation System for 5th Grade (COS-5, NICDH, 2001; Pianta *et al.*, 2008b) and Instructional Environment Observation (IEO, Stipek, 1999). These research instruments were more than sufficient to answer the main research questions

The trained researchers' classroom observational data were, however, more nuanced because the team not only collected ratings from the two research instruments but also took detailed qualitative field notes about what the teachers did and how their pupils responded. The researchers then used these notes to add fine-grained or 'thicker' descriptions of the pedagogy they witnessed in the Year 5 classrooms, and to justify the ratings they awarded on the COS-5 and IEO scales. This provides unique vignettes and concrete examples that help us to understand in more depth what teachers and pupils were doing in the classrooms, and it can help to illuminate differences in the numerical ratings.

The analyses of the extensive field notes provide both a greater understanding of the relationships between teaching and learning, and better guidance concerning excellent, good and poor teaching practice for practitioners and policymakers. The EPPSE team also conducted professional focus-group discussions and a literature review of the relevant research to identify the key factors that contribute to ECP, and to develop an analytical framework of pedagogical strategies.

The quantitative research

The quantitative research reported in two of the technical papers mentioned earlier (Sammons *et al.*, 2006, 2008c) identified a series of key findings (discussed in more detail in Chapters 7 and 8):

- There was significant variation in teachers' practice and children's responses across the 125 Year 5 classes in the focal study.
- Overall, pupils' engagement levels were relatively high, the classroom climate was generally positive and teacher detachment was fairly low.
- Pupils' behaviour tended to be worse in schools where relatively more children were eligible for FSM and where the observed classroom climate was less favourable.
- More whole-class work than individual work occurred; collaborative work and other types of group work were uncommon.
- While plenaries were only viewed in half of the literacy and numeracy lessons, observed practice was better in these classes.
- The quality of observed practice was better in schools that had been rated more highly in terms of overall school leadership, effectiveness and improvement at their last Ofsted inspection.
- In classes with a more disadvantaged intake, observation scores were lower for some areas of practice, including basic skills development, depth of subject knowledge, social support for student learning in maths, pupils' engagement and classroom routines in literacy.
- In schools with a larger proportion of pupils eligible for FSM, an indicator of a more disadvantaged intake, the scores tended to be lower for pedagogy in literacy and for subject development in numeracy.
- There was poorer behaviour and poorer quality of teaching in schools with higher levels of disadvantage in their pupil intake.

These are developed and further explained throughout the rest of this book.

These findings identify important associations around equality that are pertinent for policymakers and practitioners. The research also shows that there are statistically significant associations between a teacher's observed practice and their children's academic and socio-behavioural development, and that the variation in teachers' classroom practices predicts differences in their pupils' outcomes in reading, maths and social behaviour in Year 5. Such patterns of association help us to identify what features of classroom practice help to promote better outcomes.

The qualitative research

The qualitative Effective Primary Pedagogical Strategies in English and Mathematics (EPPSEM) research (Siraj-Blatchford *et al.*, 2011; Siraj and Taggart, 2014) extended the quantitative analyses of Year 5 systematic classroom observations by looking in greater depth at the qualitative descriptions of the classroom environments, practices and interactions that had been provided in the researchers' detailed field notes that accompanied their classroom observations. This threw light on the following:

- pedagogical strategies used in English and maths during Key Stage 2 associated with more and less effective schools
- the specific teaching behaviours in Year 5 classrooms associated with pupil outcomes
- features of the most and least effective lessons, including lesson planning, classroom interactions, teacher–pupil dialogue, and any issues of organization and behaviour.

The research team identified the different pedagogical strategies used in these schools, and matched these with the extent to which teachers' practices varied according to the level of their school's academic effectiveness and intake characteristics. This book illustrates these differences in teaching practice with many examples from the researchers' observations.

It was this detailed EPPSEM analysis (Siraj-Blatchford *et al.*, 2011) that enabled the team to better understand and explain the pattern of statistical relationships between child outcomes and observed pedagogical quality ratings that they had found. It is these patterns that reveal the particular approaches of teachers in effective schools that are most closely associated with improved pupil outcomes. The remaining chapters of this book focus on explaining the EPPSEM study processes and results.

Chapter 2

The methods of study

At the outset, the EPPSE project recruited 2,800 children aged around three years. They were drawn from 141 English pre-schools in five different geographical regions, covered by six LAs, and spread across three academic year groups. This number increased to 3,176 through the recruitment of another 300+ 'home' children who had little or no pre-school experience and who joined the study during their first year in compulsory schooling (Reception year, age 5).

During the pre-school phase of their research, the EPPSE researchers visited all 141 pre-schools and assessed them individually for quality using the Caregiver Interaction Scale (Arnett, 1989), which assessed positive relationships, permissiveness, detachment and punitiveness of the main pre-school worker (that is, their relational pedagogy). They also used the Early Childhood Environment Rating Scale-Revised (ECERS-R, Harms, Clifford and Cryer, 1998) to measure pre-school quality (Sylva *et al.*, 1999a,b). This included the following subscales:

- space and furnishings
- personal care routines
- language reasoning
- activities
- interaction
- programme structure
- parents and staffing.

In order that the more educational aspects of English practice could be assessed, the EPPSE researchers developed another scale, the **Early Childhood Environment Rating Scale-Extension** (ECERS-E, Sylv*a et al.*, 2003, 2006, 2011), which describes educational provision in terms of the following four subscales:

- language and literacy
- maths
- science and the environment
- diversity (covering gender and race awareness, and planning for children's individual needs).

Both scales are rated according to seven points, where 1 is inadequate and 7 is excellent quality. The team also studied 12 pre-schools in depth, using a qualitative case-study approach that provided more ethnographic depth than was possible by using observational rating scales (Siraj-Blatchford *et al.*, 2002, 2003). The case studies were selected according to both their quality ratings and their effectiveness in particular domains. This aspect of the research was essential because it provided information about pedagogy strategies in highly effective pre-schools (with the best child developmental outcomes), which would have been impossible to determine from only the quality ratings.

Pre-school effectiveness and quality

The case studies provided unique insights into the everyday practices and pedagogy in pre-schools that seem to make a difference to children's learning. They provided research evidence, particularly regarding the importance of sustained shared thinking, that helped to inform the development of the Early Years Foundation Stage (DCSF, 2008). They also highlighted the crucial role that pedagogy played in differentiating between good and excellent settings. Some of the 141 pre-schools were more effective than others, and the 12 case studies helped to unpick the reasons.

The EPPSE researchers' robust quality measurements of the 141 pre-schools enabled them to draw inferences about observed quality and child outcomes, and make comparisons with the home group too (Sylva *et al.*, 2004). In the context of primary schools, effectiveness is often referred to as the school's contextualized value-added score, but the EPPSE project was the first to conduct CVA analyses of pre-schools. As already seen with primary schools, effectiveness measures the extent to which a pre-school enables its children to attain beyond what would be expected of them on the basis of their entry scores and background characteristics.

This effectiveness or value-added measure of the pre-school was calculated separately from the ECERS quality rating, although, given the relationship between the EPPSE measures of quality and child outcomes, it turned out that those pre-schools that scored highly on ECERS-R and ECERS-E tended also to be identified as more effective in terms of child outcomes. This means that (given their background characteristics and baseline score) children perform beyond expectations in a highly effective pre-school, whereas they underperform and do not reach their expected level in a less effective pre-school.

As the EPPSE project's cohort of children moved into primary school, the team examined the extent to which these pupils' early experiences influenced their later development. They considered the impact of good-quality or highly effective pre-schools on the children's learning trajectories. They also investigated whether the boost a child had gained from attending a high-quality/highly effective pre-school acted as a protective factor that helped them to remain confident and successful learners if they attended a less or more academically effective primary school.

The results showed that children who had attended high-quality and highly effective pre-schools generally outperformed at age 11 those who had attended lower-quality or less effective pre-schools (Sammons *et al.*, 2008a,b; Sylva *et al.*, 2008). This is illustrated for maths in Figure 2.1.

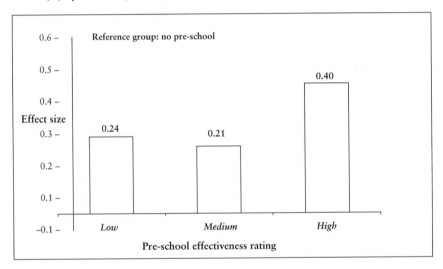

Figure 2.1: Influence of pre-school effectiveness on maths at age 11

Although Figure 2.1 illustrates only the impact of pre-school effectiveness on attainment in maths at Year 6, the full EPPSE findings demonstrate a clear relationship between effectiveness and literacy outcomes, and observed quality measures and academic outcomes. All of these comparisons are made in relation to the home group that had not attended pre-school.

Primary-school academic effectiveness and quality

It is well recognized that primary schools differ in the characteristics of the pupils who attend them (the school's intake), their academic results and their quality. To study primary-school practices properly, the EPPSE team needed to investigate a large number of primary schools to gain as full a picture as possible of the varied practices of teachers in all the differing classrooms. For the results to be meaningful and credible, the schools selected for intensive study needed to exhibit a range of social circumstances, geographical locations and different profiles in terms of their academic effectiveness and quality.

Unlike the pre-school phase, visiting all of the primary schools attended by the full sample of children to collect data on their observed quality was unaffordable and unmanageable. The cohort had moved on from 141 pre-schools in five regions to 850 primary schools in many regions. All 141 pre-schools had contained concentrated numbers of EPPSE children, whereas the primary schools to which they moved contained fewer. In fact, some schools had only one child from the EPPSE study. The researchers therefore had to devise criteria to select a subset of primary schools from the 850 for more in-depth investigation. They considered the fairest approach to be the use of a CVA measure because this effectiveness rating provides a common metric that, to some extent, already controls for important background characteristics of a school's intake and the prior attainment of pupils.

The first stage was to place the 850 primary schools into various bands of effectiveness by using value-added measures derived from analyses of data from the National Pupil Database (NPD). This database was firmly established by 1999 for children in England aged 7, 11 and 14. It includes a unique pupil number for each child (DfEE, 2000b) and all their **key stage** results from the summer of 2000 onwards. This was then linked to the Pupil Level Annual Schools Census (PLASC), which provides individual records for all pupils in England on a particular census day. It includes details about their ethnicity, first language, SEN, FSM eligibility, home postcode linked to neighbourhood poverty and so on.

Joining the NPD and PLASC databases produced a basis for analysing pupil progress that was related to pupils' demographic characteristics. This link was created through multilevel modelling (Goldstein, 1987, 1995, 1997, 2003). Having allowed for pupil and family characteristics and the features of the area that pupils lived in (by using postcodes to derive area-level variables from the national Indices of Multiple Deprivation), it produced a full set of school-level CVA residuals. The term 'residual' is often used in EER literature and refers to numerical values that indicate the impact of attending a specific school or the school's overall effectiveness score (Melhuish *et al.*, 2006). This approach to measuring primary-school academic effectiveness set new standards that were subsequently adopted by the UK's DCSF.

CVA multilevel models were used to investigate children's progress during Key Stage 2 by controlling for a pupil's prior attainment, as well as for their background. These analyses allow measurement of the extent to which children's progress can be attributed to the primary school attended. Primary schools where children make significantly greater progress than predicted (on the basis of prior attainment and background characteristics) can be viewed as more academically effective, and schools where children make less progress than predicted can be viewed as less effective. The term 'effectiveness' refers to this measure of progress. The analyses focus on academic progress in English, maths and science across Key Stage 2 (ages 7–11). The contextualized value-added models controlled for pupil background characteristics such as gender, ethnicity, EAL, FSM eligibility, SEN, measures of deprivation of the area where children live and the school-level variable of school composition (the intake). The effectiveness measures were calculated for three consecutive years. The overall academic-effectiveness measure for a school was averaged across the three subjects and across the three years (Melhuish *et al.*, 2006).

The EPPSE project's school effectiveness measures were therefore independently derived, and they indicated the academic success of the primary schools in promoting the value-added progress of all pupils in their year groups across Key Stage 2. Once the overall effectiveness score (the CVA residual) was calculated for each primary school in England, the 850 schools attended by the EPPSE children were extracted from the national data set. These focal schools were then allocated into three bands of academic effectiveness: high, medium and low. For details concerning the criteria used to determine how the schools were grouped, see Siraj *et al.* (2011, p. 14, Table 2.1a).

Table 2.1 shows that the EPPSE children who attended a low-academic-effectiveness primary school achieved an average of 98.6 in reading and 97.9 in maths, whereas those who attended a high-academic-effectiveness primary school achieved an average of 101.8 in reading and 101.5 in maths. Note that the mean for these reading and maths assessments is 100, with a standard deviation (SD) of 15. Hence a child might be expected, on average, to achieve a score of 100, and 68 per cent of children would be expected to achieve within +/–15 of this mean.

Table 2.1: EPPSE children's average academic attainment in Year 5 by primary-school academic effectiveness

Primary-school effectiveness category	NFER reading			NFER maths		
	n	Mean	SD	n	Mean	SD
Low	400	98.55	13.98	439	97.85	15.21
Medium	1670	99.21	14.77	1628	99.70	14.75
High	264	101.84	14.83	255	101.47	14.49

NFER: National Foundation for Educational Research

These results cannot be taken at face value, however, because the averages are calculated without controlling for differences in the pupil intake to different schools. To address this, further analyses were conducted for the whole EPPSE sample, which showed that, controlling for prior attainment and background characteristics, children's achievements in National Foundation for Educational Research (NFER) standardized tests in Year 5 and in national assessments carried out in Year 6 (age 11) were predicted by the overall academic effectiveness of the primary school they attended (for details, see Sammons *et al.*, 2008a,b,c). This relationship is discussed further in Chapter 8, which goes into more detail regarding the influences of teaching quality on children's academic outcomes. Having established that teaching quality and pedagogy are related to child outcomes, a further analysis was conducted of the national assessment database to extract a rating of 1–5 for national assessment effectiveness scores, and this metric was used when differentiating between the groups of schools used in the EPPSEM research.

Having established the level of academic effectiveness of all 850 primary schools attended by the EPPSE children, and their differences at school level, the research sought an additional measure of 'quality of pedagogy' at classroom level by investigating the teacher and pupil behaviours, and the pedagogical strategies, that led to better outcomes for children. How this measure was derived is dealt with in more detail in Chapter 7, which focuses on variations in classroom practice.

An important feature of the investigation involved choosing the best academic year for the focus of classroom study, to identify a group of focal primary schools for closer scrutiny at classroom level, and to find suitable observational instruments that could identify the variations in teacher and pupil behaviours that could be linked to academic and socio-behavioural outcomes.

The study year

Given that England's national assessments are conducted in Year 6 (age 11), this appeared initially to be the most appropriate age group for study. However, it presented practical problems: some head teachers were reluctant to allow intrusions into the classrooms during national assessment year, and many schools made timetable and curriculum changes during Year 6 to accommodate revision for the national assessment programme.

In the light of these considerations, the team decided that Year 5 (age 10) was the best year both to gain consent for researchers to be embedded in classrooms and to observe more typical classroom pedagogy. They could also use measures of children's academic outcomes in Year 5, collected using the NFER-Nelson tests for reading and maths, as well as socio-behavioural development profiles (Sammons *et al.*, 2007b).

The sample of focal primary schools

From among the 850 primary schools attended by the EPPSE children, the researchers identified a sample for the observation component of their research. This included approximately equal numbers of schools in a range of geographical regions with high, medium and low academic effectiveness based on the CVA analyses of progress across Key Stage 2. In addition, measures of the quality of pedagogy (excellent, good and poor) were derived from the observational instruments (COS-5 and IEO). While a school's effectiveness was the main criterion, the number of EPPSE children was also important. The team had recruited children from four successive academic year groups, with considerably larger numbers in the second and third years. It selected a sample of primary schools from those attended by the EPPSE sample in the two larger year groups. In 2004 some 1,180 children in the second year group were studying in Year 5 at 483 different primary schools. In 2005, 1,435 children in the third year group were in Year 5 at 616 different schools. The final focal school sample involved 125 schools and around 1,200 EPPSE children. The sample was also split geographically to reflect the five different regions in the original selection of six LAs (for example, rural, inner city, suburban).

The observational instruments

Having established the sample, the next challenge was to choose the measures of classroom quality. The choice of measures and instruments is extremely important in every research project (Schaffer *et al.*, 1994; Van de Grift, 2007, 2014; Van de Grift *et al.*, 2004; Devine *et al.*, 2010; Halpin and Kieffer, 2015). In educational research, it is crucial that the measures have adequate reliability and validity, and are credible within the practitioner community.

The researchers considered a range of observational instruments that they might use to explore variations in classroom processes based on measures identified as relevant in the literature from the teacher effectiveness field, including teachers' and pupils' classroom behaviour and experiences. However, they found few that contained behaviour frequency measures alongside global measures in a range of key pedagogical domains.

Two instruments were identified that offered reliability, covered a range of behaviours and would provide data that could be compared with those from existing studies, thus enhancing validity. These were the COS-5 and IEO. The COS-5 was a forerunner of the Classroom Assessment Scoring System (CLASS, see https://teachstone.com/class), which is now widely used in research projects (Pianta, 2003, 2005; Pianta *et al.*, 2008a; Pianta *et al.*, 2008b; Kane *et al.*, 2014).

At the time the research was conducted there were only a few instruments available internationally for conducting classroom observations. Since then the number has increased. While there are some overlapping dimensions, each instrument contributes uniquely to our understanding of the range and variety of classroom practices. Currently in use are the Framework for Teaching (Danielson, 2013), International Comparative Analysis of Learning and Teaching (Van de Grift, 2014), the International System for Teacher Observation and Feedback (Teddlie, *et al.*, 2006; Muijs *et al.*, 2018; Ko and Sammons, 2008) and the Mathematical Quality of Instruction framework (Charalambous and Litke, 2018).

Two instruments were chosen to provide a range of results across a wider spread of classroom behaviours. This also allowed a direct comparison of results from the two and helped to mitigate any emphasis or bias of reliance on a single instrument. It could perhaps be said that the researchers were spreading their bets, but this was justified given the complexity of pedagogy. These instruments were chosen, after much debate and discussion, for the following reasons:

- They had been devised relatively recently, specially for the primary age group.
- They covered a range of pupil and teacher behaviours.
- They offered the opportunity for comparison with other research studies in similar contexts (for example, Galton *et al.*, 1999; Clarke-Stewart, 1998).
- They had different approaches and emphases.

By using two well-respected international instruments, the team could study variations in teachers' practices that are linked to the concepts of pedagogical quality and effectiveness based on the domains covered by these instruments. (For further details of how teachers were classified into different effectiveness groups based on the observations, see Chapters 7 and 8.)

The classroom observations

A team of eight researchers and two lead trainers conducted observations in classrooms during the spring and summer terms of 2004 and 2005. The researchers had backgrounds in primary education and had previously been teachers, head teachers, advisors or inspectors. The lead trainers had backgrounds in primary education and were very experienced researchers. This team conducted their COS-5 observations across a range of academic subjects, but their IEO focused specifically on literacy and numeracy.

To prepare them to use the two research instruments, the team undertook intensive training. Initially the researchers received 12 days of training, but this was followed by many additional days spent reviewing the materials, practising the instruments by rating with videos, and working alone and in pairs observing and rating in real Year 5 classrooms unrelated to the project.

At every stage of training, the researchers had to compare their assessments with each other and to justify their judgements. This was an important part of establishing the inter-rater reliability of the observations and ensuring consistency of coding, because both the COS-5 and IEO rely on qualitative justifications for quantitative scoring.

The final stage of training involved all ten researchers simultaneously coding videos of 17 full-length lessons (11 using the COS-5 and 6 using IEO) in isolation from each other. Their results were compared to gold standard researcher scores to ensure inter-observer agreement.

The team's work followed the ethical guidelines proposed by the British Educational Research Association (BERA, 2004) in its *Revised Ethical Guidelines for Educational Research* and 'Quality Conditions for Quality Research' (BERA, 2008). The EPPSE project had been approved by the Institute of Education's Ethics Committee, and the team gave codes to participating schools to guarantee their anonymity, never using the real names of teachers or children.

The researchers observed 54 schools in 2004 using the COS-5, and 24 using IEO (one school was unable to accommodate the researcher to conduct an IEO). The sample reflected approximately equal numbers of more effective and less effective schools.

Using the same criteria, the team selected a different group of 71 schools in 2005 for both the COS-5 and IEO. They conducted COS-5 observations in all 71, making a total of 125 schools studied using COS-5. Owing to imminent Ofsted inspections, two schools could not accommodate IEO visits, so a total of 93 schools were studied using IEO (see Table 2.2).

Table 2.2: Sample of classrooms

Year	COS-5 observations	IEO
2004 (spring/summer)	54	24
2005 (spring/summer)	71	69
Total	125	93

The COS-5 had been developed by Pianta and colleagues for the Early Child Care and Youth Development study by the USA's National Institute of Child Health and Human Development. It was divided into two parts:

- behavioural coding (at classroom level, which the EPPSE project refers to as the frequency of behaviour), which focuses on observations of a target child (TC)
- observed/global coding (at child and classroom level, which the EPPSE project calls the measures of quality), which looks at the classroom more globally.

These two methods depend on observations of individual TCs lasting 20 min each. The EPPSE team used an earlier version of the COS-5 than the current one used in research and improvement, which combines the two types of observation.

Using the COS-5, the team conducted 1,009 observations in 125 primary schools. In each school they completed a minimum of eight observations. These included one start-of-day observation, one start-of-afternoon observation, two literacy observations, two numeracy observations, one science or social science/humanities observation and one observation of an additional academic subject (literacy, numeracy, science or social science/humanities, see Table 2.3).

The researchers scheduled all of their observations for the days and times when the class teacher suggested that most typical lessons would be occurring (that is, on typical school days rather than those with one-off or unusual events or activities).

The researchers prioritized the observation of core-academic subjects because these were the areas for which they had most child outcome data. Indeed, they found that the COS-5 was more awkward and less appropriate for use with non-core subjects (for example, information and communications technology, music, drama).

Table 2.3: Observation cycles

Number of cycles and number of schools					
Number of 20 min cycles	7	8	9	10	Total
Number of schools	2	113	9	1	125
Total 20 min cycles	14	904	81	10	1,009
Number of cycles by type of lesson					
Curriculum subject/time of day	Number of cycles				
Start of day	72				
Start of afternoon	71				
Literacy	153				
Numeracy	149				
Science	76				
Social science/humanities	44				
Other	3				
Total (observed in 2004)	568				
Unclassified (observed in 2005)*	441				
Total	1009				

* The 441 observations in 2005 were not classified according to lesson type. The proportional representation of each lesson would, however, have been similar to that in the 568 observations conducted in 2004 (that is, 25 per cent for literacy, 25 per cent for numeracy and around 13 per cent for science).

At the start of every 20 min observation, each researcher completed a cover sheet to provide general information about the classroom. This included details about the gender of the TCs, the lesson observed, the number of adults in the room and their designation (for example, classroom teacher, teaching assistant, learning support assistant), the number of pupils in the class, the type of room (for example, regular classroom, library, ICT suite) and the time the observation began. Whenever possible, they made sure that the TC was one of the EPPSE children.

The frequency of behaviour coding: TC observations
The first part of the COS-5 observation is frequency of behaviour coding, which takes place during the first 10 min observation segment. This includes rating the child's and teacher's behaviours across a range of classroom and curriculum settings. Throughout this section, the researchers observed and recorded the TC during a rolling sequence of ten 60 s intervals (30 s observe, 30 s record and so on).

The researchers focused on capturing information about five general areas of the TC's classroom behaviour and experience. Naturally, these general behaviours do not exhaust all of the possible pupil and teacher behaviours in classrooms. The five are:

1. **Child-level setting:** the setting in which the TC was working (whole class, individual or large/small group). To identify this, the researchers focused on the child's actual work setting rather than the teacher's intended or prescribed work setting.

2. **Content of TC's activity:** the activity in which the TC was engaged or supposed to be engaged. This includes subject areas (for example, literacy, numeracy, science, social science/humanities), subcategories (for example, word level, comprehension, computation, concept development, problem-solving), part of the literacy and numeracy hour (as described by the national strategies) and non-curricular activities (for example, enrichment, free time). The researchers focused on the particular activity that the teacher had set the TC.

    Where applicable, researchers used the subcategories in conjunction with other subject areas (for example, if, during a science lesson, a child was measuring the change in a plant's height, the researcher would code it as science and computation).

3. **Teacher behaviour:** the ways in which a teacher (or any adult in the classroom who had any contact with the TC during the observation) interacted with the child or a group of children including the TC. The behaviours include attending to TC (directly), teaching basic skills/facts, teaching analysis/inference, giving managerial instructions, monitoring/ checking work and having a positive or negative effect on discipline.

    The researchers concentrated on a select group of teaching and supporting behaviours, which, while comprehensive, were not exhaustive.

4. **Child academic behaviour:** the aspects of the TC's academic behaviour in terms of their intensity and level of involvement. These include engaged, highly engaged, unproductive/spaced out/disengaged, off-task alternative academic activity. Researchers captured the type of behaviour in which the child was engaged: learning/performing basic skills, learning/performing analysis/inference/planning, collaborative work, requesting attention/help/information, and volunteering. While some of these correspond to teacher behaviour categories, the two were coded independently.

5. **Child social behaviour:** the TC's social interactions with his/her peers and adults in the classroom, as well as any disruptive behaviour. The

researchers noted these whenever they were witnessed but they did not have to characterize the full 30 s observation. The behaviours include positive/neutral engagement with peers, negative/aggressive engagement with peers, positive/negative affect on teachers and general disruptive behaviour.

For most of these five general areas, the researchers selected the one single descriptor that best characterized their observation. For a few categories, however, such as teacher disciplines or TC volunteers, they noted the behaviour the second it was observed (for example, if a TC hit a peer, the researcher noted this immediately as negative/aggressive engagement with peers). The team called these behaviours events.

Once their ten 60 s intervals had been recorded, the researchers completed three additional ratings: teacher-sanctioned classroom setting, teacher-sanctioned collaborative work and teacher-administered test. After completing these, they continued with the second section of the COS-5 observation.

The quality-rating-scale measures: Global observations

The second part of the COS-5 observation is the global rating of measures of quality. This involves 10 min of continuous observation of the behaviours and characteristics of the TC, the teacher and any other adults in the classroom, plus the classroom environment at a wider or global level. During this section, the researchers focused on the who, what and how of everything at the classroom level. At the end of the 10 min observation, they scored 16 areas in two broad categories regarding the degree to which some prescribed behavioural, emotional and physical markers had been present. They also rated several behaviours and characteristics.

They rated the TC for seven child-level features:

1. 'positive affect'
2. 'self-reliance'
3. 'sociable/cooperative with peers'
4. 'attention'
5. 'disruptive'
6. 'activity level'
7. 'child–teacher relationships' (only with the main teacher).

They also rated the classroom overall for nine classroom-level features:

1. richness of instructional methods
2. over-control

3. chaos
4. teacher detachment
5. positive classroom climate
6. negative classroom climate
7. productive use of instructional time
8. evaluative feedback
9. teacher sensitivity (only the main teacher).

The researchers used a range of prescribed observed behaviours to rate the 16 items, as outlined in Table 2.4. After training, all of the researchers could make consistent judgements based on the frequency, range, intention and emotional tone of the interpersonal and individual behaviours seen during the observation cycle. They rated individual items on a seven-point scale (1 = very uncharacteristic to 7 = very characteristic). After rating the individual 16 features of children's behaviour and demeanour from 1 to 7, they were then able to explore these in relation to teachers' pedagogical strategies.

Table 2.4: COS-5 ratings

COS-5 global rating of overall quality: child codes	
Positive affect: the TC's level of happy mood, pleasant state and personal contentment during the interactions	**High:** shows sparkle; smiles, laughs, is enthusiastic
	Mid: is content overall; is neutral but with engagement
	Low: is flat or not content with no positive mood; is disengaged, glum, bored, detached
Self-reliance: the child's degree of autonomy, responsibility, initiative, self-direction, leadership and assertiveness	**High:** needs little adult direction; is willing to take risks, assertive with peers
	Low: lacks confidence, needs adult help before trying; dependent, passive, hesitant
Sociable/cooperative with peers: the extent of the child's positive engagement with peers and response to their initiatives	**High:** joins in, initiates talk and interaction; cooperates, sociable, shares, helps peers
	Low: is withdrawn, disengaged, no interest in peers; stubborn, bossy, obstructive, uncompromising
Attention: the child's degree of sustained, focused or directed attention to the classroom activities	**High:** shows sustained attention, is tuned in, on task
	Low: is easily distracted, creates diversions, fidgets, plays aimlessly, daydreams, needs teacher prompting, unfocused

Disruptive: a measure of the impact of the TC's behaviour on other children and adults during the class	**High:** does not follow rules, makes noises, calls out, taps pencil, annoys and disrupts others
	Mid: a few instances of inappropriate behaviour causing disruption to others
	Low: is compliant, not disruptive at all, can be inattentive when quiet but does not disrupt others
Activity level: the level of the child's activity in the class	**High:** is overactive, hyper, lots of movement, does not sit still, moves around a lot
	Mid: shows some movement but appropriate to situation; some fidgeting and shuffling
	Low: is inactive, passive
Child–teacher relationship: an assessment of the child's relationship with the teacher during the observation	**High:** responds positively to teacher, cooperates, complies, responds enthusiastically; shows respect and affection
	Mid: shows limited interaction but follows rules and instructions
	Low: exhibits negative engagements; rejects, defies, ignores, misbehaves, argues, demands, criticizes

COS-5 global rating of overall quality: classroom codes

Richness of instructional methods: a measure of the teacher's range and depth of instruction in the lesson	**High:** teacher shows a range of skills, hypothesis and depth strategies; is intellectually engaging and thought-provoking; encourages discussion, explains, models
	Mid: teacher uses no higher-order thinking skills
	Low: teacher follows a basic format
Over-control: the way in which the teacher seeks to exercise control during the observation	**High:** rigid structure, driven by teacher's agenda not child's interests; little movement, few whole-class activities, no individualization, teacher not child talk, stifled not creative, teacher directed, not necessarily successful
	Low: teacher respects child's autonomy and responsibility, sees child as active participant
Chaos: the degree of classroom chaos during the lesson	**High:** noisy, confused, unruly, chaotic, little instruction or learning, ineffectual control, misbehaviour especially during transitions, ignore sanctioned activity, disruptive or inappropriate behaviour, rude, poor discipline
	Low: organized, respectful, attentive, clear expectations

Teacher detachment: the teacher's involvement in the class or children's activity and the pupils' understanding or interest	**High:** lack of assistance and feedback; teacher does not notice off-task or poor behaviour; sits at desk, lacks interest, does not monitor children's work or behaviour **Low:** involved, responsive and alert to child's needs
Positive classroom climate: the emotional tone of the classroom – is it respectful, safe, welcoming and happy with friendships?	**High:** all listen politely, genuine respect of teacher and child **Low:** neutral climate, flat, dysfunctional, fearful, disrespect, negative
Negative classroom climate: the emotional tone of the classroom – is it a hostile, angry and punitive place?	**High:** hostile, angry, punitive, controlling; teacher is angry, irritable, lacks concern, abrupt and sarcastic; children involved in conflict; shame, hurt and humiliate each other **Low:** shows little of the above
Productive use of instructional time: how well the teacher manages the time	**High:** smooth transitions, routines followed automatically by all; good planning and well-prepared materials; efficient routines for when work complete; transition and management time limited; no waiting or disruption **Low:** time wasted, little of the above
Evaluative feedback: the frequency and quality of feedback in response to a child's performance on a particular task or skill; the presence of embellishments (repetition of child's skills; extension of child's skill)	**High:** feedback extends, consolidates and reinforces child's knowledge, understanding and skills – done often and dependably **Low:** perfunctory, occasional, lack of depth and information
Teacher sensitivity: the degree to which the teacher is alert to the children's needs and interests	**High:** teacher aware of children's needs, moods, interests, capabilities; uses sensitive discipline; takes interest in children; responses facilitate children's learning **Low:** none demonstrated

IEO

IEO, designed by Deborah Stipek of Stanford University, was the second instrument selected. This was designed for the US Center on Organization and Restructuring of Schools. The team used IEO, like the COS-5, to obtain information about variations in school processes, including teachers' and pupils' classroom behaviour and experiences.

IEO was designed to gather numerical indicators of the instructional environments experienced by pupils, and it does this by combining researcher judgements about the teacher's teaching and the pupils' learning behaviours. The team used IEO to observe literacy and numeracy teaching. They focused on these two aspects of the curriculum because they are often regarded as fundamental to children's later academic success and were receiving considerable attention as a result of the National Numeracy and Literacy Strategies in primary schools at the time of the research (DfEE, 1998a, 1999; DfES, 2001a,b).

The researchers gathered information about four main areas with 16 subscales. These are:

- general classroom management and climate ('classroom climate', 'classroom routines')
- general instruction scales ('cross-disciplinary connections', 'linkage to life beyond the classroom', 'social support for student learning', 'student engagement')
- mathematical instruction scales ('use of maths analysis', 'depth of student knowledge and understanding', 'basic skills development in the context of problem-solving', 'maths discourse and communication', 'locus of maths authority')
- reading and writing instruction scales ('reading as meaning-making', 'basic skills development in the context of reading', 'higher-order thinking in writing', 'purposeful development of writing skills', 'instructional conversations').

As with the COS-5, the team used a range of prescribed observed behaviours to code or rate the 16 items. These are outlined in Table 2.5. After their training, all ten researchers could make consistent judgements based on the frequency, range, intention and emotional tone of the interpersonal and individual behaviours seen during the observation.

Table 2.5: IEO scales of classroom behaviours

General classroom management and climate	
Classroom climate: how teacher creates classroom where pupils feel safe, respected and able to make friends, people speak respectfully and there are opportunities for collaboration; how teacher makes friends, people speak respectfully and there are opportunities for collaboration; how teacher makes and enforces rules, paces lessons, makes decisions and responds to children's ideas	**High:** respectful tones when speaking, shared smiles; welcoming; visible friendships; willing to share and help each other, ideas are welcomed and accepted, disagreements are academic not personal, teacher disciplines sensitively and deals with the behaviour rather than singling out the child; pupils have some autonomy and so on **Low:** classroom is dysfunctional, threats overheard, discipline overt and personal, children singled out when errors are made; tendency to promote 'bright' children; children show negative affect to teacher and/or each other; little evidence of respect; screaming and annoyance in the tones of adults and children; random acts of violence and so on
Classroom routines: how teacher uses instructional time, manages transitions, structures the day and lessons, prepares materials, involves children in the routine business of the day and so on	**High:** classroom resembles 'well-oiled machine' with smooth transitions; teacher's expectations clear and children understand what to do; children involved in class activities (collecting dinner money, taking register, preparing materials); learning assistants available with role defined clearly **Low:** most transitions chaotic; children walk round aimlessly during start-of-day activities; teacher's expectations unclear; learning assistant runs errands (photocopying, putting up displays) so is less available for children and so on
General instruction scales	
Cross-disciplinary connections: how teacher connects lessons and activities to multiple subject areas, with explicit and explored links between subjects	**High:** explicit connections between subjects and explored by pupils; evidence that study of one subject enriches study of another; connections explored in depth, and used to generate meaning and extend pupils' understanding **Low:** subjects studied in isolation; connections mentioned only in passing and not realized by children

Linkage to life beyond the classroom: how teacher connects lessons and activities to concerns beyond the classroom	**High:** students work on at least one topic connected directly to their personal experience or a current event; link is made explicit and meaningful, and the children show they recognize the connection and explore it in depth; tangible evidence of children's attempts to understand a topic or solve a problem
	Low: no clear connections to anything beyond the classroom; activities focus on class rather than finding relevance beyond the classroom
Social support for student learning: how teacher shapes a learning environment characterized by an atmosphere of high academic expectations for all pupils, coupled with mutual respect and support among teacher and pupils	**High:** pupils supported by high expectations conveyed by teacher for all children; children encouraged to take risks, seek challenges and learn from errors; adults value and encourage all children and treat all as contributors; all contributions taken seriously with errors explored (not glossed over) in search of the 'correct' answer
	Low: teacher puts down some children's academic efforts; pupils interfere with each other's efforts to learn with constant interruptions; children discouraged to take risks as afraid of put-downs or being laughed at
Student engagement: how teacher engages pupils in lessons	**High:** most of the time there is serious on-task behaviour, attentiveness, completion of tasks, displays of enthusiasm, initiative taken by children and accepted and extended by teacher; children contribute in whole-class and group discussions and activities
	Low: children disengaged and distracted; little attention, the disruption of some makes it impossible for others to work; much daydreaming, off-task talk and disruptive behaviour; children show little interest in the lesson

Mathematical instruction scales

Use of maths analysis: how children use mathematical analysis	**High:** children construct original ways to solve maths problems, and these methods are explored and tested seriously by teacher; they search for mathematical patterns, make conjectures with justifications, organize and evaluate work, ideas and methods; they make mathematical models to represent ideas and answers

	Low: thinking restricted to recording or reporting facts, rules, definitions; algorithms applied mechanically; much receiving, reiterating, reciting and performing routine procedures; little evidence of maths analyses
Depth of student knowledge and understanding: how maths knowledge is treated in depth in class	**High:** development of systematic and integrated understandings of mathematical concepts; pupils produce new knowledge when connecting topics, solving problems, making conjectures, justifying hypotheses and making conclusions; teacher engages children to show how they grasp and solve complex problems
	Low: concepts treated superficially; only one way to solve a problem; teacher and children present fragmented pieces of information; knowledge not used to make clear distinctions, arguments, solutions; little attempt to make connections between concepts; much rote memorization and basic recitation
Basic skills development in the context of problem-solving: how pupils learn basic skills in the context of problem-solving	**High:** pupils take time out from solving problems to learn the meaning of specific terms in the problem, to use a particular tool, to represent quantities symbolically, to perform a basic skill that is then used in solving a problem; teacher makes in-depth attempts to link basic skills teaching in the context of problem-solving
	Low: few basic skills taught with instruction isolated from problem-solving; children drilled with flash cards or rapid verbal questioning; focus on memorization or recitation; much repetitive computation (worksheets/sums) with little attempt to link this skills development to actual problem-solving
Maths discourse and communication: how classroom discourse creates a shared understanding of maths	**High:** considerable teacher–pupil and pupil–pupil discourse about mathematical ideas, which promotes understanding; discourses make distinctions, apply ideas, form generalizations and raise questions; unscripted sharing of ideas; dialogue builds coherently to promote improved, shared understanding of maths topic

	Low: teacher mainly lectures; communication seems scripted; teacher controls destination of lesson and ideas; common pattern of teacher question, chosen child's response, teacher feedback statement; children mainly report experiences, facts, definitions, procedures; much oral fill-in-the-blank and short-answer questions
Locus of maths authority: how teacher supports a shared sense of authority and responsibility for validating pupils' mathematical reasoning	**High:** teacher and students hold each other accountable for convincing them and each other that their reasoning is sound and answers correct; teacher answers questions with a question or offers instrumental help to push pupils to make their own decisions; children turn to themselves or each other for help before consulting teacher
	Low: teacher and textbook are only source of maths authority, they validate correct methods, explanations and answers; children accept an answer as correct only once teacher has validated it; teacher controls discourse and often treats pupil questions as digression; children turn to teacher for help, not each other

Reading and writing instruction scales

Reading as meaning-making: how pupils try to derive meaning from the texts they read	**High:** teacher creates atmosphere of enjoyable, purposeful reading, asks open questions, encourages pupils to read what interests them; children's reading involves understanding text's meaning, guessing meaning of unfamiliar words by context, using prior knowledge to predict what is coming, looking for patterns among works
	Low: children engaged mainly in activities that require decoding, choral reading, recitation, memorization or application of phonics rules; little focus on meaning of what is being read; teacher focuses on decoding not content, and corrects children's misreading of words without discussing the words' meanings

Basic skills development in the context of reading: how teacher passes on the skills to understand what is read (for example, phonics, voice, tense, sentence structure, syllabification, syntax, grammar, vocabulary) within the activity of reading for meaning	**High:** children take time out of reading to grasp the meaning of a word, phrase or literary device, based on the text, rather than asking teacher; pupils develop their own dictionaries made of words encountered during reading; teacher explains a basic skill that will appear in the passage to be read, and makes explicit connection
	Low: reading skills taught in isolation; few connections made between skills instruction and the text being read
Higher-order thinking in writing: how teacher helps pupils to plan, edit, revise and use higher-order thinking when they write, beyond merely practising the spelling of words, learning grammar rules and filling in blanks with pre-specified answers	**High:** children have a story to tell, a point to make or message to communicate to a desired audience; they plan, create outlines, edit and revise their work; teacher provides age- and skill-appropriate opportunities for different kinds of writing, appropriate scaffolding, substantive feedback (on ideas, not only grammar and spelling); children listen to, and offer suggestions for improving, their peers' work
	Low: teacher passes on literacy skills in isolation from writing; children learn vocabulary lists and spellings without using the words in a substantive way; they practise fill-in-the-blank activities without actually writing something meaningful
Purposeful development of writing skills: how teacher helps pupils to learn basic writing skills as they write, and to write for different specific purposes	**High:** pupils take time out to correct an invented spelling while writing, they write new words into a personal dictionary and use this to support their writing; teacher links a writing skill instruction directly and explicitly to the writing activity that follows the instruction
	Low: teacher provides writing skills in isolation as bits of information, the purpose of which is not made clear to children; connections between skills and writing are unexplored or unmentioned; children memorize lists of vocabulary and spelling but do not use these in their writing

Instructional conversations: how classroom conversations are devoted to creating or negotiating a shared understanding of the content	High: considerable teacher–pupil and pupil–pupil interaction about the ideas of a topic; talk is reciprocal about the content being studied, sharing ideas and explanations; children make distinctions, apply ideas, form generalizations and raise questions in complete sentences
	Low: children simply report experiences, facts, definitions and procedures; teacher controls the conversation and asks closed questions, and children respond with short answers; little genuine dialogue

Note: For details of the scales, see NICHD (2001) and Stipek (1999).

The team rated each IEO scale between 1 (low) and 5 (high). Their agreed rule-of-thumb guidelines for rating were as follows:

1 = stereotype of conventional (formal/didactic) and/or undesirable environment

2 = minimal intensity to mark a shift from the conventional environment, could be limited to the teacher or to a few students

3 = greater and/or uneven intensity in shift from conventional, including some students

4 = substantial and intense shift from conventional, including many to most students

5 = very intense, including most to almost all students.

Field notes

As noted earlier, the EPPSE researchers reported the findings of the observational part of the research in three technical publications (Sammons *et al.*, 2006, 2008c; Sylva *et al.*, 2008). These reports focused solely on the numerical scores given by the researchers on the COS-5 and IEO scales during their visits to schools.

However, the researchers also took detailed observation notes (a running record) before scoring each COS-5 and IEO scale, and these notes were the primary source of evidence for their rating. They reviewed each scale before beginning each observation to help them to focus their note-taking on the relevant evidence, which would support their numerical rating. This distinguished those teachers working in the classroom with higher scores on the quality rating scales. They made notes about the behaviour of both the teacher and the TC, the levels of pupil engagement, the children's interactions with each other and with the adults in the classroom, the types of question overheard and so on. One of the strengths of both research instruments is that they provide both quantitative data from the rating-scales judgements and qualitative data from the researchers' field-note analyses.

The three reports referred to above did not include evidence from the researchers' field notes that justified their scores on the observational scales. Following publication, it became apparent that the richness of the qualitative information and notes collected by the field team provided insights into life inside Year 5 classrooms far beyond that gleaned from the simple numerical scores. It was the field notes that provided the rich data that enabled the subsequent EPPSEM substudy (Siraj-Blatchford *et al.*, 2011) to identify the specific pedagogical practices of teachers working in effective schools. The field notes brought the numerical scores to life. Brief extracts from these notes are used in some of the chapters.

Investigating classroom practices

Armed with three sources of data – a school effectiveness measure (from value-added national assessment data), classroom-quality measures (the COS-5 observations and IEO) and qualitative researchers' observational field notes – the EPPSE team were finally in a position to start examining full data relating to the pedagogical practices across the 125 schools with differing levels of academic effectiveness and pedagogical quality. This book is therefore based on a mixed-methods research design based on a combination of quantitative data from systematic observations, and value-added assessment and rich qualitative data from field notes, which complement and extend our understanding of classroom practice. By bringing these various sources of data together, we have been able to establish an understanding and explanations of what underpins effective primary practice in Year 5 classes.

In addition to the systematic observation and qualitative field-note data, the research design for the in-depth study involved sampling schools according to their overall effectiveness. Three distinct groups of typical schools were identified using nationally derived CVA scores based on three years of national assessment data (for details of the distribution of CVA scores for all primary schools in England, see Melhuish *et al.*, 2006, Appendix 4) plus schools' most recent Ofsted ratings. Within the observational sample with full data sets, three groups were identified:

- a group of ten academically highly effective schools with good-quality pedagogy based on the Year 5 systematic observation data
- a group of nine medium-academic-effectiveness schools with medium-quality pedagogy
- a group of ten low-academic-effectiveness schools with poor-quality pedagogy.

Eight schools did not fit into any clear category so were excluded from the subsequent analysis. The other schools fell between or around these three distinct groups. Each of the three contained schools from a variety of settings (inner city, suburban and rural) and had a range of levels of advantage of pupil intake (that is, higher and lower percentages of pupils eligible for FSM).

The researchers aimed to identify schools that were typical of these three, and then to analyse, compare and contrast the pedagogical strategies used within all three groups of typical Year 5 classrooms based on the field notes. This provided a clearer picture of what was happening both at the two extremes of the continuum and in typically average classrooms. By applying the criteria of each group stringently, three clear groups that were almost equal in size emerged.

The first group: Academically highly effective schools with good-quality pedagogy

To identify those pedagogical strategies being used in the classrooms in schools that were particularly effective, the analyses were undertaken in three stages. The first involved returning to the effectiveness rating of the school taken from the CVA scores of national assessment outcomes. Given that the observations had focused on English and maths teaching, the value-added scores for these key curriculum areas were of special interest.

The second stage entailed assembling the Year 5 classroom's observed quality as assessed by the COS-5 and IEO. The last stage involved collating the school effectiveness data alongside the scores taken from the observations.

To be included in the top group, a school's English and maths national assessment residual scores (RSs, the school's effectiveness derived from national tests) had to be high (≥ 4) in both subjects, or high (≥ 4) in one subject and medium ($= 3$) in the other. The schools in this top group were also required to be rated as at least medium (IEO = 2); COS-5 = 3) for 'teaching quality', with one or both ratings in the high-quality category

(IEO = 3; COS-5 = 5 ≥ 4, see Table 2.6). The categorizations are discussed in more detail in Chapter 8.

The only exception was for schools with medium ratings on both pedagogical quality scales whose English and maths RSs were both rated as high (RS ≥ 4). Any school whose 'quality of pedagogy' on both scales was medium (IEO = 2; COS-5 = 3) and whose RSs were both high (RS ≥ 4) would also have been included in this group. However, no school fell into this category.

Table 2.6: Criteria for academically highly effective schools with good-quality pedagogy

Source	Possible scores (low to high)	Criteria
School effectiveness: national assessment effectiveness scores	1–5	RS ≥ 3 in both English and maths AND at least one RS ≥ 4
IEO	1–3	IEO ≥ 2 if COS-5 = 5 OR IEO = 3 if COS-5 = 3 or 4*
COS-5	1–5	COS-5 ≥ 3 if IEO = 3 OR COS-5 = 5 if IEO = 2*

* Schools where quality of pedagogy on both scales was medium (IEO = 2; COS-5 = 3) but both RSs were high (RS ≥ 4) would also have been included in this group. However, none of the schools fell into this category.

The researchers' criteria were stringent, so only ten schools (12 per cent) were placed in this academically highly effective, good-quality pedagogy group (see Table 2.7). Henceforth, this book identifies these ten as Group A and describes them as excellent schools.

The second group: Medium-academic-effectiveness schools with medium-quality pedagogy

The second group were the schools with average results (that is, scores at the median values) for all measures. Once again, the team applied their criteria stringently. To be included in this group, a school's English and maths effectiveness scores had to be rated medium (= 3), and scores on both classroom observation scales also had to be medium (IEO = 2 and COS-5 = 3, see Table 2.8). The team placed nine schools in this medium-academic-effectiveness, medium-quality pedagogy group (see Table 2.9). This book refers to these nine as Group B and describes them as good schools.

Table 2.7: Characteristics of academically highly effective schools with good-quality pedagogy

School identity	IEO	COS-5	National assessment effectiveness scores		Disadvantaged intake (% pupils eligible for FSM)
			Maths	English	
S01	3	5	3	4	0
S02	3	3	5	4	22
S03	2	5	4	4	32
S04	3	4	3	4	31
S05	3	4	3	5	16
S06	3	3	5	3	3
S07	3	4	3	4	18
S08	3	4	4	4	12
S12	3	3	3	4	31
S13	3	4	4	3	49

Table 2.8: Criteria for medium-academic-effectiveness schools with medium-quality pedagogy

Source	Possible scores (low to high)	Criteria
School effectiveness: national assessment effectiveness scores	1–5	RS = 3 in both English and maths
IEO	1–3	IEO = 2
COS-5	1–5	COS-5 = 3

Table 2.9: Characteristics of medium-academic-effectiveness schools with medium-quality pedagogy

School identity	IEO	COS-5	National assessment effectiveness scores		Disadvantaged intake (% pupils eligible for FSM)
			Maths	English	
S25	2	3	3	3	35
S26	2	3	3	3	7
S27	2	3	3	3	11
S28	2	3	3	3	5
S29	2	3	3	3	3
S30	2	3	3	3	7

School identity	IEO	COS-5	National assessment effectiveness scores		Disadvantaged intake (% pupils eligible for FSM)
			Maths	English	
S31	2	3	3	3	19
S32	2	3	3	3	42
S36	2	3	3	3	14

The third group: Low-academic-effectiveness schools with poor-quality pedagogy

The third group were the schools whose English and maths effectiveness scores were low (≤ 2) in both subjects or low (≤ 2) in one subject and medium (= 3) in the other.

Again, the criteria were strictly applied and ten schools were placed in this low-academic-effectiveness, poor-quality pedagogy group. These included seven with a medium pedagogical quality in the rating scales (IEO = 2; COS-5 = 3) and at least one rating in the poor-quality category (IEO = 1; COS-5 ≤ 2), and three schools with medium ratings on both pedagogical quality scales but whose English and maths RSs were low (RS ≤ 2, see Table 2.10). This book identifies these ten schools as Group C and refers to them as poor schools (see Table 2.11).

Table 2.10: Criteria for low-academic-effectiveness schools with poor-quality pedagogy

Source	Possible scores (low to high)	Criteria
School effectiveness: national assessment effectiveness scores	1–5	RS ≤ 3 in both English and maths AND at least one RS ≤ 2
IEO	1–3	IEO ≤ 2 if COS-5 = 1 OR IEO = 1 if COS-5 = 2 or 3*
COS-5	1–5	COS-5 ≤ 3 if the IEO = 1 COS-5 = 1 if the IEO = 2*

* Schools where quality of pedagogy on both scales was medium (IEO = 2; COS-5 = 3) but both RSs were low (RS ≤ 2) were included in this group. Three schools fell into this category.

Table 2.11: Characteristics of low-academic-effectiveness schools with poor-quality pedagogy

School identity	IEO	COS-5	National assessment effectiveness scores		Disadvantaged intake (% pupils eligible for FSM)
			Maths	English	
S73	1	3	2	3	8
S74	2	3	2	2	10
S75	2	3	2	2	39
S76	1	1	1	2	53
S77	2	1	2	2	12
S78	2	1	3	2	13
S79	2	3	2	2	60
S80	1	2	2	1	40
S81	1	1	2	3	15
S82	1	1	3	2	16

For the final part of the analysis, after identifying the three distinct groups containing typical schools, the team gathered the remaining schools loosely into three general categories, which occasionally overlapped. These were those schools that did one of the following:

- fell between the highly effective and medium-effectiveness groups
- fell between the medium- and low-effectiveness groups
- did not quite meet the criteria of the medium group but were very close (for example, IEO = 2, COS-5 = 3, maths residual = 3, English residual = 2).

These schools were an important part of the analysis, and the team included examples from their classroom observations in the EPPSEM report to illustrate the pedagogical strategies that they had identified.

Identification of key pedagogical strategies

The development of the analytical framework of pedagogical strategies involved combining professional focus-group discussion with a literature search to ensure both breadth and depth to the observed classroom practices.

This resulted in a provisional list of more than 40 pedagogical strategies, many with similar features. This initial analytical framework was interrogated through further focus group discussion, which referred back to the literature review. This helped to identify overlapping and duplicated strategies and resulted in the collapsing of some areas.

The qualitative data were then systematically analysed and refined until a saturation point was reached. This was where no new strategies emerged. This process determined which examples confirmed or confounded the theoretical themes that were emerging and it resulted in 11 pedagogical areas with some qualifications or subheadings.

The analytical process followed many progressive stages of deduction and verification, thus making it grounded. It involved inductive processes and constant iteration between qualitative data, theory and empirical evidence. Table 2.12 records the final list of 11 effective pedagogical strategies. These are justified, developed and applied in later chapters.

Table 2.12: Key pedagogical strategies

Category	Pedagogical strategy
1. Organization	• Well-organized teaching time, no time wasted, good pace, good classroom routines, children are self-reliant • Teacher support for children's learning • Teacher provision of a safe, supportive environment
2. Classroom climate	• Positive classroom climate, teacher–pupil and pupil–pupil interactions/relationships • Teacher's in-depth knowledge of, enthusiasm for and confidence in teaching subject
3. Clear objectives, shared goals	• Clear, shared objectives with specific guidance on how to achieve them
4. Behaviour management	• Effective behaviour management
5. Collaborative learning	• Use of groups for a specific, collaborative purpose • Peer tutoring
6. Personalized learning	• Appropriate and considered differentiation • Scaffolding • Variety and richness of teaching resources
7. Dialogic teaching and learning	• Sustained shared thinking • Open-ended questions used to develop deeper understanding rather than for summative evaluation • Teaching and encouraging analytical thought • Children's talk/conversations encouraged and moderated
8. Assessment for learning	• Ongoing formative assessment for learning and as learning

Category	Pedagogical strategy
9. The plenary	• Use of the plenary
10. Making clear links	• Builds on prior pupil knowledge and looks forward to the next steps in the curriculum • Makes cross- and extracurricular links explicit • Practical teaching activities to teach testing and application of knowledge and problem-solving
11. Homework	• Some use of homework

Classroom organization and climate

Chapters 3–6 are more practical than the preceding two and follow a new shared structure. Each begins by summarizing differences in the three groups of schools (excellent, good and poor) in terms of the quantitative observational measures. After establishing some significant differences between the three, these chapters delve deeper into the researchers' field notes to provide detailed qualitative descriptions of why individual classrooms were rated higher or lower for any one measure. For example, statistical tests showed that the groups differed significantly in the degree to which they made 'productive use of instructional time' (see Table 2.4). To understand how schools differed regarding this quantitative measure, the researchers' field notes were explored because they provide concrete examples of rating a classroom higher or lower on the measure.

Chapters 3–6 draw on the rich qualitative observational data from researchers' field notes to explore the most important features of excellent teaching in effective primary schools across the 11 strategies (see Table 2.12). Taken together, they seek to increase practitioners' and policymakers' general understanding of what constitutes excellent teaching by describing in more detail the 11 pedagogical strategies identified at the end of Chapter 2. These have been grouped together and are presented across the four following chapters as described below.

Chapter 3 considers how Year 5 teachers in three distinct groups of excellent-, good- and poor-quality primary classrooms varied in their organization. It also summarizes the research findings in relation to 'classroom climate', 'child–teacher relationships', 'teacher support for children's learning' and 'teacher provision of a safe, supportive environment' (Siraj and Taggart, 2014).

Strategy 1: Organization

The classroom environment must be well organized if effective teaching is to take place. Teaching time needs to be well planned, and routines must be second nature so that children know what they have to do, how they should do it and what they should do if they need help.

Through the COS-5 and IEO research instruments, the EPPSE team gained a great deal of quantitative information about the classroom organization and lesson planning of the Year 5 classrooms they observed in detail.

The researchers used the COS-5 to measure the following:

- how well teacher resources were organized
- how suitable they were for the particular teaching activity
- how productively teaching time was used
- how clear the teachers were about what they expected the children to do in their activities
- how much class time was spent on transitions between activities and on classroom business
- the TCs' responsibility for managing their own time and materials.

IEO was used to measure the following characteristics of classroom routines:

- structure
- organization
- management
- pre-preparation
- lesson pace
- efficiency.

This revealed how well organized the teacher and classroom were, how well established the classroom routines were, and how well the children understood and met the teacher's expectations.

In their field notes, the researchers recorded teacher resources and detailed illustrations of overall classroom organization. These included classroom routines, how the teacher managed transitions and other classroom business, the pace of the lesson, and whether or not children were perceived to be self-reliant.

The team found that the excellent Group A (high academic effectiveness and good-quality pedagogy) schools and the good Group B (medium academic effectiveness and medium-quality pedagogy) schools had very similar ratings for many features, and they were often rated significantly higher than the poor Group C (low academic effectiveness and poor-quality pedagogy) schools. Table 3.1 shows that, although Group B's scores were consistently lower than those of Group A and higher than those of Group C, they were usually closer to those of Group A.

For all items, however, Group A schools were rated highest for organization and Group C schools were rated lowest. Many of these differences are statistically significant ($p < 0.05$).

Table 3.1: Classroom 'organization' and groups of schools

Characteristics of classrooms in schools with:	Group A	Group B	Group C
Productive use of instructional time	Very high	High	Medium
Teacher's resources well organized and fit for purpose	Excellent*	Very high	High
Children's self-reliance	High	Medium	Medium
Clear teacher expectations	Very high	Very high	High
Children spending time on transitions/management/business	Very low†	Very low†	Low†
Classroom routines	Very high†	High†	Medium
Children being responsible for time and resources	Medium	Medium	Low

Note: Unless otherwise stated, different quantitative scores indicate significant differences ($p < 0.05$) between groups.

* As the mean score for Year 5 classrooms in Group A was equal to the maximum score for this feature, and significantly higher than the mean score for Group B, the additional qualitative description of excellent was used for this one item.

† The difference between these groups was not significant.

Lessons and teaching resources in the Group A and B classrooms were generally well planned and managed, and both learning, and behavioural objectives and expectations, were shared by all members of the class. All Group A and B classrooms were rated highly for how well the teachers had established routines. The children knew what to do, how to do it and how to seek extra help when required. They had, and showed, greater agency.

The researchers' notes recorded a sense of smooth, quick transitions, with children moving purposefully from one activity to the next, little wasted time and self-reliant pupils. For example, their IEO field notes from lessons in two Group B schools state:

> *Transitions are routine for almost all children. The teacher packs a lot into the lesson. Everyone knows what is expected of them.* (School 26, Literacy IEO)

> *No time was wasted in moving from set literacy table places to the carpet at the start and the end of the lesson. The teacher was*

very well prepared with an [overhead projector image] of the poem and interactive board sentences and the worksheets. The teacher's expectations are very clear as to what to do and what time they have to complete the task. The teaching assistant role is with a group of 8 children – less able; this is clearly defined, and they (the teacher and the teaching assistant) have planned prior to lesson. Equipment all available. (School 28, Literacy IEO)

The phrase 'no time wasted' recurs throughout the field note observations of the Group A schools. It is clear that the children in these excellent classrooms were completely familiar with the classroom routines, and that these had been designed to minimize disruption and maximize teaching time. For example, the researchers noted:

A quick pace from the very beginning. No time lost whatsoever. (School 1, Literacy IEO)

Difficult to see how any more could have been squeezed in. (School 1, Numeracy IEO)

No sense of any time wasted. (School 1, COS-5)

Children immediately sat on carpet as arrived in room. Routine to brainstorm in pairs as class went smoothly. (School 2, Literacy IEO)

Little time wasted. Children settled quickly to the task and a high percentage were on task. (School 3, COS-5)

No time lost. Very quick start to literacy. Finally all cleared up quickly. They knew what to do and they did it. (School 4, Literacy IEO)

In these excellent schools, when children did occasionally stray off task, or there were signs of disorganization, the teachers quickly regained control so that the lesson could move forward.

Most of the teachers in the Group A schools excelled at the following:

- preparing and organizing suitable, high-quality teaching, and for their lessons, which were thoughtfully adapted to meet the individual needs of their pupils
- using every second of available teaching time effectively
- encouraging their children to be self-reliant and giving them responsibility for their own time and resources.

These three characteristics appear to be key markers of this group of teachers in effective primary schools. For example, the field notes from these class observations reported the following:

> *Routines very efficient; monitors for everything to help the teacher. No disruption.* (School 5, COS-5)

> *Well established routine.* (School 6, COS-5)

> *Children familiar with routines. They knew what to do when they returned from assembly.* (School 6, Numeracy IEO)

> *Couldn't have been smoother.* (School 7, Literacy IEO)

> *A well-oiled machine. Happy confident children moved easily from one activity to the next.* (School 7, Numeracy IEO)

> *No time lost ever. Great routines which all followed.* (School 8, Literacy IEO)

Although the researchers rated most Group C classes as medium or good on most items, they scored them significantly lower than Group A and B classes for the following:

- how well teachers organized their resources
- the fitness for purpose of their resources
- how productively teachers used instructional time
- the clarity of teachers' expectations, including classroom routines
- the children's independence and self-reliance.

For example, the researchers' notes from classes in Group C schools typically describe the following:

> *Time is not well managed. Lessons run over leaving no time for the next lesson.* (School 76, Numeracy IEO)

The team observed organizational difficulties in Group C classrooms right from the very beginning of lessons. Instead of a crisp, sharp start, they began slowly, without any sense of urgency or brisk pace. In one school, for example, the notes report that the teacher appeared to be resigned to a slow and disorganized start to the lesson and apparently did not see the need to change this:

> *Children take a long time to respond and are often late arriving for sets. Teacher does not seem to mind this.* (School 76, Numeracy IEO)

Even when good planning took place, and the teacher put a lot of effort into effective delivery, lessons in these Group C classrooms were often seen to be disorganized. For example, one teacher, despite good planning and a great deal of effort on his part, was unable to establish control of his class or set a good teaching pace. The researcher noted:

> *The teacher strives for control and to make himself heard. He can get involved with individuals and the SEN (Special Educational Needs) group, but then becomes completely detached. He shouts for control then ignores the behaviour for long periods. His presentations are very hurried as though 'This is what I said I'd do and I'm going to do it', but once he's done that, he doesn't really seem to care about the children's work. He doesn't monitor children's work in any depth nor is there feedback.* (School 79, Literacy IEO)

The researcher's notes go on to describe the teacher's losing battle and increasing despair, his desperation to maintain control and teach his pupils something, anything. However, the inevitable failure of his efforts was obvious from the start.

The notes from these Group C classrooms paint an overall picture of inadequately prepared resources, poor understanding of behavioural and learning expectations, general disorganization, and children who are not encouraged to function independently and become self-reliant.

Pupils in Group A schools were rated as significantly more self-reliant ($p < 0.05$) than those in Group B and C schools, with no significant differences between Group B and C schools. This suggests that the production of self-reliant children is another key marker of teaching in effective schools.

The finding that the three groups of schools did not differ significantly in the time spent on classroom business and management activities (for example, taking the register, lining children up for assembly) was something of a surprise. Although children in Group C schools did spend a little more time on management and classroom business activities, the time devoted to these administrative tasks across all groups was relatively small. It is possible that this similarity exists because IEO recorded events at the beginning of lessons, when all teachers spent roughly equal amounts of time on class business. If IEO had included an overall lesson measure, the recorded differences between the groups might have been closer to other research on effective teaching (Mortimore *et al.*, 1988).

Overall, the team found that children in Group A learnt in very well-organized classrooms. Their teachers were clear about what they needed to achieve in their lessons and how they should do it. They encouraged their pupils to be self-reliant, and responsible for managing their own time and resources.

In particular, the teachers in Group A schools gave a great deal of thought to the resources they used. They prepared them ahead of time, managed them well during lessons, and ensured that they were fit for purpose and tailored to their pupils' individual needs. They made productive use of instructional time by maintaining a good pace and ensuring that every second of the lesson counted. Their pupils always had the highest ratings for self-reliance.

In summary, the researchers rated virtually 100 per cent of Group A teachers' lessons as follows:

- well planned
- with all resources fit for purpose
- well organized before the start of the lesson.

They noted that there were very few instances of chaos in their classes, and almost all of the instructional time was carefully planned and well used.

Although the team found that teachers in Group B schools were close to the standards of those in Group A, the teachers fell short of excellence in the following three important areas:

- their resources were not so well organized and fit for purpose
- they made less productive use of instructional time
- they did not encourage children's self-reliance to the same extent.

By contrast, the researchers rated Group C teachers significantly lower than those in Groups A and B in the following six areas:

- organization of resources
- resources' fitness for purpose
- productivity of instructional time
- clarity of teachers' expectations
- classroom routines
- children's independence and self-reliance.

Overall, they found that the classroom organization in these poor schools was average or below average. In many areas the researchers gave these classes the lowest possible ratings, and they failed to award any Group C teacher the highest rating for any of them.

The lessons that the team observed in these poor schools were slow to start, the pace was not maintained and time was wasted during transitions. Pupils in the classes received the lowest ratings for self-reliance, and they had significantly less responsibility for managing their own time and resources: they often did not understand what they were supposed to do or how they should do it. The teachers used resources that were not well prepared, and there were often insufficient copies of handouts or computer resources failed to work properly.

Group C teachers changed their minds, sometimes mid-sentence, about what they wanted their children to do. Many provided activities whose sole purpose seemed to be filling time. Only a third managed time efficiently around teaching and learning. Although the levels of chaos in these lessons were not consistently high, some classes had very high ratings, and the overall ratings for chaos were significantly higher in Group C schools than in the other groups.

Strategy 2: Classroom climate

The COS-5 and IEO provided the researchers with a wealth of information about the classroom climate. This is a technical name for the overall atmosphere in the classroom that is characterized by the teacher–pupil and the pupil–pupil relationships. The researchers recorded the feeling of each classroom through their field notes from the lessons witnessed for the IEO ratings and from the positive classroom climate section of both research instruments. Taken together, these gave the team a clear insight into the relationships between teachers and pupils.

The COS-5 also provided further opportunities for researchers to record their observations of the classroom relationships and environment, through notes such as 'teacher behaviour: displays positive affect', 'children's social behaviour: positive affect towards teacher', 'positive affect: child–teacher', 'children well liked and respected by peers', 'over-control', 'teacher detachment' and 'teacher sensitivity'.

Following the data analyses, outlined briefly in Chapter 2 and in more detail in Chapter 7, the researchers identified four main elements of classroom climate taken from the two observation instruments, as follows:

- overall classroom climate
- child–teacher relationships
- teacher support
- safe, supportive environment.

These are described in more detail below.

Overall classroom climate

The overall picture regarding classroom climate was clear. Teachers in excellent schools had the highest rating for positive classroom climate, followed by good schools. Both groups had very low ratings for negative classroom climate. Poor schools were rated significantly lower for positive classroom climate, and significantly higher for negative classroom climate, than schools in Groups A and B (see Table 3.2). Indeed, the researchers rated excellent classrooms exceptionally highly for positive classroom climate: they found that the pupils were well liked and respected by their peers, that there were strong child–teacher relationships, and that the teachers showed sensitivity and provided a safe environment.

Table 3.2: Results for overall 'classroom climate'

Characteristics of classrooms in schools with:	Group A	Group B	Group C
Positive classroom climate	Very high	High	Medium
Negative classroom climate	Very low	Very low	Low

Note: Unless otherwise stated, differences in quantitative scores indicate significant differences (p < 0.05) between groups.

No classroom in the poor category received the highest possible score for positive classroom climate on either research instrument, while some received the lowest possible score. In contrast, no good or excellent classroom received the lowest score for positive classroom climate, and some received the highest score. In addition, on the IEO scale, all excellent schools scored at least the median (3 on a 1–5 scale), and the pupils in these classrooms worked in a positive classroom climate in all of the observed sessions.

The mean score for 'classroom climate' in poor schools was below the median on both scales (COS-5 = 4; IEO = 3). This indicates that a 'positive classroom climate' was often missing and that, in general, it only approached the median rating. In contrast, the mean scores in excellent and good schools were towards the top end of the scales.

The mean score in good schools was between the top two scores on each scale (COS-5: 6.25 on a 1–7 scale, IEO: 4.75 on a 1–5 scale). This suggests, again, that pupils in good classrooms were likely to experience a 'positive classroom climate'.

As expected, the reverse was true for scores for 'negative classroom climate' on the COS-5. The overall ratings were significantly higher for poor classrooms, and there was no significant difference between good and excellent schools. Although the mean rating for negative classroom climate in poor schools was just below the midpoint (3.21, median = 4), the mean scores for excellent and good schools were only just above the lowest possible score (1.30 for good schools, 1.14 for excellent schools = 1.14, minimum score = 1). This is a striking difference. Poor schools scored near the average rating, whereas there were almost no instances of any negative classroom climate in both good and excellent schools. This difference between some and none seems important.

In summary, the overall 'classroom climate' in poor schools was often rated as very low. Pupils in these classes were less likely to experience a positive climate and more likely to experience a negative one. Meanwhile, pupils in good schools were generally learning in a positive climate, and the fortunate few who attended excellent primary schools were by far the most likely to experience an unceasingly positive classroom climate.

Descriptions in the field notes from Group A schools include the following:

A strong feeling of respect for each other. A mature attitude.
(School 1, Literacy IEO)

Firm but friendly and supportive teaching approach with high expectations. Children feel very secure in terms of both learning and socially. (School 1, Numeracy IEO)

Very positive feeling. A quiet buzz of work. All respect each other.
(School 3, COS-5)

Child–teacher relationship

The quality of the relationship between teachers and pupils is plainly important. Mutual respect is a significant part of any classroom ethos and was evident in the observations of all Group A lessons. In these classrooms, children's opinions and feelings were valued, and they were expected to respect the opinions and feelings of everyone in the classroom. Instances of disciplinary problems were rare and, when they did occur, were sensitively handled by the teacher without belittling the child. In other words, the relational pedagogy of the teachers was exceptionally good.

Examples of this sort of high-quality teaching was represented in the field notes, as follows:

A feeling that children were enjoying their learning and confident. A feeling of respect between children and teacher. Very aware of children. A warm supportive attitude, which reflects a child-centred approach. No need to discipline. (School 1, COS-5)

The teacher is happy and jokey with the rest of the class. Lots of smiles are shared. Mentors different groups – praise-encouragement. Obvious affection seen. (School 2, COS-5)

The teacher established firm, friendly control and the children responded. They clearly enjoyed their learning and all were respectful. Lots of praise, encouragement for the children. (School 3, Numeracy IEO)

Demeanour of teacher: relaxed, does not raise her voice, lots of smiles, laughed with children. Very proud of children's achievements. (School 5, Literacy IEO)

Such mutual respect allows children to confidently share their writing with the class. Everyone listens intently as others read. Class teacher makes positive comments, but also some fair criticisms well received. (School 7, Literacy IEO)

The researchers measured the relationships between teachers and pupils in several ways. They recorded instances of positive or negative interactions in the first part of each COS-5 observation cycle and measured the overall relationship between the teacher and the TC in the second COS-5 cycle (see Table 3.3). This second measure allowed the researchers to add their own qualitative observations.

Table 3.3: Results for 'child–teacher relationships'

Characteristics of classrooms in schools where:	Group A	Group B	Group C
Teacher displays positive affect	Very low	Very low	Very low
Teacher displays negative affect	Very low	Very low	Very low*
TC displays positive affect	Very low	Very low	Very low
TC displays negative affect	Very low	Very low	Very low
Child–teacher relationships	High	Medium	Medium

Note: Unless otherwise stated, differences in quantitative scores indicate significant differences ($p < 0.05$) between groups.
*   Although all scores for teacher displays negative affect were very low, Group C teachers scored significantly higher on this item than those in Groups A and B.

Some of these ratings were very low because the team recorded very few displays of positive or negative interactions between teachers and children in the first part of each COS-5 cycle. It is significant, however, that there is a difference in the number of times teachers displayed negativity. Group C teachers, for example, were observed displaying negativity towards the TC more often than teachers in Groups A and B.

The minimum and maximum scores for each group provide compelling evidence. The team observed no display of negativity at any excellent school, a maximum of one negative display at each good school, but up to five at each poor school. This means that pupils in Group C schools were more likely to experience disapproval, reprimands or an expression of the teacher's dislike than their peers at good or excellent schools.

The COS-5's overall measure of child–teacher relationships showed that relationships between the TCs and their teachers were generally good in all schools, but that the relationship in excellent schools was at a quite different level.

The teachers in Group A schools seemed happy to be in their classrooms with their pupils, and genuinely to enjoy the time that they spent with them. One field note records as follows:

Happy and relaxed children. Children smile lots at the teacher. She has a lovely attitude and obvious fondness for the children. (School 2, Literacy IEO)

The researchers frequently commented on the affection that they observed Group A teachers showing their pupils, which implies that this is another key feature of teaching in effective schools. For example:

Good relationships seen, affectionate. Teacher praises the way they are all getting on with each other. Target child cooperates all tasks all session. (School 5, COS-5)

Relaxed, well prepared. Never raised voice. Lots of smiles and pats on back to children. (School 5, Numeracy IEO)

Genuine respect by children and teacher for all in the class. (School 6, COS-5)

Teacher support
To support their pupils effectively, teachers need to be fully involved with them and acutely sensitive to their needs. The observational instruments provided the researchers with three quantitative measures of teacher support (see Table 3.4). The COS-5 measured 'teacher detachment' and 'teacher sensitivity', plus the researchers could record qualitative evidence

to support their numerical judgement. IEO measured 'social support for student learning in literacy'. The field notes contain many descriptions of teacher support and some cases of its absence.

Table 3.4: Results for 'teacher support'

Characteristics of classrooms in schools with:	Group A	Group B	Group C
Teacher detachment	Very low	Very low	Low
Teacher sensitivity	Very high	High	Medium
Social support for student learning in literacy	High	High	Medium

Note: Unless otherwise stated, differences in quantitative scores indicate significant differences (p < 0.05) between groups.

The results present an overall picture of teacher support that is encouragingly good (low 'teacher detachment', high 'teacher sensitivity' and high levels of 'social support for student learning in literacy'). They demonstrate that most primary teachers are involved with their pupils and provide a high level of social support for their learning.

Again, however, the quality of teacher support varied between the three groups of schools. Teachers in poor schools were rated significantly higher than those in excellent and good schools for 'teacher detachment', and significantly lower in 'teacher sensitivity' and 'social support for student learning in literacy'. There were no significant differences between excellent and good schools for teacher detachment and social support for student learning in literacy.

However, teachers in excellent schools stood out by demonstrating significantly greater 'teacher sensitivity'. Although teachers in good schools were significantly more sensitive to the needs of their pupils than those in poor schools, teachers in excellent schools scored the highest. This demonstrates that excellent teachers consider relational pedagogy alongside intentional teaching.

Group A teachers knew their pupils exceptionally well, and they adapted their approach and activities to suit them. They provided considerable and consistent encouragement to the children, and this was demonstrated through their frequent use of appropriate praise. In this way, teachers communicated genuine respect for the children's achievements and encouraged them to continue to improve their work.

The field notes show that respect between teachers and children was a significant part of the ethos in Group A schools. These were classrooms where children's opinions and feelings were valued, and where they were expected to respect the opinions and feelings of everyone. Discipline problems were very rare and, when they did occur, they were handled sensitively by the teacher without belittling the child. For example, a researcher recorded the following:

> *Target child started lesson looking glum. Teacher sat next to him for part of observation to make sure he was on task and participating in the group work. Child very attentive during the time teacher with his group. Teacher questioned him about the work, smiled at him and used positive body language.* (School 8, COS-5)

The team's overall impression of Group A teachers' attitudes towards their children, and the level of support and concern they provided, was overwhelmingly positive. The teachers working in effective schools appeared to know their pupils well, to provide a safe, supportive and encouraging learning environment, and to communicate their concern and genuine affection for the children clearly.

Safe, supportive environment

Children learn best in an environment where they feel safe and supported, and where there is a culture of mutual respect. The COS-5 provides quantitative measures ('TC displays positive/negative affect towards peers', 'TC demonstrates positive affect', 'TC is sociable/cooperative with peers', 'children are well liked and respected by peers') and qualitative evidence that, along with the researcher's field records from IEO, gave the team clear insight into how safe and well supported children felt in their classrooms (see Table 3.5).

The children appeared to be equally happy in their classrooms, and with each other, regardless of their school's level of academic effectiveness or quality of pedagogy. The team found no significant differences between the three groups of schools on the COS-5 measure regarding the TC's attitude in general or towards his/her peers. Encouragingly, in all three groups, children showed many more positive than negative attitudes towards their peers.

However, the team found a difference in the level of sociability and cooperation between the TCs and their peers. Although not all differences were significant, TCs in excellent schools were significantly more sociable and cooperative than their peers in poor schools.

Table 3.5: Results for 'safe, supportive environment'

Characteristics of classrooms in schools where:	Group A	Group B	Group C
TC displays positive affect	High	High	Medium*
TC displays positive/neutral affect towards peers	Low	Low	Low
TC displays negative/aggressive affect towards peers	Very low	Very low	Very low
TC is sociable/cooperative with peers	Medium†	Medium	Medium†
Children are well liked and respected by peers	Very high	High	Medium

Note: Unless otherwise stated, differences in quantitative scores indicate significant differences (p < 0.05) between groups.
*   Although they fall into different qualitative categories, the differences between Group C and the other groups are not significant.
†   Although all three groups fall into the same qualitative category, classes in Group C are at the low end of this category and those in Group A are at the high end. The difference between these groups is significant (p < 0.05).

The teachers in excellent schools showed consistent respect, social support and concern for their pupils. This was shown through their relationships with the pupils and the pupils' relationships with each other, which seemed to be shaped by the classroom ethos and the teacher's example. The degree to which pupils felt safe – both physically secure and safe enough to take risks – is associated with their learning. If a child feels sufficiently safe to risk giving a wrong answer then they must feel well supported by their teacher.

The researchers rated children in excellent schools the most highly (p < 0.01) for being 'well liked and respected by peers', and children in good schools significantly higher than their counterparts in poor schools. In their qualitative descriptions, the researchers referred regularly to the safe and supportive feeling in excellent classrooms and how this seemed to facilitate the children's confidence and approach to their learning. For example, they noted the following:

> *The classroom seemed totally safe. The children were confident, comfortable and enjoying each other's company; also respectful towards the teacher who they obviously liked.* (School 3, Literacy IEO)

> *A very safe classroom, the children are secure and confident. Teacher maintains firm, friendly and supportive control. All respect each other – adults, children. The children are enjoying their learning.* (School 4, Literacy IEO)

> *This classroom is a safe place to take risks and make mistakes.* (School 7, COS-5)

In classes taught by these teachers, there appeared to be a genuine feeling of mutual trust, which helped the children to concentrate their energy on their learning and allowed them to take the risks that would further their understanding.

The researchers often rated the 'classroom climate' in Group C schools as unpleasant. They found that the teachers were more likely to display negativity (for example, disapproval, reprimands, expression of teacher's dislike) and the children were less sociable and less cooperative than in other schools. In contrast, Group A schools had happy, safe, industrious classrooms, with an overall climate that combined a strong work ethic, a positive and supportive approach, and respectful relationships. The comparison serves to reveal that teachers in Group C schools had poor relationships with their children.

Every classroom in the Group A schools was rated very highly for the respect, social support and concern that teachers showed their pupils, and this revealed an exceptionally positive and supportive, learning climate. The researchers commented frequently in their notes about these teachers' obvious affection for their pupils, the mutual respect between all members of their classroom community, and how this created a happy and productive learning environment. For example:

> *Good evidence of mutual support between children. Class teacher and teaching assistant are both encouraging and listen respectfully to children's suggestions.* (School 6, Literacy IEO)

> *Respect obvious. Children work well in groups, negotiate roles, share work and help others.* (School 8, Literacy IEO)

> *Lovely atmosphere. Obvious affection for children. Children laugh and smile.* (School 8, COS-5)

In summary, the research findings regarding 'classroom climate' are as follows:

- The classroom climate was much more positive in good and excellent schools.
- The teachers were more detached, and there was a greater level of over-control, in poor schools.
- The teacher sensitivity to pupils' individual needs and interests, and the children's respect for each other, was greater in good and excellent schools.
- The children in good and excellent schools were more engaged with their learning.

The team's research and analysis in this area underscores the idea that teachers working in effective primary schools excel at providing an extremely positive classroom climate, at sensitively responding to the needs of their pupils, and at creating an environment where children are well liked and respected by their peers.

Chapter 4

Clear objectives and behaviour management

Effective learning is facilitated by teachers and pupils who work together towards common, shared goals that are agreed and understood by all concerned. Children need to know what they are supposed to be learning, and how much they should aim to achieve in a defined period of time. They need to internalize these goals as their own.

Teachers need to ensure that their pupils understand the learning objectives, the key learning concepts and the ideas required to meet these targets. Teachers in effective schools check that every one of their pupils understands all the concepts and ideas presented in lessons. They intervene when this understanding is not clear or is incomplete, even when it means changing the lesson or activity part-way through.

Strategy 3: Clear objectives, shared goals

The COS-5 includes two quantitative measures of how well goals are shared and whether teachers ensure that they make their key concepts and ideas clear to their pupils. In addition, both the COS-5 and IEO provide quantitative insight into whether or not teachers share their learning objectives explicitly with their pupils, and how thoroughly they check pupils' understanding of key ideas.

Once again, the field notes provide further information about how clearly teachers communicated their lesson objectives and key learning concepts. The researchers noted when teachers wrote learning objectives on the board and whether or not they referred to them during the lesson. The team described the teachers' explanations and approaches to new ideas and concepts, how they handled any difficulties or misconceptions, and the children's reactions to these.

Analysis of the data again showed that the classrooms varied in practice and results. Teachers in Group A schools were rated most highly for sharing learning goals with their pupils. Group B teachers were rated significantly higher than Group C teachers, both for making the learning intentions of their lessons clear to pupils and for how thoroughly they explained their key learning concepts and ideas (see Table 4.1).

Table 4.1: Results for clear objectives and shared goals

Characteristics of classrooms in schools where:	Group A	Group B	Group C
Learning intentions of the lesson/ activity are clear to all children	Very good	Good*	Good*
Teacher ensures concepts and ideas are clear to all children	Very good	Very good	Good

Note: Unless otherwise stated, differences in quantitative scores indicate significant differences (p < 0.05) between groups.
* Year 5 teachers in Group B were rated significantly higher than those in Group C.

The team rated virtually all teachers in excellent and good schools extremely highly for ensuring that the lesson objectives and activity concepts and ideas were clear. The teachers usually achieved this by writing the lesson objective on the board and making sure that pupils understood what they were expected to achieve in each lesson. It was standard practice in these schools for lesson objectives to be on the board, for teachers to check that children understood the activity's main ideas, and for them to intervene when understanding was not clear or complete.

The team found that both teachers and pupils in excellent and good schools were clear about what should be happening in the classroom at all times and were committed to ensuring that the goals were achieved. In Group A schools, the teachers were particularly good at ensuring that every child grasped the objectives of the particular lesson or activity, and the pupils were always clear about what they were expected to achieve and how much time they had to do so.

The field notes capture this approach, as follows:

The teacher changed her lesson when she realised her pupils had not grasped one of the main principles needed to complete a symmetry activity. After introducing symmetry (the children had been working on this in Art as well as Maths), the children were asked to work in pairs and create patterns for each other to repeat. The patterns had to contain two lines of symmetry and a perpendicular line.

Despite a careful introduction to the task, and the teacher modelling how to approach it, the children were still not sure what to do (there was much confusion over how to draw a perpendicular line). When the teacher realised that the confusion

was widespread, she stopped the lesson, re-explained the task and then asked the children to have another go. (School 2, Numeracy IEO)

By contrast, teachers in poor schools did not make their objectives and learning concepts clear to their pupils. These teachers were slower to check and, when necessary, to correct their pupils' understanding of key concepts and ideas. Although the children in poor classrooms were aware of their lesson objectives, it was not obvious to the researchers whether they understood them or knew how to achieve them, and there was much less focus and drive to meet the goals of the classes.

In summary, the researchers found that most teachers, regardless of the academic effectiveness or pedagogical quality of their school, ensured that they sought to share the learning intentions of their lessons with their pupils, although those in poor schools were not rated as highly on this as teachers in good and excellent schools. They also determined that teachers in excellent and good schools were better at ensuring that their pupils understood the learning intentions, and the ideas and concepts presented in their lessons.

This suggests that another key characteristic of teaching in effective schools is that teachers always provided children with clear learning objectives and ensured that each pupil knew what they were expected to learn during each lesson and activity.

Strategy 4: Behaviour management

It is widely agreed that effective behaviour management in the classroom is crucial for successful teaching and learning. For pupils to make good progress, both teachers and children need to feel safe and to work in a peaceful environment that is conducive to learning.

The COS-5 provides a number of quantitative measures of behaviour management, such as how often the teacher has to discipline the TC, the child's level of disruptive behaviour, and the degree of over-control and chaos in the classroom. IEO contains a measure of the children's engagement with their learning, and the researchers' notes provided a rich vein of information about how behaviour is managed (see Table 4.2).

The results revealed clear differences between the three groups of schools. Children in Group A and Group B schools were less disruptive and rarely needed to be disciplined. When the teachers did need to correct behaviour, they used humour or a quiet reminder, as follows:

> *Teacher has to discipline him once. Does so in jokey manner by saying all he will remember is the colour of the carpet.* (School 2, COS-5)

> *In whole session, no disciplinary problems. Only one very minor disagreement by three boys, which was settled amicably.* (School 3, Literacy IEO)

Table 4.2: Results for 'teacher support'

Characteristics of classrooms in schools where:	Group A	Group B	Group C
Teacher disciplines	Very low	Very low	Very low*
Frequency of TC's disruptive behaviour	Very low	Very low	Very low
TC's overall level of disruptiveness	Low	Very Low	Low
Engagement	High	High	Medium
Over-control	Very low	Very low†	Low
Chaos	Very low	Very low	Very low‡

Note: Unless otherwise stated, differences in quantitative scores indicate significant differences (p < 0.05) between groups.

* Instances of the class teacher disciplining pupils were very rare. However, Group C teachers disciplined their pupils significantly more often than Group A or Group B teachers.

† The only significant difference regarding over-control was that Group C teachers were rated significantly higher than those in Group B.

‡ Group C classrooms were rated significantly higher for chaos than Group A or B classrooms.

Frequency of disciplining and levels of disruptive behaviour

Overall the researchers noted few instances of teachers disciplining pupils, and of pupils displaying disruptive behaviour. Less than 20 per cent of their COS-5 observations included instances of a teacher disciplining a pupil. Poor schools fared less well and their children were disciplined by their teacher significantly more frequently than those in good and excellent schools. The incidents of chaos were also more numerous in Group C classrooms.

However, the maximum scores were more revealing. While the team recorded no disruptive behaviour in any excellent school, they reported many in poor schools, with some incidents during the first half of the observation time (maximum = 5, maximum score possible = 10).

Interestingly, the scores for 'over-control' and the 'TC's overall level of disruptiveness' were significantly different only between Group C and

Group B schools. Both measures of disruptiveness rated children in poor schools as more disruptive than those in good schools.

The qualitative evidence clarifies the nature of the differences. Group A classrooms were consistently rated highly for their teachers' management of classroom behaviour. The researchers report friendly banter between teachers and children, but this took place within a well-established framework of acceptable behaviour. The banter may even account for the slightly higher level of disruptiveness recorded for this group. Examples from the field notes are as follows:

> *The whole class and all children are on task, but control is established by involving children in their learning. There was no sense of over-control.* (School 1, COS-5)

> *The teacher has a strong presence and maintains a high profile throughout. Feeling of teacher and children jointly seeking progress. Control by expectation, involvement in learning. Teacher is firm and friendly.* (School 1, Literacy IEO)

> *The teacher uses his name several times – compliments him on his eagerness to volunteer and participate. Praises for correct answers. He smiles back at her several times. Eye contact.* (School 2, COS-5)

Children in Group A classrooms were often encouraged to participate actively in their lessons through discussion, practical activities and even, in one case, a classroom debate. However, there was always a clear sense of the children knowing exactly how far to take things. Ratings for 'chaos' in Group A classrooms were consistently very low, suggesting that teachers were confident in their behaviour-management techniques and that children respected the rules.

The researchers commented as follows:

> *There was a true sense of friendly/firm control with a feeling of the teacher and children jointly seeking progress.* (School 4, COS-5)

> *Control is by expectation and involvement in learning. The teacher is firm and friendly.* (School 1, Literacy IEO)

> *The teacher maintains firm, friendly and supportive control.* (School 4, Literacy IEO)

> *Teacher experienced and in control. Talks at normal volume, children listen attentively. She allows lots of quiet on-task*

discussion in pairs and with whole class. Children on task, no disruptions observed. (School 5, Numeracy IEO)

The researchers observed teachers in good schools disciplining pupils on only ten occasions (and seven of these were in School 30). They saw only two incidents at a good school of a teacher disciplining a child more than once during the same observation. Most of the disciplinary incidents at good schools were observed in one mixed Year 5/6 class. The researcher noted:

The classroom climate is quite difficult. Although the teacher endeavours to maintain a positive ethos, the number of children who challenge her authority, ignore her and create restlessness (sometimes through challenging each other) is large. I note that the majority of the disengaged children are Year 6. (School 30, Literacy IEO)

These difficulties appeared to relate mostly to the Year 6 pupils. The researcher wondered whether the older children resented being taught with the younger ones. Apart from this one school, discipline was not a real concern in good schools.

Classes in Group C schools accounted for about three-quarters of the total observed disciplinary incidences. While the teachers involved generally disciplined only once or twice during a single observation, there were two observations in School 79 when the teacher spent half of the time disciplining pupils. At another school in this group, the team saw the teacher disciplining pupils in more than half of the observations. In this school, the teacher usually had to discipline pupils more than once during each observation.

Although levels of indiscipline were generally low in the majority of poor schools, the children were more disruptive and the teachers disciplined them more frequently. Pupils shouting inappropriately was a distinctive feature of poor classrooms, and the discipline was often public and sometimes involved threats, personal attacks, shaming or belittling children. The degree of chaos and teacher over-control (rigid approaches designed to meet the teacher's rather than the children's needs) was also significantly higher in poor schools.

Behaviour-management strategies
The three groups not only varied in their frequency of disciplining but also differed in the way they handled discipline. Group A and Group B schools managed behaviour mainly by keeping pupils focused on their work, and

the children were significantly more engaged in their learning than those in Group C schools.

When teachers in excellent and good schools disciplined a pupil, it was usually handled sensitively and sometimes with humour. For example, the researchers' noted as follows:

Only one child disciplined gently by the teacher. (School 8, COS-5)

Teacher is very relaxed and organised. No discipline problems. All on task and enthusiastic about all of the lesson. (School 8, Literacy IEO)

This firm but relaxed approach is shown by the following:

Teacher manages 'over-the-top' responses to reproduction firmly and effectively. (School 27, COS-5)

Indeed, when an incident occurred during a literacy lesson in School 27 between a child with autism and another child, the teacher quietly took them both aside to sort out the difficulty. Rather than allowing the situation to get out of control, the teacher maintained calm and order without adding to the chaos or belittling the children.

Many teachers in excellent and good schools used the strategy of questioning children who were not listening or were misbehaving (for example, flicking or chatting). In one numeracy lesson in School 31, a boy at the back of the class started throwing something in the air. Instead of addressing this directly and drawing attention to the child's poor behaviour, the teacher asked the pupil to answer part of a maths question that the class was working on, then waited until he was able to provide the correct answer. The teacher's waiting was presumably intended to ensure that the pupil stayed on task, and it was an effective way of quickly and quietly helping the boy to stop misbehaving and get back on track.

Discipline was handled very differently in poor schools. The teachers often appeared to be fighting for control, sometimes using shouting, anger and humiliation to deal with inappropriate behaviour. For example:

Teacher strives for control and to make himself heard. Shouts, lengthy lectures, public castigation. (School 79, Numeracy IEO)

The researcher noted that this particular teacher seemed almost afraid of losing complete control of his class, and hurried through his lesson so quickly that, at times, the children (and the researcher) could not understand him.

Threats, even for the wrong answer, were a large part of this teacher's discipline-management strategy. At one point he threatened a boy with putting his name on the board if he shouted an answer that the teacher did not want. Shouting was a big problem in this class, and, when one child complained about another who had been shouting answers, the teacher replied that he was 'not interested, and not in the mood for you'.

The situation in this classroom became so difficult that the researcher felt obliged to help some children who were struggling. At the end of the lesson, both teacher and children were out of breath and exhausted from their struggle. Once the children had left the room, the teacher confided in the researcher:

> These children don't change. The trouble is, only about four of them have been through school together; the rest have joined at different times. Each one is like a spinning top, fine on their own, but together they just bounce off each other. These children have no respect.

The researcher felt that this teacher's sense of futility was palpable.

In one class in School 82, the researcher observed the teacher using personal attacks to discipline her pupils. Her response to a restless child was to say: 'Right, I'm getting sick of you. Really, really sick. You haven't stopped talking since you came in the class.' She sent another child out of a numeracy lesson just for being restless. Reponses to discipline issues in this poor classroom were public, and the punishments were extreme for the level of misdemeanour. Indeed, the levels of 'over-control' and 'chaos' were significantly higher in poor schools than in the other two groups.

The overriding image of these Group C schools that emerges from both the data and researchers' notes is of chaotic classrooms where teachers try to overcompensate for poor behaviour and disorganization by applying too much control. The contrast with excellent schools is stark, with the filed notes describing calm, orderly and productive classrooms, as follows:

> *Calm, quiet and firm discipline – mainly by expectation.* (School 3, COS-5)

> *No chaos/poor discipline etc. Occasional quiet reminder of rules. All well organised.* (School 4, COS-5)

> *You can hear a pin drop in this class as children work out factors of 42 – and such a buzz of enthusiasm.* (School 7, COS-5)

In summary, the team found the following:

- Although instances of teachers disciplining children were rare, teachers in poor schools disciplined students much more frequently than those in the other groups.
- The TCs they observed in poor schools had higher levels of general disruptive behaviour than those in the other two groups.
- The level of chaos, although still low, was much higher in poor schools than in the other groups.
- The classrooms in excellent and good schools were indistinguishable in terms of behaviour management. The differences between them were not statistically significant.

Taken together, these findings reveal yet another key marker of teachers in effective schools: they manage behaviour by setting high expectations, by involving children in their own learning, and by handling any discipline issues both privately and sensitively. They respect children and avoid humiliating them in public.

Chapter 5

A mixture of learning approaches

For primary-school teaching to be truly effective in supporting good child outcomes, it needs to involve a rich mixture of practices and approaches. Teachers in effective schools had high-quality interactions and conversations with their pupils regardless of the type of settings and provided them with feedback to improve their learning. These teachers also engaged children in learning dialogues that helped them to rehearse their lessons, to follow arguments, to improve their reasoning and to reach their own conclusions. In doing this, teachers in effective schools used a variety of learning resources, which they selected and prepared with great care and then personalizes for their pupils. In this chapter the findings for collaborative and personalized teaching as well as for dialogic teaching and feedback for learning are discussed.

Strategy 5: Collaborative learning

As described in earlier chapters, the researchers studied the EPPSEM children working in three main types of setting: individual, group and whole class. In recent years, the precise impact of group work on children's learning has been the focus of much discussion. Group work implies much more than sitting children near to each other and asking them to work together. Real group work requires them to work collaboratively, and this includes sharing roles, ideas and information. Each child usually has a specific job in a group, and the aim is for all children in a group to achieve their personal learning objectives by working together and helping each other.

Working collaboratively, either as part of a group working with a shared remit or as part of a peer-tutoring scheme, provides children with excellent learning opportunities. In these settings there is a greater likelihood of children developing deep, long-lasting understanding because they have to consult each other, share knowledge and understanding, and analyse and improve each other's ideas. In these types of setting, children had opportunities to teach each other.

Time spent working in groups

Through the COS-5 and IEO, the team gathered a great deal of information about how often children worked in groups, but with less detail about the specific purpose of their group work. The COS-5 requires researchers to record the time that the TC spends working individually, in groups and in a whole-class setting, as well the time spent on collaborative work (see Tables 5.1 and 5.2). Because the COS-5 focuses on the start of lessons, and group work commonly takes place later in lessons in UK schools, the reported incidence of collaborative group work is lower than if a whole lesson were measured.

The COS-5 results show that group work and collaborative learning were relatively rare (all means were less than 1; maximum score = 10), with no statistically significant differences between the three groups of schools. Interestingly, although the difference between the groups is not significant, the means shows a distinct pattern: both excellent schools and poor schools had slightly higher instances of group work than good schools. In fact, group work was recorded by the COS-5 in only three good schools.

Table 5.1: Results for collaborative learning: time TC spent working in a group

Characteristics of Year 5 classrooms in schools where:	Group A	Group B	Group C
TC works in a group	Very low	Very low	Very low
TC is involved in collaborative work	Very low	Very low	Very low

Note: Unless otherwise stated, differences in quantitative scores indicate significant differences (p < 0.05) between groups.

The team noted more instances of collaborative learning on the IEO scale, which records the events in an entire lesson, and observed group work in about half of the lessons. IEO requires researchers to note whether any collaborative group work occurs but does not require them to record how much time is spent working in this way. Further information depends on the researchers including observations in the comments sections or in their field notes. This means that there may have been some collaborative group work that is not evident in the data.

Table 5.2: Results for collaborative learning: frequency of group work observed

	Academic effectiveness and quality of pedagogy	No	Yes	Total*
IEO: group work seen (no or yes)	Group A: excellent	8	6	14
	Group B: good	9	7	16
	Group C: poor	9	7	16

* Two observations per school. Totals are smaller than twice the total number of schools in each group because this measure was made only during the second year of observations.

Although the use of group work was inconsistent, and relatively infrequent compared with whole-class and individual work, the researchers' field notes recorded more details of collaborative group work in excellent schools. This collaborative work often took place spontaneously during whole-class activities.

The field notes typically describe collaborative group work in excellent schools in these positive terms:

> *Child worked closely with peers, discussing work and approach to the problem.* (School 1, COS-5)

> *Children were working collaboratively. The classroom was a buzz of activity.* (School 1, COS-5)

> *Children made excellent progress in using and applying their knowledge of place value in this whole class activity. Good teaching – and opportunities to learn from contributions of others.* (School 7, COS-5)

Children were generally put into one of three groups:

- for a specific, collaborative purpose (for example, to complete a project or provide constructive feedback for each other)
- for ability-setting: differentiation
- to facilitate peer-tutoring.

These are described in more detail below.

Groups for a specific, collaborative purpose

When children in excellent schools spent time working collaboratively, they were often asked to act as a sounding board for each other, or to comment on each other's work. There were also times when they worked in groups to solve a problem.

For example, during an observed numeracy lesson in School 3, the teacher gave the pupils the imaginary task of ordering desks for everyone at the school. The children had to work together in groups to share their understanding of measurement, develop their skills in measuring, agree a common understanding of 'middle number' and plan the work.

The lesson began with sharing the objectives of the task. This was followed by group work to solve the problem. The exercise concluded with the groups sharing their findings with the entire class. The result was a lesson filled with questioning and discussion among the children in each group. The researcher saw a class of busy, communicative children working together to solve a complicated problem that required every child's effort and skill.

Groups for ability-setting: Differentiation

Teachers in Group A schools did not generally group their children by ability in literacy. None of them grouped their pupils at a whole-class level (for example, one class for higher ability, a second for middle ability and a third for lower ability). Some schools were too small for this. School 1, for example, consisted of only four classes, but even the larger Group A schools, which grouped children by ability for maths, did not all do this for literacy.

In classrooms, only a few Group A schools grouped pupils by ability for literacy, and those that did only seated children of similar ability next to each other. By contrast, about half of the Group A schools grouped pupils by ability for numeracy. One school did this at the whole-class level and the others by ability in the classroom.

Teachers in Group A schools used differentiation more frequently than their counterparts in the other groups. They often used differentiated groupings to provide further teaching or extra support for a particular group of pupils. In one observation, for example, a teacher in School 8 was explaining subtraction sums to the whole class. Once the rest of the class began working on the differentiated worksheets that she had provided, the teacher sat with the lowest-ability group to provide extra teaching and support.

Groups to facilitate peer-tutoring

Although peer-tutoring was not specifically recorded by the COS-5, there was some information about it in the IEO. Two sections of the numeracy IEO ('maths discourse and communication' and 'locus of maths authority') provided information about whether or not peer-tutoring took place. The 'instructional conversations' section of the literacy IEO also provided data. Once again, the field notes were a rich source of information about classroom practices, as follows:

> *Talking, working with peers. At times the child takes the lead in discussion.* (School 1, COS-5)

> *Clear evidence of good positive relationship with peers, with 'response' partner, and others on the table.* (School 1, COS-5)

> *Children worked with response partners.* (School 1, COS-5)

> *Cooperates well in group reading – takes turns in group, no arguments. Listens well to peers read.* (School 2, COS-5)

> *Children are encouraged to discuss with their partner during the mental introduction to the lesson to decide on the two-step process needed to multiply by 20.* (School 2, Numeracy IEO)

It is clear from the researchers' reports that children in excellent schools were used to helping each other, and that they often had response partners with whom they worked regularly. For example, in a School 1 literacy lesson, the teacher checked to make sure each child's response partner was present before setting a task for pairs to tackle. The teacher asked the pupils: 'You're going to work with response partners. Anyone have a problem because their response partner is not here?' The children were obviously used to working in this way because they set straight to work without any chaos or confusion about what they needed to do.

Overall, the team reported the following:

- Instances of genuinely collaborative learning (not merely sitting next to one another) were rare in all three groups of schools, and, because the number of observations was small, they found no significant differences.
- Although the differences were not significant, collaborative learning was referred to more frequently in the researcher's field notes in excellent schools.
- Group work was used most often for collaborative learning, differentiation and peer-tutoring.
- The children appeared to enjoy and benefit from the experience of collaborative learning.

These field researchers' notes suggest that teachers in effective schools provided better evidence of group work that requires genuine collaboration. The teachers encouraged pupils to work as response partners in peer-tutoring situations, and they used group work to allow them to devote more time to a particular group of children.

Strategy 6: Personalized learning

Teachers in effective schools adapt every aspect of their classroom practice to the specific needs of the individuals within their classroom. They recognize their pupils' particular personal needs by developing a good understanding of all the children in their class. They then design or select, develop and deliver learning materials that are suitable for their children's range of identified needs. They scaffold and differentiate the work they set for them and the outcomes that they expect from them (West and Muijs, 2009).

The researchers investigated this feature of pedagogy through the COS-5, which refers specifically to personalized teaching and learning (see Table 5.3), and rates teachers for the following:

- 'sensitivity' and 'detachment'
- 'richness of instructional materials'
- 'social support for student learning' differentiation.

These are discussed in more detail below.

The researchers' qualitative comments about the COS-5 and IEO, together with their field notes, provided more detailed descriptions of the teachers' attempts to personalize their pupils' learning.

Table 5.3: Results for personalized learning

Characteristics of classrooms in schools with:	Group A	Group B	Group C
Teacher detachment	Very low	Very low	Low
Teacher sensitivity	Very high	High	Medium
Richness of instructional materials	High	Medium	Low
Social support for student learning in literacy: differentiation	High	High	Medium

Note: Unless otherwise stated, differences in quantitative scores indicate significant differences (p < 0.05) between groups.

The analyses showed that the three groups of classrooms were divided again into two, with the poor schools rated significantly worse on all elements of personalized learning. Excellent and good schools were rated similarly, but with excellent schools rated significantly higher on several items.

Teachers in poor schools were rated as low or medium on all items. They showed greater detachment and less sensitivity to their pupils' needs. Their teaching materials were also not as varied or well adapted to their pupils' specific needs.

By contrast, teachers in Group A schools were much more attuned to their pupils. They were involved with their learning and acutely sensitive to their needs. In particular, they were exceptionally good at producing and providing learning materials that were adapted to the interests and abilities of their pupils.

Teacher sensitivity and detachment

Effective, accurately personalized learning is rooted in teachers' sensitivity to individual pupil needs and their deep involvement in their children's learning. Group A schools scored significantly higher for 'teacher sensitivity' than those in good and poor schools, and lower for 'teacher detachment'.

The researchers' observations underlined how well the teachers in excellent schools knew their students and how involved they were with their learning. Again and again, they noted that the teachers seemed to know every child as an individual, and they adapted their approaches and expectations accordingly. For example, the field notes reported as follows:

> *Teacher encourages all to contribute ideas throughout. Children listen well to each other. Teacher uses children's names to get them to contribute.* (School 2, Literacy IEO)

> *Teacher says to all about boy at front, 'Very good boy spending his time reading whilst he's waiting.' This is one of very shy boys, less confident. She boosts his confidence here.* (School 5, Literacy IEO)

Poor schools were generally rated around the median for 'teacher detachment' (although two schools received very low scores) and below the midpoint for 'teacher sensitivity'. This indicates that the teachers generally maintained a physical and emotional distance between themselves and their pupils, and that they were either unaware of or did not react to the children's different personal needs.

Richness of instructional materials

The three groups of schools differed considerably for this measure. Teachers in excellent schools used better resources than those in good schools, and both of these sets of teachers used significantly better resources than their counterparts in poor schools. The research did not have information about levels of resourcing across schools, so no inferences can be made about whether excellent schools had more money to spend on resources or spent money more wisely.

The teaching resources in excellent schools were often extremely flexible and adaptable. For example, a maths game in School 7 involved children calling out times-table questions to each other to help them to learn to recall their tables quickly. Because of the way in which the game was designed, the caller had to know the answer before asking the question, so the level of question varied according to the complete ability range of the children in the class.

Without exception, poor schools received ratings below the median on the variety and richness of the teaching resources used during lessons. The team reported frequently that worksheets (not necessarily a poor resource) appeared to be used as a time-filling activity rather than as a learning experience.

Social support for student learning: Differentiation

Teachers in Group A schools scored higher for 'social support for student learning' than those in Group C. Schools and teachers can differentiate between pupils by using differentiated tasks and/or by ability-setting. The team found that the more academically effective the school, the more likely its teachers were to use carefully differentiated learning materials. For example, in School 8, the teacher wanted her pupils to develop a deep understanding of a poem that she had read with them. She began by asking them to visualize and draw a character from the poem, a task that all of the children could complete together.

Then she asked the children to choose between two tasks with different difficulty levels. They could write either a continuation of the poem that kept to the original poem's style, or (for those who needed an easier task) a letter to the postman asking for his help (pretending that they were locked in a house and needed to escape).

One researcher noted that several lower-ability children chose to attempt the more difficult task, even when the easier task was suggested.

Social support for student learning: Scaffolding

The COS-5 and IEO provide no direct measures of scaffolding, but the team's analysis suggests that scaffolding was far more likely to take place in excellent and good schools.

For example, children in School 32 were learning how to write persuasive letters to support a cause. The teacher provided both a checklist of qualities that the children should look for in their own writing and a framework that showed them how their letters should be set out. This level of scaffolding may have been unnecessary for the more able children, but, by providing such supportive resources, the teacher was able to ensure that all children, whatever their ability, could attempt the task.

In summary, the team found that Group A and Group B schools met their children's needs through their teachers' friendly approach, high expectations, and appropriately challenging and differentiated tasks. They also found that excellent schools were outstanding at providing a rich variety of teaching and learning resources, and were particularly tuned to their pupils' personal needs.

The teachers in Group A and Group B schools were also more likely to personalize their pupils' learning experiences, and they did this by being sensitive to individual needs and providing richly varied learning materials. They were rated low on 'teacher detachment' (for example, noticing children's behaviour and needs, and distancing themselves from their pupils by staying at their desks), and scored particularly highly for providing 'social support for student learning' in literacy. This is frequently captured by the field notes. For example:

> Sure of her understanding of the children, their levels and needs. Also in her ability to extend appropriately. (School 1, Literacy IEO)

> Clearly knows children well. Gives sensitive support and realistic feedback as she moves round the room. (School 6, COS-5)

> Teacher is very aware of children's strengths and weaknesses and gives appropriate support and asks questions to suit those she chooses to answer, often naming them rather than choosing volunteers. (School 7, COS-5)

> Knows children well. Directs some questions – and frames some for particular children. (School 7, COS-5)

By contrast, the researchers found that teachers in Group C schools provided teaching and learning resources that were less varied, less engaging and less likely to be appropriately differentiated. These teachers were less sensitive to their pupils' individual needs and more detached from their learning experiences.

Overall, the EPPSE team found that the quality and variety of teaching resources was better in excellent and good schools than in poor schools. Teachers in Group A and Group B schools were more involved with, and aware of, their pupils' individual needs, and they offered them more social support with their learning.

Strategy 7: Dialogic teaching and learning

Dialogic learning refers to those situations where teachers and pupils participate together in an enriching interactive discourse, or dialogue, about the learning in order to extend pupil thinking and understanding. This means more than teachers simply imparting knowledge because it is a questioning and challenging two-way discussion in which both teachers and pupils have a stake.

The best dialogic teaching includes higher-order thinking skills that challenge the learner, so this practice can work both ways. Its objective may be to increase the pupils' understanding, but it is often the teacher who learns through this approach.

Compared with other pedagogical strategies, the team observed few examples of dialogic teaching. Possibly because of this, they found few differences between the three groups of schools. The exception was in numeracy, where teachers in excellent and good schools were rated significantly higher for dialogic teaching (for their use of analysis in maths, and in the depth of their pupils' knowledge and understanding). In literacy, they were rated higher for 'instructional conversations'.

The COS-5 provided insights into the extent of dialogic teaching. The first part of the observation, in both the language and numeracy sections, divides teaching into analysis and meaning-making activities (where dialogic teaching is likely to take place), and basic skills activities (where it is less likely to occur). The team recorded the time the teacher and child spent on these two elements, and this indicated the proportion of time when dialogic teaching might have been used.

The second part of the observation gives further insight into the use of dialogic teaching. Alongside awarding numerical ratings for a number of factors, the researchers recorded their qualitative observations about the learning and teaching, including the 'richness of instructional methods', 'classroom climate', 'productive use of instructional time', 'evaluative feedback' and 'teacher sensitivity'. All of these provided evidence for dialogic learning and teaching.

The IEO instrument also illuminates the teachers' use of dialogic learning and teaching. Researchers recorded their numerical ratings and qualitative observations of 'use of maths analysis', 'depth of student knowledge and understanding' and 'maths discourse and communication'. They did likewise for 'reading as meaning-making', 'higher-order thinking in writing', 'purposeful development of writing skills' and 'instructional conversations'. These are all areas where dialogic learning and teaching commonly take place.

However, the data showed that very little time was spent on teaching and learning analysis, inference or planning (the scores were all low or very low), and that there was only one significant difference between the groups (see Table 5.4). Children in Group A schools spent much more time performing analysis and using inference skills than those in Group B schools.

Table 5.4: Results for dialogic teaching and learning: comprehension and analysis activities overall

Characteristics of classrooms in schools where:	Group A	Group B	Group C
TC is learning/performing analysis or inference	Low*	Low*	Low
Teacher is teaching analysis, inference or planning	Low	Low	Very low†

Note: Unless otherwise stated, differences in quantitative scores indicate significant differences (p < 0.05) between groups.
* Difference is significant (p < 0.05).
† Differences are not significant.

The team found few differences between the three groups' results for literacy and numeracy. There were no significant differences for any literacy measure ('comprehension', 'reading as meaning-making' and 'higher-order thinking in writing'). However, in numeracy, children in Group C schools spent significantly less time than their counterparts in other schools on 'use of maths analysis', 'depth of student knowledge and understanding' and 'locus of maths authority'. This suggests that the way in which maths is taught is particularly important.

The team also found some important differences in patterns of communication. Children in Group A schools spent significantly more time in 'instructional conversations' than their peers. In addition, these children, as well as those in good schools, spent more time on 'maths discourse and communication' (see Table 5.5). Not surprisingly, communication, and the specific type of communication, is critically important for effective dialogic teaching and learning.

Table 5.5: Results for dialogic teaching and learning: communication

Characteristics of classrooms in schools with:	Group A	Group B	Group C
Instructional conversations in literacy	Very high	High*	Medium*
Maths discourse and communication	High	High	Low

Note: Unless otherwise stated, differences in quantitative scores indicate significant differences ($p < 0.05$) between groups.
* Difference is not significant.

Concept development, and problem-solving and analysis, are important parts of dialogic learning, and the team observed them in more than half of the lessons. While some of these instances were brief, about three-quarters involved sustained episodes of dialogic teaching. This indicated that although dialogic teaching was far from the principal pedagogical strategy, it was used consistently and to good effect.

One field note, for example, describes a teacher in School 5 preparing pupils to work on some money problems as a real-life application of maths. She told the children not to worry about their answers, explaining that she was more concerned about their identifying the operations (and, by implication, the strategies required to solve the problems) than calculating the answers.

At one point in the lesson, she asked the children to write down the operations required to solve a problem and told them that they were not allowed to write down the answer. Some children found this hard, and the teacher reassured one by saying: 'You look quite hesitant. Don't worry about the answers; you are very good at maths. Write down the operations only.'

This teacher went beyond offering her pupils the opportunity to focus on strategies rather than answers by insisting that they did not work out the answers. She encouraged them to discuss their solutions with each other, and there was a great deal of sharing of ideas and strategies between the children.

A teacher in School 8 was rated very highly on concept development and problem-solving, which implies good dialogic learning and teaching. In one lesson, the researcher noted that the children were not stifled but felt free to ask questions, request feedback, and discuss their work with each other and the teacher. Although the children were tackling basic maths skills (number bonds to 100), the teacher encouraged them to work in small groups and discuss their strategies with each other. A researcher wrote that the teacher encouraged two boys with SENs to participate in the whole-class activity, and used questioning and humour to keep the entire class engaged in the lesson.

The researcher noted that the same teacher also spent a great deal of time during numeracy and literacy observations asking her children questions. During a numeracy data-handling lesson, she frequently asked them to explain concepts: 'What is the mode? Explain what the data mean. How will we deal with all the data?'. She then used their answers to clarify the data's meaning. During a literacy poetry lesson, she paused often to ask them about inferences that could be drawn from the poem, and whether they could justify their interpretation of a character from what was written.

The observational data showed that children attending poor schools spent less time learning and carrying out analysis than their peers in excellent and good schools. Teachers in poor schools were less likely to do the following:

- encourage discussion, analysis and depth of understanding of mathematical concepts
- share the responsibility for learning with the children
- support and promote discussion for a deeper understanding in literacy.

By contrast, children in excellent schools spent significantly more time on the following than children in good and poor schools:

- learning
- performing analysis
- using inference skills.

They were also significantly more engaged in instructional conversations.

The findings demonstrated a clear distinction between approaches to maths in poor schools and in excellent and good schools. Teachers in excellent schools encouraged discussion, analysis and a deep understanding of mathematical concepts, and they shared the responsibility for learning with the children. Additionally, in literacy, they supported and promoted discussion to promote a deeper understanding, whereas this approach was rarely used by teachers in poor schools.

Strategy 8: Assessment for learning

Assessment or feedback for learning helps pupils to understand how well they are performing and gives them detailed guidance on how to improve. Teachers in effective schools do this by providing feedback to the entire class (for example, as part of the plenary), to groups of children and to individuals. This type of assessment can be delivered immediately, during an activity, by the teacher or the child's peers, or after the activity, perhaps as part of marking the child's work. It is often called formative assessment as opposed to summative assessment, which can often be just a score on a test (see Black and Wiliam, 1998a,b).

The COS-5 provides two indicators of assessment for learning: a numerical rating of 'evaluative feedback' and a researcher's qualitative rating according to whether children could reflect on their learning through review (see Table 5.6). It should be noted that the term 'evaluative' in the COS-5 relates to formative feedback because it is commonly understood in the more recent literature. Researchers also recorded when a plenary took place. This is the obvious point in the lesson for teachers to feedback to pupils, and for children to feedback to each other about their work.

By contrast, IEO offers more opportunities to note and comment on teacher feedback in 'maths discourse and communication', 'locus of maths authority' and 'instructional conversations'. These are areas where assessment, questioning and feedback from teachers and/or peers take place naturally.

Table 5.6: Results for assessment for learning

Characteristics of classrooms in schools with:	Group A	Group B	Group C
Evaluative (formative) feedback	Medium	Medium	Low
Children reflecting on learning through review	Medium*	Low*	Medium*

Note: Unless otherwise stated, differences in quantitative scores indicate significant differences (p < 0.05) between groups.

* Because the scale was so small (1–3), it was difficult to reflect significant differences in the qualitative terms as they related to the means. Group C was not significantly different from Group B but was rated significantly lower than Group A.

Predictably, the researchers found that teachers in the academically highly effective schools with good-quality pedagogy (Group A) and those in medium-academic-effectiveness schools with medium-quality pedagogy (Group B) provided more evaluative feedback than those in the low-academic-effectiveness schools with poor-quality pedagogy (Group C), and they offered more opportunities for the children in their classes to reflect on their learning. In addition, teachers in Group A schools provided greater opportunities for their pupils to reflect on their learning through review than teachers in Groups B or C, who did not differ in this area.

The researchers noted that, in excellent schools, assessment for learning involved feedback at both the individual and the class level. Here they saw both depth and breadth to the feedback. The teachers often encouraged children to evaluate their own handwriting, used children's answers to model correct answers and gave individual feedback as they moved round the classroom.

The key findings regarding assessment for learning are that good and excellent schools provided much more evaluative feedback to their pupils than teachers in the poor schools.

Taken together, these findings provide several more distinguishing features of teachers in effective primary schools. They teach in a mixture of settings; they provide a good variety of high-quality learning resources; they understand and respond sensitively to their children's needs; they give pupils opportunities to learn and practise analysis; they encourage discussion, analysis and a depth of understanding in maths; they share the locus of maths authority with their pupils; they support and promote discussion to promote a deeper understanding in literacy; they ensure that assessment for learning is part of every lesson; and they create opportunities for their children to reflect on their own learning.

Chapter 6
Plenaries, making clear links and findings on homework

This chapter reports on a bundle of pedagogical strategies that, while seen less frequently during the observations, were nevertheless evident across the range of excellent, good and poor schools.

Strategy 9: The plenary

Chapter 1 reported that the national strategies in England stressed that plenaries should be an integral part of primary-school lessons. The plenary is the technical term for the time, usually at the end of the lesson, when teachers gather pupils together to review that lesson and consolidate their learning. It is an opportunity to explore how far their objectives have been achieved and to identify the next stage of learning to be addressed. This pedagogical approach is consistent with contemporary good practice.

Although the research team observed plenaries in only 56 per cent of primary schools, their quantitative analysis revealed that the quality of teaching was significantly higher in schools where the teacher used a plenary in both literacy and maths, and lowest where no plenary was observed in either subject (see Chapter 7). Undoubtedly this was linked to the fact that teachers in Group A and B schools included plenaries in their lessons almost twice as often as those in Group C schools.

IEO provided detailed information about the length, content, focus and depth of plenary sessions, and it showed that there was considerable variation in all of these dimensions. The sessions ranged from a few minutes, when the teacher merely checked basic understanding, to a deeper exploration of issues raised during the lesson.

In addition, the researchers found that teachers in excellent schools were more likely to use the plenary to provide opportunities for further discussion, to explore issues in more depth, and to extend work and concepts covered in the lesson. This finding confirmed and extended earlier research, which revealed a statistically significant link between the use of the plenary and independent measures of observed quality (Sammons *et al.*, 2008c).

In Group A schools, 75 per cent of the lessons scrutinized using IEO included plenaries. The teachers in these schools used them for the following:

- to informally assess children's understanding of basic concepts and skills
- to provide an opportunity for children to share their work and receive feedback
- to resolve issues arising from the lesson and provide a forum for collaborative problem-solving.

In Group B schools, 50 per cent were observed using plenaries but many of these sessions were rushed and superficial. There were few opportunities for sharing work and deepening understanding. It seemed to the researchers that the teachers included a plenary because they knew they should but did not make time to plan or deliver the session properly. Most plenaries were shorter than 5 min, while the longest (about 15 min) was really only a continuation of the main lesson with children solving slightly more difficult problems. Most teachers checked answers with the children or questioned them about their work, but not in depth, with the purpose of sharing strategies, or to provide an opportunity for higher-order thinking or insightful questions.

The percentage dropped to 25 per cent in Group C schools and, when a plenary did take place, it was generally short and used only to check answers to work that had been completed during the lesson. The team observed no in-depth discussion, extension or reflection in any of these school's plenary sessions.

One researcher's field notes describe a good example of a 10 min plenary at the end of a literacy poetry lesson (School 31). The pupils had been working individually on rhyme, alliteration and onomatopoeia, and composing their own verse. Towards the end of the lesson, the teacher gathered the children and asked them to work together to write a class chorus for their individual verses. She said that the chorus had to include both alliteration and the sound of a lorry trundling along a road.

By letting the children lead and improve each other's suggestions, the whole class contributed to this part of the exercise. The teacher then asked a few individual children to add the verses that they had written to create a whole-class poem. This well-managed plenary was so effective that the children were disappointed when it ended for break time. It allowed pupils to consolidate their understanding of poetry techniques, to work collaboratively by helping each other to improve, and to extend their knowledge and skills by considering their own work.

Informal assessment during the plenary

The researchers often observed teachers in excellent schools using the plenary as an opportunity, quickly and informally, to assess their children's understanding of basic concepts and skills. A class in School 8, for example, had worked in groups to collect data, produce a tally and then make a bar chart that represented each group's findings. In the plenary, the teacher displayed all of the bar charts and asked the children, as a whole-class activity, to identify the mode.

In Schools 1 and 4, teachers used short plenary sessions to check answers at the end of their numeracy lessons. This suggested that these Group A teachers considered the plenary to be a useful tool. Its inclusion in a lesson, even in a shortened and simplified form, helped them to gain feedback on pupil understanding and consolidation of learning.

Opportunities for children to share their work during the plenary

Many teachers in excellent schools used the plenary as a forum for children to share their work, which usually included some feedback from the teacher. In School 2, for example, the teacher used a 5 min plenary session to provide feedback to the whole class by asking three children to read aloud the hobbit character profiles they had just written. She offered a little feedback to the individual children about their written work but mainly used the plenary to address issues around the task's difficulty level. Many children had found it very hard, so the teacher reassured them, encouraged them to keep trying and offered some commendable suggestions to try (for example, using more semicolons in their writing).

A teacher in School 4 used a similar technique at the end of a literacy lesson. Her pupils had just written poems about their school environment and, although most would be sharing their work with the class the following day, the teacher provided some immediate, general feedback by reading out some of the children's work at the end of the lesson.

One researcher noted a particularly striking example of a plenary in School 1. The children had been working on writing haiku poems containing a chronological sequence. The teacher spent the final 10 min of the lesson asking pupils to read their haikus out to the class, then offering very specific suggestions for improvement.

The quality of the plenary feedback was different in this lesson because the focus was on finding ways to improve the work rather than providing praise and encouragement. This gave every pupil the chance to reflect critically on their own and each other's work and to consider what worked well. It also provided them with clear suggestions for improving their haiku. The Group A teacher exemplified how developing a learning community culture engages learning.

Resolving issues during the plenary

In some excellent schools, the plenary session was used to resolve issues arising in the lesson and to provide a forum for collaborative problem-solving. A teacher in School 3, for example, had asked the children to create an imaginary desk order for the class. They had to consider a number of factors, including the desks' dimensions. The children's measuring had yielded mixed results, so the teacher used the plenary session to resolve this difficulty through a discussion of averages and middle numbers. The children shared their results with each other and then discussed the options for finding the most representative measurements (median, mode, mean). The teacher encouraged them all to 'argue for their point of view' in the plenary.

Overall, the researchers found the following:

- Teachers in poor schools rarely used plenaries. Even when they did, the sessions were usually brief and used only to check work done in lessons.
- Teachers in excellent and good schools used plenaries more often than teachers in poor schools.
- Teachers in excellent schools used plenaries to deepen children's understanding and to allow opportunities for reflection and feedback.

Strategy 10: Making clear links

IEO rates and records what researchers witness regarding 'cross-disciplinary connections' and 'linkage to life beyond the classroom' (see Table 6.1), while the COS-5 instrument provides information about the different activities and discussions teachers use to link their pupils' learning in a particular lesson to other subjects and to life outside the classroom.

The researchers recorded the explicit links and connections that teachers made both in their field notes and in their assessments of the teachers' 'richness of instructional methods', 'sensitivity', 'social support for student learning', 'basic skills development in the context of problem-solving', 'maths discourse and communication', 'purposeful development of writing skills' and 'instructional conversations'.

Table 6.1: Making clear learning links

Characteristics of Year 5 classrooms in schools with:	Group A	Group B	Group C
Cross-disciplinary connections	Low*	Very low	Very low
Linkage to life beyond the classroom	Low	Low	Low

Note: Unless otherwise stated, differences in quantitative scores indicate significant differences ($p < 0.05$) between groups.
* Only the difference between Groups A and B was significant.

Because the researchers did less IEO, statistically significant differences were less likely. Despite this, they found that the differences between academically highly effective schools with good-quality pedagogy and low-academic-effectiveness schools with poor-quality pedagogy approached significance ($p < 0.055$, $p < 0.065$) on both the IEO literacy and numeracy measures for 'cross-disciplinary connections' and 'linkage to life beyond the classroom'. This difference was particularly clear when the mean, minimum and maximum values were studied. These results were treated with caution because of the relatively small numbers in the three groups of schools in these analyses, particularly as in the mixed-method design the qualitative field notes are accorded more weight in seeking to understand differences in practice. In the qualitative analysis the data-reduction process similarly involves studying patterns of practice and their associations.

Overall, teachers in all schools were rated better at making 'linkages to life beyond the classroom' than 'cross-disciplinary connections'. Teachers in the Group C schools were rated particularly poorly at making 'cross-disciplinary connections'. Their mean rating was just above the minimum score ($x_ = 1.29$, minimum = 1), while the highest rating any teacher in a Group C school received was 3 (maximum score = 5). Teachers in the Group B schools were rated between the other two groups ($x_ = 1.62$), and their maximum score of 4 was also exactly between the maximum scores of the other groups. Although teachers in Group A schools were rated the highest for making 'cross-disciplinary connections', and some of them were given the highest rating of 5 (maximum score = 5), their mean score was still below the midpoint of the scale (average score = 3, $x_ = 2.25$). Even though these teachers were normally observed to be better at making 'cross-disciplinary connections' clear to their pupils, they still had much room for improvement in this area.

Although all teachers scored better for 'linkage to life beyond the classroom', the overall rating for poor schools was below the midpoint score of 3 ($x_ = 2.21$). Once again, no teacher received the highest score of 5. Teachers in good schools were rated between their peers in excellent and poor schools, although they were closer to the former. Some teachers in good schools, like many in excellent schools, received the highest possible rating of 5. Finally, teachers in excellent schools were rated as slightly above the midpoint ($x_ = 3.44$) in their ability to link learning in the classroom to life beyond it.

The researchers often observed teachers in excellent schools making cross-subject and extracurricular links for their pupils. They saw teachers explaining connections between what their children were doing in one lesson and what they were learning in another, and with the world outside school. These teachers did this in the lessons (for example, suggesting children might enjoy rereading the stories they are writing now later in their lives) and by using practical activities that linked the lesson's objective to the outside world.

On one occasion, IEO at School 4 captured how, in only 90 min, the teacher connected literacy, geography, science, and personal/social and health education (a road-safety aspect) and linked them with the children's lives. At the start of the lesson, the teacher told the children to write a poem using ideas from a previous geography lesson, which considered how people affect the environment. In that lesson, the children had begun looking at the school's environment and the surrounding area, and they had gone onto the school roof to look at their city. To strengthen the link between subjects, the teacher told the children to write their poems in their geography books.

The children began by sitting in debating groups on the carpet, brainstorming words for 'environment'. The teacher then wrote the keywords for the lesson on the board, the children discussed their previous work on the topic in a whole-class session, and then they enjoyed a lively class debate, full of questions and astute arguments. The researcher was very impressed by the quality of debate and how well the children followed the rules.

After this, the children watched a short film and then returned to their tables to begin writing their poems about the school environment and the impact of people on it. IEO gave a sense of children experiencing an enormous number of activities, especially given the short time, all designed to demonstrate the links between academic subjects and the environment around the school. In pedagogical terms, the lesson also illustrated how teachers need to consider, plan and respond to pace and variety in learning.

During IEO of literacy in School 1, a researcher's notes described how the teacher had used the children's prior knowledge to extend their understanding of one topic and not only to link it to a second but also to strengthen their understanding of both topics. The teacher had been working on haiku poems with her mixed Year 5/6 class. She began the lesson by praising the children for their work on haikus the previous day. She then explained that she was setting them a bigger challenge: they had to write another haiku, and this had to show chronological change (for example, growing up, months of the year). By the end of the lesson, the children had worked through the difficulties of incorporating sequential events into the haiku's restrictive format and had also presented their work to the rest of the class. The researcher's notes indicated that the children were highly engaged throughout the lesson, and that the teacher spent a great deal of time supporting individual children.

The team often observed excellent teachers reminding children about their previous work to help them with a similar task. In School 2, for example, the teacher asked the children to recall a character profile they had previously written about – Dickens's Scrooge – to help them write a profile of a Tolkien hobbit. Similarly, in a School 5 lesson, the teacher linked numeracy and literacy with earlier work on Donizetti's opera L'elisir d'amore (*The Elixir of Love*). The class began with the teacher asking the children why real-life problems are important and explaining the meaning of 'cross-curricular'. The pupils then had to create some money problems for each other that were linked to the opera. They invented issues involving the price of the elixir, food, drinks and flowers for the opera's wedding. The researcher commented that the children were very engaged and enthusiastic throughout the lesson.

Overall, the team found the following:

- Teachers placed little emphasis on making clear links between subjects or between life inside and outside the classroom.
- However, when teachers did make links, they were more likely to do so when referring to life inside and outside the classroom rather than to connections between academic subjects.
- Teachers in poor schools made the fewest links with life outside the classroom.
- Teachers in excellent schools were consistently better than other teachers at making clear links, especially to life outside the classroom.

It should be noted here that plenaries have the potential to provide opportunities for making learning links explicit. During such sessions, discussions that consolidated learning could be enhanced with examples across subjects and to life outside the classroom.

Strategy 11: Homework

The COS-5 and IEO, with their emphasis on what happens inside classrooms, do not record information about homework. The researchers did note all references to homework in the lessons they observed, but they could only use these to gain an insight into whether homework was a regular expectation, how it was used, and the quantity and quality of work assigned.

During the observations, homework was mentioned in only 30 per cent of Group A schools, where it appeared to serve two purposes. First, it provided pupils with opportunities to learn and practise basic skills (learning spellings was the most commonly mentioned homework) and, presumably, asking children to complete tasks at home freed up class time for other learning activities. Second, it linked to what the children were learning in class, either as extension work or, again, to allow more class time for other topics. The researchers noted that teachers in these schools took care to explain the homework so that the children could get the most out of it.

The team observed homework in only 11 per cent of Group B schools. In School 27, for example, it was used to clarify some teaching points. The children were learning how to measure irregular shapes, and the teacher used homework to consolidate the pupils' understanding.

Some schools used an informal approach and set small amounts of optional work that could be done in breaks. In School 30, for example, a bottom-set literacy group had been working on the 'true' story of 'The Three Little Pigs'. The teacher asked them to think about whether they believed the wolf's or the pigs' side of the story before the next lesson. In School 31, the teacher offered pupils, who had enjoyed a poetry lesson, a house point (that is, an additional incentive/bonus often placed on something like a 'group star chart') if they wrote another verse during the break.

Although the homework in these cases was very informal, it is highly likely that some children completed it. The task in School 30 was an interesting extension to the class activity and was easily achievable by a group of pupils who struggled with literacy. The children in School 31 enjoyed writing their poems, so the opportunity to continue, combined with the incentive of a house point, meant that they were likely to do so.

This informal approach avoided the confrontation that can arise over incomplete homework. Children who completed the tasks were rewarded (for example, by praise, by being better prepared for a class discussion, by a house point), but those who did not were not singled out for punishment.

It could be argued, of course, that these tasks are not really home work, and that their informality arises from teacher laziness (no marking, no consequences to follow through on) or is simply the result of an unplanned opportunity seized by the teacher. However, setting work outside class time in this way means that all pupils have an equal opportunity to benefit (regardless of their home circumstances), and that reprimands for not completing the work are eliminated.

The team noted that, in poor schools, teachers appeared to set homework because they were required to. The teachers seemed to be very concerned with the actual setting and collecting of homework (and punishing when incomplete), but the work itself was rarely linked to what the children were learning in class. Further, the team did not observe a single example of a teacher using an opportunity that arose during a lesson to set different or more homework than they had already planned.

Overall, despite the researchers being unable to measure the use of homework systematically, their notes about instances when homework was set show the following:

- Teachers in excellent and good schools appeared to set homework that was more meaningful and directly linked to what the children were learning than teachers in poor schools.
- Teachers in excellent and good schools had a more flexible, informal and optional approach to assigning homework, and this was sometimes on top of timetabled requirements.

In addition, although the data from the COS-5 and IEO plainly cannot provide any definitive evidence of teachers' intentions around the homework they set, the EPPSE questionnaire completed by teachers in the focal schools (see Chapter 9) indicated that pupils made more progress in the schools whose teachers reported a greater emphasis on homework.

This notion is supported by the EPPSE 3–14 study, which showed that students in secondary school, after controlling for SES, who spent two or more hours per night on homework (compared with children who spent no time on homework) showed better progress in maths and, to a slightly lesser extent, in English. The EPPSE 3–14 project also found that this level of homework in secondary schools was associated with a positive effect on socio-behavioural outcomes from age 11 to 14 (Sylva *et al.*, 2012).

Taken together, the findings about the learning approaches considered in this chapter add the final few distinguishing markers of teachers in effective primary schools. They show that these teachers did the following:

- ensured plenary sessions took place
- used plenary sessions to provide their pupils with opportunities to deepen their understanding
- provided opportunities for pupils to reflect on their work and receive feedback
- made clear links to areas, topics and subjects beyond the immediate lesson
- created connections between subjects and links to life beyond the classroom
- provided small amounts of meaningful, relevant and flexible homework.

By employing these pedagogical strategies, the teachers provided higher-quality classroom experiences for their children.

Chapter 7

Investigating variations in classroom practice

Chapters 3–6 explored in depth the findings from the qualitative field notes of practices in Year 5 classrooms of effective and less effective primary schools according to the three group categorization of schools as Groups A, B or C. Chapters 7 and 8 return to the quantitative strand of the mixed-methods study. They are more technical than the previous chapters but they are particularly important because they describe the wide variation in practice in terms of the two international systematic observation schedules used and how this relates to children's outcomes. This contextual information is very valuable.

This chapter presents findings from systematic observations of classroom practice and is based on the subsample of 125 schools drawn from the 850+ schools attended by the EPPSE children in the main study. It summarizes the variation in observed practice and identifies patterns and associations, for example, such as how practices vary by school context measured by the level of social disadvantage of the pupil intake (see Sammons *et al.*, 2006).

The observations were conducted during the spring and summer of 2004 and 2005. These were years when the new National Numeracy and Literacy Strategies (DfEE, 1998a, 1999; DfES, 2001a,b) were becoming embedded in classroom practice. There was a growing policy emphasis on raising standards and reducing the number of poorly performing schools. There was renewed focus on accountability via the publication of schools' results, target-setting and Ofsted's inspection findings. There were also increases in teachers' pay and in provision of continuous professional development (CPD), which shaped school performance and professional practice (see Sammons, 2008).

This chapter provides a short description of the sample of schools and details the COS-5 and IEO instruments. It focuses on the extent to which the observation tools identify variation between teachers' practices and children's observed responses in different classrooms. This is important because there was a great deal of variation between teachers in different schools, and from this the researchers were able to identify teachers who exemplified practices for further study (as discussed in Chapters 3–6).

The relationships between the Ofsted indicators of school quality and the COS-5 and IEO measures are explored. It was hypothesized that more effective schools and those that Ofsted judged to be of higher quality would also show more positive classroom practices (Teddlie *et al.,* 1989).

In addition, the extent to which variations in classroom practices might be associated with the school context was explored by linking this with the percentage of pupils in each school's intake who were eligible for FSM, an indicator of poverty. The results of this investigation have implications for policies seeking to use education as a means to combat social exclusion and improve social mobility, because social disadvantage may act as a moderating influence on some classroom processes. Over the years, past research has found that teachers in schools in different FSM contexts can have different expectations of pupils (for example, lower expectations of disadvantaged groups). Also, research has consistently found that the pupil composition (% FSM) is associated with poorer progress for all pupil groups in schools with high concentrations of disadvantaged pupils (Sammons *et al.,* 1997; Teddlie and Reynolds, 2000).

The rest of this chapter is divided into four linked sections.

Section 1 provides information about the various elements of the COS-5 and IEO instruments and the independent measures of school quality from Ofsted inspections. It describes the focal school sample and gives details of the Ofsted measures.

Section 2 covers findings on variations in classroom practices using the COS-5, including descriptions of classroom settings, curricular activities, teachers' and children's behaviours, and the quality of child–teacher interactions. It reports on the qualities of classroom practices and processes, as well as the underlying dimensions of classroom processes that were identified. It also details findings on variations in literacy and numeracy practices assessed with IEO.

Section 3 explores the relationships between classroom practice and Ofsted ratings. It draws special attention to whether variations in practice are associated with school disadvantage context.

Section 4 draws conclusions and discusses implications.

1. Observations and Ofsted measures of school quality
The classroom observation instruments
Two systematic observation instruments were used to explore variation in classroom processes. The use of two such tools had a number of advantages.

It enabled exploration of validity and reliability, and it allowed more practices to be studied. The COS-5 was employed in Year 5 classes in 125 schools, and IEO in a subset of 93 of the same classes and schools. A brief description of the two instruments is given in Boxes 7.1 and 7.2.

IEO CRITERIA

Researchers observed one complete literacy and numeracy lesson. IEO tackles four main areas:

- general classroom management and climate scales for both subjects
- general instruction scales for both subjects
- mathematical instruction scales for numeracy
- reading/writing instruction scales for literacy.

Literacy

- classroom climate
- classroom routines
- cross-disciplinary connections
- linkage to life beyond the classroom
- social support for student learning
- student engagement
- reading as meaning-making
- basic skills development in the context of reading
- higher-order thinking in writing
- purposeful development of writing skills
- instructional conversations.

Numeracy

- classroom climate
- classroom routines
- cross-disciplinary connections
- linkage to life beyond the classroom
- social support for student learning
- student engagement
- use of maths analysis
- depth of knowledge and student understanding
- basic skills development in the context of problem-solving
- maths discourse and communication
- locus of maths authority.

Box 7.1: Criteria used for IEO

THE COS-5

This is divided into two main parts:
- frequency of behaviour coding (TC)
- measures of quality coding (global).

Frequency of behaviour coding

Frequency of behaviour coding is used in the first of two 10 min observations. It includes coding child and teacher behaviours across a range of classroom and curriculum settings. During these observations a TC is observed and recorded during a sequence of ten 60 s intervals (30 s observe, 30 s record), during which the focus is on information in five general areas of the TC's classroom behaviour and experience, as follows:

Child-level setting: the classroom setting in which the TC is working:
- whole class
- large group (>6)
- small group (≤6)
- individual

Content of TC's activity: the nature of the activity, including:
- subject areas (for example, literacy, numeracy)
- subcategories within a subarea (for example, word level and comprehension in literacy)
- part of literacy and numeracy hour, as described by the National Literacy Strategy (adapted for use in the UK)
- non-curricular activities (for example, enrichment and free time).

Teacher behaviour: interaction with the TC:
- attending to TC (directly)
- teaching basic skills
- teaching analysis
- managerial instructions
- monitoring and checking work
- displaying positive or negative affect and discipline.

Child academic behaviour:

Type of behaviour
- learning/performing basic skills
- learning/performing analysis
- collaborative work
- requesting attention/help/ information
- volunteers.

Degree of involvement
- engaged
- highly engaged
- unproductive
- off-task or alternative academic behaviour.

Child social behaviour: social interactions with peers and adults in the classroom:
- positive/neutral engagement with peers
- negative/aggressive engagement with peers
- positive affect in interactions with teacher
- negative affect in interactions with teacher.

Measures of quality coding

This part is dedicated to 10 min of continuous observation of behaviours and characteristics of the TC and the teacher in the classroom at a global level. It contains two broad categories: child and classroom codes. Under these main headings there are a number of subheadings or constructs (behaviours, characteristics) that must be rated.

Child codes
- disruptive
- self-reliance
- sociable/cooperative with peers
- child–teacher relationships
- positive affect
- activity level
- attention.

Classroom codes
- richness of instructional methods
- teacher detachment
- positive classroom climate
- productive use of instructional time
- evaluative feedback
- teacher sensitivity (main teacher only)
- chaos
- negative classroom climate
- over-control.

Items are rated on a seven-point scale (1 = very uncharacteristic to 7 = very characteristic).

Box 7.2: Criteria used for the COS-5

A number of items in the COS-5 are devoted to the measurement of the nature of interaction between teacher and TC. Observations are made from the perspectives of both the child and the teacher. Four behavioural measures are recorded, each of which comprises a pair of observations, one pertaining to the child and the other to the teacher:

- teacher attends to TC/TC requests attention
- teacher displays negative affect/TC displays negative affect
- teacher displays positive affect/TC displays positive affect
- teacher disciplines/TC displays disruptive behaviour.

The use of systematic observations was intended to complement the use of more detailed qualitative field notes, which provide more fine-grained and nuanced accounts of practice (see Chapter 2).

The sample

As discussed in Chapter 2, the researchers identified a purposive school sample totalling 125 schools and around 1,200 EPPSE children. The selection was based on indicators of primary-school academic effectiveness (derived from the CVA analyses of pupil progress across Key Stage 2, Melhuish *et al.*, 2006) and the number of EPPSE children enrolled (four or more in the school). The sample was chosen to include approximately equal numbers of academically effective, typical and ineffective schools.

Ofsted's inspection evidence of school quality

Ofsted's inspection grades available for the 125 focal schools (those closest to the most recent observations; that is, 2003 or 2000) were matched with the systematic observational measures. The Ofsted data included judgements of 'overall school effectiveness', 'improvement since last inspection', 'effectiveness of school leadership', 'quality of teaching and learning in Key Stage 1 and Key Stage 2' and pupil measures (for example, 'exclusions', 'attitudes to school' and 'attendance').

In schools judged to be more effective or showing more improvement across the last inspection cycle, the researchers expected to find evidence of more positive classroom practice. However, in exploring the associations between the classroom observation measures and inspection judgements, it must be remembered that inspection data were collected at different time points, reflecting the national inspection cycle, and that they apply to the whole school, whereas the classroom observations were conducted in 2004–2005 and were based on specific days of observation in one class only. The findings can thus provide only a guide to possible associations.

2. Variations in classroom practices
The IEO scale

IEO has a strong focus on pedagogical practices associated with learning in literacy and maths (see Box 7.1). This instrument was used to observe 93 literacy lessons and 93 numeracy lessons.

Literacy

Figure 7.1 shows the variation across different domains for the IEO literacy quality ratings.

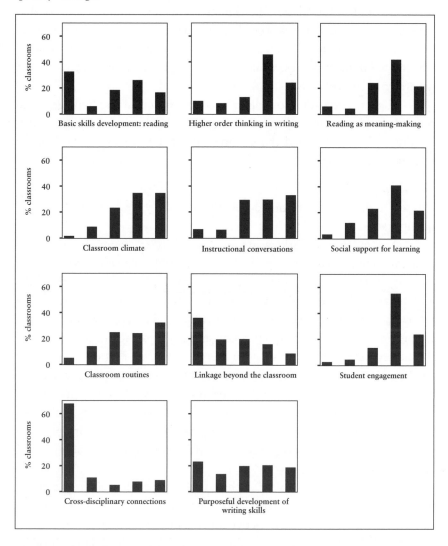

Figure 7.1: Distribution of IEO literacy scores (% classrooms plotted against the five-point quality-rating scale)

Most variation between classes was found for seven scales: 'cross-disciplinary connections', 'linkage to life beyond the classroom', 'reading as meaning-making', 'basic skills development in the context of reading', 'higher-order thinking in writing', 'purposeful development of writing skills' and 'instructional conversations' (see Figure 7.1).

The emphasis on 'basic skills development in reading and writing' showed a particularly wide spread, with more than a third of classes being given the lowest rating. By contrast, 'reading as meaning-making' showed few classes receiving a low score. Approximately 70 per cent of classes were rated favourably for 'classroom climate'. The IEO findings suggest that 'student engagement' levels were high in the majority of literacy classes/lessons. The extent to which teachers made 'cross-disciplinary connections' was limited in most classes, while 'social support for student learning' was generally rated positively.

Higher scores for 'cross-disciplinary connections' and 'linkage to life beyond the classroom' indicate the extent to which teachers seek to widen interest in literacy beyond the confines of the subject and make it more relevant to their pupils.

Numeracy

Figure 7.2 shows the variation across the numeracy dimensions of the IEO quality ratings.

The greatest variations among teachers were found for teaching/pedagogy items, particularly in 'use of maths analysis', 'basic skills development in the context of problem-solving' and 'locus of maths authority' (see Table 7.1a). The lowest mean scores on the numeracy scales reflect the extent to which teachers provide a wider context for material learned in class. 'Cross-disciplinary connections' and 'linkage to life beyond the classroom' had the lowest mean scores, indicating that the majority of teachers infrequently connected numeracy with other subjects or activities. The low ratings for 'linkage to life beyond the classroom' (60 per cent of classes received the lowest rating) reveals that many teachers make few references to real-life contexts, and they may be missing opportunities to enhance pupil awareness of the wider applicability of maths concepts and approaches.

'Basic skills development in the context of problem-solving' showed wide variation, with a minority (a little more than 20 per cent) rated very low on this aspect and only 10 per cent being rated very highly. The pattern for 'use of maths analysis' was very similar. As in the literacy lessons, 'student engagement', 'classroom climate' and 'social support for student learning' were generally highly rated in most classes.

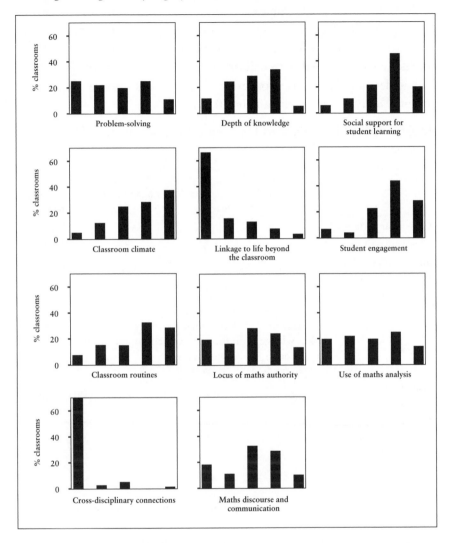

Figure 7.2: Distribution of IEO numeracy scores (% classrooms plotted against the five-point quality-rating scale)

Interrelated domains

The researchers examined the associations between the items in IEO using **correlations**. A correlation provides a measure of the extent to which different features of a teacher's practice are interrelated. In statistical terms, this is called co-variation (expressed by r, the value of which ranges between 1 and −1). The higher the positive correlation, the stronger the association.

119

This means that if a teacher scores highly in one domain they are likely also to score highly on the other. For instance, as indicated in Table 7.1b, basic skills development (in the context of problem-solving) is strongly associated (r = 0.69) with 'depth of student knowledge and understanding'. This means that teachers who paid a lot of attention to basic skills (problem-solving) also developed with children better 'depth of student knowledge and understanding'. The strongest correlation was between 'classroom routines' and 'classroom climate' (r = 0.81).

Table 7.1a&b: Correlations between different features of classroom practices

Table 7.1a	Classroom routines	Social support for student learning	Student engagement	Locus of maths authority
Classroom climate	0.81	0.75	0.74	0.58
Classroom routines	-	0.70	0.77	0.62
Social support for student learning	0.70	-	0.76	0.58

Table 7.1b	Depth of student knowledge and understanding	Basic skills development in the context of problem-solving	Maths discourse and communication	Locus of maths authority
Use of maths analysis	0.75	0.67	0.68	0.68
Depth of student knowledge and understanding	-	0.69	0.80	0.68
Maths discourse and communication	0.80	0.65	-	0.68

Note: The domains shown exhibited some of the strongest associations.

These analyses reveal the extent of similarity and, by contrast, differences in the classroom experiences of children taught different classes. They also provide information about variation in quality and emphases that may provide valuable clues regarding areas of weakness or CPD for teachers to improve the quality of the teaching and the learning experiences of pupils in upper primary school (Key Stage 2 in England).

Underlying dimensions in classroom processes
Given all the variation in observed practices identified and described above, it was important to explore the underlying dimensions to help make sense of

the wealth of data. A data-reduction technique called principal components analysis was used to further explore patterns of association among our different measures of teachers' observed classroom practice. This revealed a number of distinct dimensions (factors) for both the COS-5 and IEO. For further discussion of the principal components analyses, see Sammons *et al.* (2006).

Underlying dimensions of IEO

Data from the literacy and numeracy scales of the IEO instrument were analysed separately to identify the underlying dimensions. Analysis of both literacy[1] and numeracy yielded three similar dimensions – 'pedagogy', 'subject development' and 'learning linkages' – explaining 73 per cent of the variance in the individual literacy items and 76 per cent of the variance in the numeracy items. The literacy and numeracy items that form particular factors are given in Box 7.3.

IEO DIMENSIONS

Literacy
Pedagogy
- classroom climate
- classroom routines
- social support for student learning
- student engagement
- instructional conversations.

Subject development
- higher-order thinking in writing
- purposeful development of writing skills.

Learning linkages
- cross-disciplinary connections
- linkage to life beyond the classroom.

Numeracy
Pedagogy
- classroom climate
- classroom routines
- social support for student learning
- student engagement.

Subject development
- use of maths analysis
- depth of knowledge and student understanding
- basic skills development in the context of problem-solving
- maths discourse and communication
- locus of maths authority.

Learning linkages
- cross-disciplinary connections
- linkage to life beyond the classroom.

Box 7.3: Underlying dimensions of IEO

The factor structures underlying the IEO literacy and numeracy data were found to be conceptually similar. Three factors were identified for each set of data relating to the 'subject development', 'pedagogy' and 'learning linkages' dimensions. The items most closely associated with the 'learning linkages' factor were the same for both literacy and numeracy. The items loading on 'pedagogy' were again the same, with the exception of 'instructional conversations', which was an additional item to load on literacy. The 'subject development' factors were subject specific. These provide a helpful way to analyse and summarize the differences in observed literacy and numeracy teaching at Key Stage 2. Importantly, classes where scores were higher for these three factors provided higher-quality educational experiences for the children.

The COS-5: TCs observations (frequency of behaviours)

The COS-5 was a forerunner of the Classroom Assessment Scoring System (CLASS), now widely used in research projects (see http://info.teachstone.com/blog/author/bob-pianta-phd) and having a strong focus on the general classroom environment (see Box 7.2).

Overall, 1,009 observations were conducted in the 125 classes. For each class, the researchers completed a minimum of eight 20 min observation cycles. These included the following:

- one start-of-the-day observation
- one start-of-the-afternoon observation
- two literacy observations
- two numeracy observations
- one science or social science/humanities observation
- one additional academic subject (could be another literacy, numeracy, science or social science/humanities observation).

The researchers scheduled their observations to take place on a typical day and focused on the experiences of the TCs.

Classroom organization

The observations were categorized according to whether the TC was seen as part of a whole-class, group or individual activity. The most dominant classroom organization was whole class, with individual working accounting for 36 per cent of the time. Observations of large- and small-group settings were generally limited. The use of whole-class working was most common during science (64 per cent). Large- and small-group working were also most likely to occur during science (11 per cent). Individual working was most frequent during literacy (37 per cent), followed by numeracy (35 per cent), and was less common in science (25 per cent).

The proportion of whole-class working identified during the observations was higher than that reported by Galton *et al.* (1999), who found that children were engaged in whole-class work during science only for a third of the time. There are a number of possible reasons for this apparent difference. One is likely to relate to definitions of whole-class activity. In Galton *et al.*'s (ibid.) research, the definition was based on observations of teachers' communication patterns (whether an interaction was made with the whole class, an individual child or a group), whereas the observations of whole class refer to instances where the whole group of children received the same instruction from the teacher.

Individual and whole-class working generally dominated classroom organization. However, there was still considerable variation between individual classes with regard to teachers' use of different forms of organization.

During the second round of data collection, an addition was made to the IEO instrument to record all parts of the literacy and numeracy lessons observed by the researchers, including the plenary (because the 20 min observation schedule did not fit with the typical lesson length). For IEO, complete lessons were witnessed. A plenary occurred in only half of the full lessons observed (50.7 per cent in literacy and 47.8 per cent in numeracy). The National Numeracy and Literacy Strategies (DfES, 2001a,b) had recommended that teachers use the plenary to provide opportunities to review lesson aims and offer feedback to help consolidate learning (see Chapter 6). The absence of a plenary session in literacy and numeracy lessons in around half of the classes observed suggests that some teachers may not be aware of the purposes and value of plenaries, or may indicate a weakness in classroom planning or organization where a plenary was intended but earlier activities in the lesson overran.

Teachers' pedagogical behaviour

Considerable variations in teachers' behaviour were observed between classes. There were large variations in the time spent teaching basic skills. By contrast, the time devoted to teaching analysis skills was less variable. On average, teachers were observed to be teaching analysis skills for about a third of the time, whereas on average they spent 67 per cent of classroom time teaching basic skills. The distribution of analysis teaching was skewed, with little or none observed in around 30 per cent of classes. Similarly, teachers' use of monitoring and managerial instructions varied, it being a prominent feature of only a minority of classes.

Child academic behaviour

Four types of child academic behaviour were identified in the observations: engaged, highly engaged, unproductive and off task. TCs were judged to be productively engaged in their lessons for approximately 78 per cent of the time (64 per cent engaged, 14 per cent highly engaged). On average, only 3 per cent of off-task behaviour was observed, and in more than half of the classes the researchers saw none. This incidence of off-task behaviour is less than that reported by Galton (1997), Galton *et al.* (1980), Galton and Simon (1980) and Mortimore *et al.*, (1988), who used the Oracle observation instrument. When Galton *et al.* (1999) studied the same schools 20 years, he found a significant decrease in off-task behaviour, suggesting that pupil engagement had increased between 1977 and 1997.

Overall, unproductive behaviour (for example, queuing) accounted for an average of 19 per cent of the time observed. A large proportion of unproductive time may be an indicator of poor organization by teachers. Unproductive behaviour was much more common than off-task behaviour, being a significant feature of some classes and taking up around a third of observed time (that is, 3 min or more of every 10 min in 20 per cent of classes). Episodes of unproductive and off-task behaviours were more common in literacy lessons (21 per cent) than in maths (16 per cent) and science (17 per cent).

Child–teacher interaction and child social behaviour

Four measures were used for child–teacher interactions:

- TC requests attention, help or information/teacher attends to TC.
- Teacher or TC displays negative affect.
- Teacher or TC displays positive affect.
- TC displays disruptive behaviour and teacher disciplines.

Overall, teachers attended to children more frequently than pupils requested help. This may reflect teachers' skills in identifying potential need and helping to reduce off-task behaviours.

Children showed a 'positive affect' (for example, smiling, enthusiasm) more often than teachers, with many classes showing no incidence of 'positive affect' (> 75 per cent) on the teacher. This suggests that TCs received very little direct positive teacher interaction. Previous observational studies (in the 1970s and 1980s) have indicated that teachers' use of positive comment and feedback is limited, and the present study worryingly also points to a similar pattern.

Global measures of classroom practice with the COS-5

The experiences of the TC, described above, showed wide variation in classroom practices. Variability was also evident when more global dimensions of classroom practices were recorded, as reported below.

Child behaviours (global dimensions)

Classroom practices varied widely across a number of areas, including 'attention', 'sociable/cooperative with peers', 'self-reliance' and 'child–teacher relationships'. 'Sociable/cooperative with peers' showed the most variation (it had the highest SD), which suggests that teachers vary in the extent to which they encourage pupil cooperation (see Figure 7.3). 'Activity level' (covering activity, restlessness and fidgeting) had the lowest level of variation.

The charts in Figure 7.3 show that some observed behaviours vary more than others. Where the results are highly skewed in one direction, this means that there was little difference observed in most classes. For example, limited 'disruptive' behaviour was seen in most classes, so the distribution is skewed towards the low end.

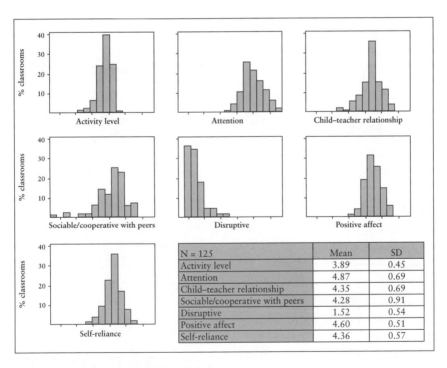

N = 125	Mean	SD
Activity level	3.89	0.45
Attention	4.87	0.69
Child–teacher relationship	4.35	0.69
Sociable/cooperative with peers	4.28	0.91
Disruptive	1.52	0.54
Positive affect	4.60	0.51
Self-reliance	4.36	0.57

Figure 7.3: Variations between classes in children's observed behaviour (COS-5 global dimensions; % classrooms plotted against the seven-point quality-rating scale)

Teachers' classroom practice and processes

There were nine global codes for classroom practices, which showed different amounts of variation (see Figure 7.4).

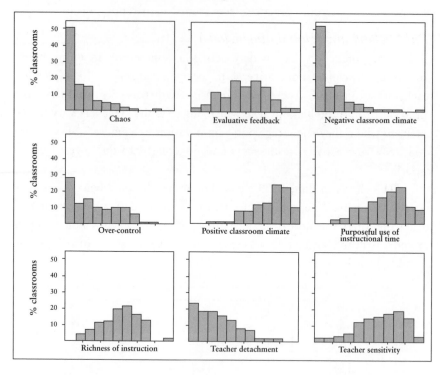

Figure 7.4: Distribution of classroom practice and processes (COS-5 scales; % classrooms plotted against the seven-point quality-rating scale)

The largest variation was for the scale 'over-control'. Some 40 per cent of classes were rated low on this scale, but there was quite a spread. Only 4 per cent had very high scores for this.

Ratings for 'evaluative feedback', 'teacher sensitivity', 'richness of instructional methods' and 'productive use of instructional time' showed a wider spread across classes. This indicates that there was much more variation between teachers in these features of their classroom practice. This is an important finding because, where a lot of variation occurs, this may help to account for differences in effectiveness in promoting children's progress (explored in Chapter 8).

By contrast, 'chaos' and 'negative classroom climate' both showed highly skewed distributions, indicating that in most classes these aspects were very rare. More than 50 per cent of classrooms received the most favourable rating on these scales.

The extent of variation between classes is also important because it indicates that children have very different classroom experiences in specific features of pedagogy that may affect their learning, motivation and achievement.

Underlying dimensions of the COS-5

Given all of the variation in observed practices that we identified and have described above, it was again important to explore the underlying dimensions to help to make sense of the wealth of data. As shown with IEO earlier in this chapter, principal components analysis illustrates how different items in the COS-5 cluster together. It revealed five distinct dimensions (factors), as shown in Box 7.4.

COS-5 DIMENSIONS
Quality of pedagogy
- classroom code: richness of instructional methods
- classroom code: teacher detachment
- classroom code: positive classroom climate
- classroom code: productive use of instructional time
- classroom code: evaluative feedback
- classroom code: teacher sensitivity

Disorganization
- child code: disruptive
- classroom code: chaos
- classroom code: negative classroom climate

Child positivity
- child code: self-reliance
- child code: sociable/cooperative with peers
- child code: child–teacher relationship

Positive engagement
- child code: positive affect
- child code: activity level

Attention and control
- child code: attention
- classroom code: over-control

Box 7.4: Underlying dimensions of the COS-5

The first factor, 'quality of pedagogy', represents general classroom processes and pedagogy. It is associated with six of the classroom quality measures: 'richness of instructional methods', 'teacher detachment', 'positive classroom climate', 'productive use of instructional time' and 'teacher sensitivity'.

'Disorganization' was formed from three quality measures: child's 'disruptive' behaviour, 'chaos' and 'negative classroom climate', the clustering of which indicates that disruptive behaviour and negative or chaotic classroom atmosphere are likely to coincide. However, whether a chaotic atmosphere in the classroom produces disruptive behaviour or whether it is caused by it cannot be ascertained. It seems likely that the two tend to reinforce each other.

The third factor, 'child positivity', was formed from another three quality measures: 'self-reliance', 'sociable/cooperative with peers' and 'child–teacher relationships'. This grouping suggests that in classes where children are observed to be more self-reliant, they are also more likely to demonstrate the social skills of cooperation.

'Positive engagement' was made up of two quality measures: 'positive affect' and 'activity level'. This clustering indicates that in classes where children are observed to be occupied, they are also more likely to be rated as happy.

The fifth factor, 'attention and control', brought together two further quality measures: 'attention' and 'over-control'. This is in many respects the inverse of the 'disorganization' dimension.

3. Relationships between classroom measures, school FSM and Ofsted ratings

The relationships between the socially disadvantaged pupil intake (% FSM), Ofsted school quality ratings and the underlying factors (dimensions) of that relate to aspects of teacher and pupils' classroom behaviours were investigated.

Interestingly, the level of disadvantage of the school's intake (% FSM) showed little association with Ofsted's judgements, and correlations were not statistically significant. This finding provides little evidence to support the view that inspection judgements are biased against schools in more challenging, highly disadvantaged contexts. Attendance was the only Ofsted rating that was significantly correlated with FSM ($r = 0.51$). Many studies have found that attendance rates tend to be poorer among pupils of low SES, and the Ofsted ratings are likely to reflect this pattern. (Inspectors refer to schools' attendance data and look at registers to make their assessments.)

IEO

The correlations between the school quality measures and the IEO literacy and numeracy factors, as well as the individual literacy and numeracy items, were investigated. These measures tended to show a clearer pattern than those found for the COS-5 factors. There were no associations for the 'learning linkages' factor.

As can be seen in Table 7.2, Ofsted's judgements of 'school effectiveness' were moderately positively correlated with the 'pedagogy' and 'subject development' factors in literacy ($r = 0.24$ and $r = 0.25$) and numeracy ($r = 0.25$ and $r = 0.22$). These moderate to weak but consistently positive patterns of association indicate that observed practice in our study tended to be rated more positively in schools that were previously rated more favourably by inspectors. It should be noted that the Ofsted inspections did not necessarily take place in the same year as the classroom observation, nor would they have focused on Year 5 classes as this research study did. The correlations are reported only to illustrate whether overall Ofsted school judgements might be associated with the observed quality of pedagogy, as defined by the two international instruments analysed in this research. The findings confirm that there are indeed positive associations.

Table 7.2: Correlations between IEO factors, Ofsted ratings and school disadvantage

Ofsted's judgements and school characteristics	IEO: literacy factors		IEO: numeracy factors	
	Pedagogy	Subject development	Pedagogy	Subject development
% FSM	−0.36†	ns	ns	−0.23*
School effectiveness	0.24*	0.25*	0.25*	0.22*
Improvement since last inspection	ns	0.27*	ns	ns
Leadership	ns	0.28*	0.23*	ns
Teaching Key Stage 1	ns	0.27*	ns	0.27*
Learning Key Stage 1	ns	0.29*	ns	0.29*
Teaching Key Stage 2	ns	0.24*	ns	ns
Learning Key Stage 2	ns	0.23*	ns	ns
Attitudes to school	0.24*	ns	ns	ns
Attendance	0.23*	ns	ns	0.30†

ns: not significant.
* Correlation is significant at the $p < 0.05$ level (two-tailed).
† Correlation is significant at the $p < 0.01$ level (two-tailed).

Ofsted's judgements of 'improvement since last inspection' were also positively correlated with 'subject development' in literacy (r = 0.27). Of the two items associated with this factor, only the 'purposeful development of writing skills' item on the literacy scale was correlated with 'improvement since last inspection' (r = 0.38). During the period 2001–2005, schools became more confident in the implementation and development of the National Literacy Strategy, and there was an increasing focus on writing, especially for boys in the later years of Key Stage 2 (DfES, 2001b). The correlation between the extent of school improvement previously identified by inspectors in the focal schools and observation evidence regarding this aspect of literacy suggests that the most improved schools may have placed more emphasis on developing teachers' practice in literacy and particularly on writing development.

Ofsted's judgement of school 'leadership' was positively correlated with 'subject development' in literacy (r = 0.28) and 'pedagogy in numeracy' (r = 0.23). These findings again support the view that school influences may have an indirect impact on teachers' classroom practice, providing evidence that schools with more effective leadership tend to have better-observed classroom practice in several areas.

Ofsted's judgement about the quality of 'teaching' and 'learning' during Key Stage 1 correlated with 'subject development' in both curriculum areas. The quality of 'teaching' and 'Learning' during Key Stage 2 was significantly correlated with 'subject development' in literacy but not in numeracy. Again, these results suggest that despite the different timescales and frames of reference, there is evidence of better-observed practice in specific aspects of teaching in schools that were judged more favourably in Ofsted inspections. Thus both research and inspection findings in this study suggest that better school leadership and overall school quality can provide a more supportive environment for the practice of individual class teachers.

Pupil attitudes and attendance

There were positive associations between the 'pedagogy' literacy factor and Ofsted's judgements of pupils' 'attitudes to school' (r = 0.24) and 'attendance' (r = 0.23). The literacy item, 'classroom routine', was correlated with two out of three Ofsted measures of pupil outcomes, namely 'behaviour including exclusion' (r = 0.30) and 'attitudes to school' (r = 0.38). 'Classroom climate' was correlated with the inspection rating of pupils' 'attitudes to school' (r = 0.29). There was also a significant positive association between 'attendance' and 'subject development' in numeracy. All five items loading on this factor ('use of maths analysis', 'depth of student knowledge and understanding', 'basic skills development in the context of problem-solving', 'maths discourse and communication' and 'locus of maths authority') were moderately to strongly correlated with Ofsted's 'attendance' measure. 'social support for student learning' was similarly correlated with 'attendance'. In addition, 'classroom climate', 'classroom routine' and 'use of maths analysis' were positively correlated with pupils' 'behaviour including exclusion' and 'attitudes to school' (see Sammons *et al.*, 2008c).

Disadvantage context (based on % pupils eligible for FSM)

The 'pedagogy' factor in literacy was negatively correlated with the level of social disadvantage of pupil intake in the school (% FSM, r = −0.36). In literacy, four items were loaded on the 'pedagogy' factor ('classroom climate', 'classroom routine', 'social support for student learning' and 'student engagement') and were negatively correlated with FSM. For literacy, these aspects of pedagogy seem to be sensitive to pupil context and may reflect the influence of teacher expectations and/or pupil behaviour. By contrast, for numeracy it was the more specific aspects of maths teaching, such as 'depth of student knowledge and understanding', 'maths discourse and communication' and 'locus of maths authority', that were correlated with the level of social disadvantage rather than the more general aspects of classroom pedagogy, such as climate and routine. The 'subject development' factor in numeracy (on which these items load) was similarly negatively correlated with disadvantage, but the association was fairly weak (r = −0.23).

The findings indicate that a number of important features of classroom practice are associated with the level of social disadvantage of a school's pupil intake. Though only modest, the associations tend to be negative, indicating a tendency for poorer practice to be observed in schools where levels of disadvantage are higher. This may reflect problems such as lower teacher expectations, less experienced or poorer teachers, or greater difficulties relating to pupil behaviour, attitudes and attendance. The findings warrant further investigation, given concerns about the attainment gap related to pupil background, which has been shown to increase as children progress through school. Part of the explanation may be that disadvantaged children are, for a range of reasons, likely to experience poorer teaching at Key Stage 2, and/or that they pose more challenges for teachers and schools. The present research points to those areas of classroom practice and pedagogy that are worth investigating.

The COS-5

The level of social disadvantage of school context (% FSM), 'school effectiveness' and 'improvement since last inspection' also showed some significant correlations with COS-5 factors and items. Ofsted's judgement of overall 'school effectiveness' was also positively correlated with the 'quality of pedagogy' factor, but the correlation was weaker (r = 0.18, p < 0.06) and just missed statistical significance (see Table 7.3). There were no associations for the 'positive engagement' factor.

Table 7.3: Correlations between COS-5 factors, Ofsted ratings and school disadvantage

Ofsted's judgements and school characteristics	Quality of pedagogy	Disorganization	Child positivity	Attention and control
% FSM		0.36*		
School effectiveness	0.18 p < 0.06			0.20†
Improvement since last inspection			0.21†	
Attendance		−0.22†		

* Correlation is significant at the p < 0.01 level (two-tailed).
† Correlation is significant at the p < 0.05 level (two-tailed).

The 'attention and control' factor was correlated with Ofsted's judgements regarding the schools' effectiveness. The individual item correlations showed that while 'attention' was correlated with Ofsted's school effectiveness judgement (r = 0.26), 'over-control' was not. 'Attention' was also correlated with 'improvement since last inspection' (r = 0.24) and school 'leadership' (r = 0.22). This suggests that in schools judged to have achieved greater improvement and to have better leadership, pupils experience classes where they are more likely to be engaged with their work. Conversely, in primary schools where inspectors judge that there has been less improvement, pupils show lower levels of engagement in class.

The 'child positivity' factor (based on the 'self-reliance', 'sociable/cooperative with peers' and 'child–teacher relationships' factors) correlated with Ofsted's judgement of 'improvement since last inspection' but not with 'school effectiveness'. However, the 'self-reliance' item in this cluster was correlated with Ofsted's judgements of 'school effectiveness' (r = 0.36) and 'improvement since last inspection' (r = 0.39) in the analysis of the individual items, as well as 'teaching and learning at Key Stage 2' (r = 0.20

for both). The observation item 'self-reliance' was also weakly correlated with the school value-added residuals for maths but just failed to reach significance.

'Self-reliance' is an observational measure of the extent to which pupils display autonomy, take responsibility, and show initiative and leadership in class. It could be argued that this is more likely to be observed in classrooms where teachers create a climate that encourages children to demonstrate and develop these traits. 'Self-reliance' appears to be more evident in classes in schools that have been identified by inspectors as more effective and having shown greater improvement.

The measuring classroom 'disorganization' factor was positively correlated with FSM (r = 0.36). All three items in this factor ('chaos', 'disruptive behaviour' and 'negative classroom climate') correlated with this measure. Again, this supports the view that teaching in highly disadvantaged schools is likely to be more challenging as a result of poorer pupil behaviour. Further analyses are needed to see whether disorganization is also greater where teachers are less experienced, since highly disadvantaged schools may find teacher recruitment and retention more problematic than less disadvantaged schools. (The teacher questionnaire explores this aspect further.)

'Disorganization' (and its associated items) was also negatively correlated with Ofsted's judgement of schools regarding pupil 'attendance'. 'Attendance' was more favourably correlated in schools where 'classroom climate' was positive (r = 0.22) but less favourably correlated in schools where 'classroom climate' was observed to be negative (r = −0.26) or where classes where chaotic, where time was wasted repeating instructions and the establishment of smooth routines and transitions between activities was problematic (r = −0.30). Ofsted's judgements of pupils' 'Attitudes to school' were better in schools where the EPPSEM study found that teachers made 'productive use of instructional time' (r = 0.24, an item loading on the 'quality of pedagogy' factor). This suggests that pupils' 'Attitudes to school' are less positive where classroom organization is poor and potential learning time is lost. It may be that poorer attitudes and attendance are a reflection or symptom of less effective teaching practices. Equally in schools with poorer pupil attitudes and attendance, it may be harder for teachers to create productive classroom routines and a positive climate.

These findings indicate that social disadvantage, school quality judgements and teaching quality are interlinked, and that their relationships need to be studied by those seeking to promote school improvement and foster high-quality classroom practice.

Plenary sessions in literacy and numeracy: Quality and effectiveness

Given the evidence that around half of the classes observed for a full lesson did not use a plenary session for literacy or numeracy lessons, further analyses were conducted to see whether schools in which the plenary was adopted differed in terms of our extra measures of school quality and context. There is evidence that inspectors rated those schools in which the researchers observed the use of the literacy plenary more favourably regarding a number of aspects. Ofsted's judgements for overall 'school effectiveness', 'improvement since last inspection' and 'ongoing assessment' were more positive in schools where the literacy plenary was observed, and the differences were statistically significant.

Similarly, classes in which the plenary was seen showed significantly higher scores for IEO 'pedagogy' factors for both literacy and numeracy. Differences between groups were also found for a number of the items loading on this factor, thus indicating a more positive climate in classrooms where children have the opportunity to review, reflect and consolidate their learning in a plenary session. The absence of a plenary may indicate poorer planning or less classroom organization, and possibly less attention to the use of interactive whole-class teaching, consolidation and review.

Further comparisons were made between classrooms where both literacy and numeracy plenaries were witnessed and those where none were observed. In all, just over a quarter of the teachers observed used both literacy and numeracy plenaries, while a similar proportion used neither in the lessons we witnessed (see Table 7.4). Data were available for 69 classes to make these comparisons.

Table 7.4: Comparison of use of plenaries in literacy and numeracy sessions

		Plenary numeracy		Total
		No	Yes	
Plenary literacy	No	19	15	34
		27.5%	21.7%	
	Yes	17	18	35
		24.6%	26.1%	
Total		36	33	69

There was a clear pattern of higher mean scores for classes using plenaries in both literacy and numeracy lessons (based on independent sample t-tests). There were also significant differences in the 'classroom climate', 'social support for student learning' and 'instructional conversations' items in literacy. Differences for a number of additional items approached significance. These included 'purposeful development of writing skills', 'classroom climate' and 'social support for student learning' in numeracy. In addition, Ofsted's judgements of overall 'school effectiveness', 'improvement since last inspection' and 'ongoing assessment' were more positive in primary schools where the Year 5 teacher was observed using a plenary. For all measures, the differences indicated that observed practice was rated most favourably in classes that used a plenary in both literacy and numeracy lessons, and least favourably in classes where no plenary was used for either subject. (For details, see Sammons *et al.*, 2006, p. 46, Table 4.2.1a.)

Key messages and conclusions

This chapter provides an account of observations of variations in teachers' classroom practices based on a bigger sample than that used to study strategies in depth, as described in Chapters 3–6. It is important to document this wide variation because results showed that teachers differ quite markedly in their behaviour, and not all are equally effective. These findings show that children do not receive a common experience in Year 5.

Overall, levels of student engagement were relatively high, and classroom climates were positive. Teacher detachment was generally fairly low, but in a small number of classes this general pattern was not seen.

In a substantial proportion of classes there was little use of the plenary. This is of some concern because this part of the lesson is intended to give opportunities for feedback and to consolidate learning. By missing out the plenary, teachers may be reducing the opportunity to provide such consolidation. In particular, the use of more demanding, higher-order communication is typically more common in plenary sessions. Better practice was more common in lessons where teachers adopted a plenary in both literacy and numeracy. The lowest ratings were given to classes that did not use a plenary in either subject. This finding is striking because the observation instruments are international and were not predicated on the National Literacy and Numeracy Strategies used in England at the time of the research (DfES 2007).

Some aspects of teacher and child behaviour were associated with, and appear to be influenced by, the level of social disadvantage of the pupil intake. Child behaviour tended to be worse in schools where there were a larger proportion of pupils eligible for FSM. Also, the observed teaching quality was poorer in classes where the school context was more disadvantaged. This may reflect the impact of more challenging pupil behaviour, lower teacher expectations and/or less experienced or capable teachers in such schools (since teacher recruitment and retention tends to be more problematic in these contexts).

The findings indicate that Ofsted's judgements of overall features, such as 'school effectiveness' and 'leadership', are significantly correlated with better observed practice. This suggests that school and teacher effectiveness are not independent but interdependent. Teachers' classroom practice was observed to be of a higher quality if they taught in a school that had previously been rated by Ofsted as of higher quality. This may reflect the influence of better leadership, higher expectations, greater collaboration between teachers and consistency in approaches in more effective schools. The classroom practice of teachers in a more effective school may be influenced by the school (indirectly or directly). In such a school, teachers may receive more CPD or guidance that supports their teaching. Of course, it is also possible to conjecture that effective schools may have other effective practices that help to explain these associations, such as attracting or retaining more effective teachers.

SER has indicated that the school culture and leadership can affect teacher expectations and behaviour, and more effective schools may be better at recruiting/retaining better teachers (Mortimore *et al.*, 1988; Sammons *et al.*, 1997; Hopkins, 2001; Leithwood *et al.*, 2006). These are key aspects that SER and inspection evidence have identified as important in promoting better outcomes for pupils (Sammons, 1999; 2007; Teddlie and Reynolds, 2000; Ko *et al.*, 2013; Ofsted, 2000). These findings lend support to the conclusion that overall school effectiveness can affect individual teachers' classroom practice. Some schools may be more and others less supportive in fostering high-quality teaching.

4. Summary of key findings regarding variation in Year 5 classroom practices and behaviours
Pedagogy

- There was significant variation in teachers' practices and pupils' behaviours that distinguished better and poorer quality in the educational experiences of pupils.
- Levels of student engagement were relatively high and classroom climates were generally positive. Teacher detachment was generally low and there was less pupil off-task behaviour observed than in previous classroom studies.

- Classroom experiences varied considerably, with some children attending poorer-quality settings. This has implications for the promotion of equal educational opportunities.
- Teachers' pedagogical practice and classroom organization varied (for example, the teaching of analysis and emphasis on basic skills, classroom climate, organizational routines).
- Most teachers generally followed the format of the National Literacy and Numeracy Strategies except for their use of the plenary, which was not observed in nearly 50 per cent of classes.
- The quality of teaching was consistently higher in classes where a plenary was used in both literacy and numeracy lessons, and lower where no plenary was used in either.

School context

- Pupil behaviour and classroom organization were worse in schools with higher levels of social disadvantage.
- The quality of pedagogy was poorer in schools with higher levels of social disadvantage.

Classroom practice and measures of effectiveness

- Observed practice was better in schools that had previously been rated more positively by Ofsted (particularly for leadership and school effectiveness). This suggests that the practice of teachers in more effective schools is related to the overall quality of the school and its leadership.
- Significant though modest positive associations were found between Ofsted's judgements of overall school effectiveness, the school's improvement since the last inspection and Year 5 teachers' use of the plenary in literacy and numeracy lessons.

In Chapter 8, data regarding the EPPSE children's progress and the measures of classroom practice are linked to see whether better observed practice (the COS-5 and IEO) predicts better progress for pupils' academic outcomes.

Endnote

[1] The analysis of the literacy scale included only 9 of the 11 items. The two remaining items – 'reading as meaning-making' and 'basic skills development in the context of reading' – were not included because these two activities were mutually exclusive and would rarely co-occur within the same observation cycle. Consequently, the number of observations for these items was too small to include.

Chapter 8

The influence of school and teaching quality on children's progress

This chapter builds on the findings described in Chapter 7, which provided descriptions of the COS-5 and IEO, the extent to which they identified variation in teachers' practice and pupils' observed responses, and the associations between these and judgements made by Ofsted (school quality and effectiveness).

This chapter examines patterns of associations between the COS-5 and IEO ratings and EPPSE children's progress in the 125 focal schools. It provides a more detailed analysis, using multilevel statistical models to predict individual children's outcomes having controlled for their background characteristics (for example, gender, parental qualifications, the HLE) so that the net influence of school and classroom quality as predictors of child outcomes can be explored.

The analyses focus on a subsample of nearly 1,200 (1,160) children in 123 of the 125 focal schools (two schools were excluded owing to insufficient data for child outcomes). Further details of the attainment, progress and socio-behavioural development of the full EPPSE sample in Year 5 have been given in separate reports (Sammons *et al.*, 2007a,b; Anders *et al.*, 2011), with a particular focus on the influences of child, family, the HLE and pre-school experiences. The team investigated in more detail the potential influences of classroom practices by using the observation data collected in the focal primary schools and discussed in Chapters 2 and 7. This quantitative strand uses a large amount of data regarding child outcomes to establish whether observed differences in classroom practice predicted differences in these outcomes. It complements and extends the qualitative strand of the EPPSEM study, which explored, in depth, pedagogical strategies that were evident in more effective schools (Chapters 3–6).

For the quantitative analysis of child outcomes, value-added multilevel models were used to study children's academic progress across Year 1 to Year 5 using only those child and family factors previously found to be statistically significant predictors. This means that this study of the effects of classroom measures controls for intake differences at the pupil level. Therefore the estimates of the effects of these classroom measures are reported net of the impact of background influences, including prior attainments in Year 1. This means that the effects of classroom measures are calculated net of the effects of other influences (predictors) in the statistical models.

A range of information has been drawn on. This includes the NFER's standardized assessments of attainment for reading and maths in both Year 1 and Year 5), and information about child, family and HLE characteristics collected from parental interviews when children were recruited to the study and again in Key Stage 1.

As discussed in Chapter 7, data from the COS-5 and IEO were used to identify a number of factors. Five factors were identified for the COS-5 and three identified from IEO. These were tested in the multiple regression models to see if they predicted the variation in child reading and maths outcomes.

Teachers' views of school policies and organization, and different aspects of their practice, were collected via a questionnaire with a 94 per cent (n = 118) response rate.

The remainder of this chapter is divided into four sections and describes how overall measures of 'teaching quality' (and other dimensions) are associated with child outcomes. The outcomes tested were academic progress between Year 1 and Year 5 in reading and maths. Although the EPPSEM study also reported on children's socio-behavioural development, only the academic outcomes are analysed here. For full details of EPPSE children's social behaviours, see Sammons *et al.* (2007a).

Section 1 compares the background characteristics of the children in the EPPSEM subsample with those in the full EPPSE sample. It was important to establish that the subsample was similar in background to the main sample and therefore typical of children in the main study.

Section 2 discusses how data from the COS-5 and IEO factors were further analysed to create overall summary indicators of 'teaching quality'.

Section 3 describes the results of multilevel statistical analyses of children's academic progress between Years 1 and 5 in reading and maths, and how this relates to the overall measures of 'teaching quality' and different dimensions observed. Multilevel analysis is a statistical method that recognizes the complexities in analysing clustered data where children are nested within classes and schools (Goldstein, 1995, 2003). It also enables the research to control statistically for the effects of different child, family and neighbourhood characteristics that predict children's educational outcomes (attainment and progress). The results of the multilevel analyses support the hypothesis that child progress is associated with attending a school with better-observed quality of teaching. In addition, a number of measures from the Year 5 teachers' questionnaire are tested and point to some significant relationships.

Section 4 summarizes the main results and conclusions.

1. The sample

As explained in the 'The sample of focal primary schools' in Chapter 2, the main EPPSE child sample spans four academic year groups, with the middle two (cohorts 2 and 3) containing the largest groups of children.[1] The classroom observation subsample was selected from schools attended by children in these two larger cohorts, ensuring that each school had four or more EPPSE pupils and that there were approximately equal numbers included of relatively more effective and relatively less effective schools (as defined by the school's value-added scores) (see Sammons *et al.*, 2006, 2007a).

The children in the Year 5 observation sample were compared with the full EPPSE sample to make sure that the two groups were not significantly different. Table 8.1 compares the background characteristics of the children.

Table 8.1: Characteristics of Year 5 children and classroom observation data compared with the total EPPSE sample at entry to primary school

Characteristics	COS-5 sample n = 1,160		IEO sample n = 823		Total sample n = 3,172	
	n	%	n	%	n	%
Gender						
Male	582	50.2	407	49.5	1,636	51.6
Female	578	49.8	416	50.5	1,536	48.4
Ethnicity						
White UK heritage	862	74.3	585	71.1	2,295	72.4
White European heritage	39	3.4	27	3.3	122	3.8
Black Caribbean heritage	30	2.6	25	3.0	116	3.7
Black African heritage	17	1.5	12	1.5	66	2.1
Indian heritage	20	1.7	17	2.1	93	2.9
Pakistani heritage	25	2.2	85	10.3	67	2.1

Characteristics	COS-5 sample n = 1,160		IEO sample n = 823		Total sample n = 3,172	
	n	%	n	%	n	%
Bangladeshi heritage	89	7.7	13	1.6	177	5.6
Mixed heritage	17	1.5	43	5.2	40	1.3
Any other ethnic minority heritage	59	5.1	14	1.7	192	6.1
EAL	139	12.0	113	13.7	354	11.2
Child needs EAL support at Year 5	56	4.8	45	5.5	98	3.1
No. of siblings						
siblings	204	17.6	132	16.0	624	19.7
One sibling	738	63.6	529	64.3	1955	61.6
Two-plus siblings	198	17.1	145	17.6	483	15.2
Pre-school home learning Environment (HLE) Index (missing 4%)						
0–13	110	9.5	84	10.2	308	9.7
14–19	249	21.5	176	21.4	665	21.0
20–24	259	22.3	189	23.0	727	22.9
25–32	374	32.2	264	32.1	960	30.3
33–45	133	11.5	83	10.1	346	10.9
Mother's qualifications						
None	247	21.3	179	21.7	647	20.4
Vocational	173	14.9	129	15.7	442	13.9
16 academic	461	39.7	314	38.2	1118	35.2
18 academic	78	6.7	49	6.0	257	8.1
Miscellaneous	9	0.8	7	0.9	25	0.8
Degree and higher degree	156	13.4	114	13.9	533	16.8
Father's qualifications						
None	199	17.2	144	17.5	484	15.3
Vocational	141	12.2	110	13.4	346	10.9
16 academic	310	26.7	203	24.7	676	21.3
18 academic	69	5.9	47	5.7	223	7.0
Degree or equivalent	123	10.6	90	10.9	378	11.9
Higher degree	37	3.2	28	3.4	165	5.2
Other professional/ miscellaneous	12	1.0	10	1.2	32	1.0
Father absent	246	21.2	173	21.0	757	23.9

Characteristics	COS-5 sample n = 1,160		IEO sample n = 823		Total sample n = 3,172	
	n	%	n	%	n	%
Family highest SES						
Professional non-manual	80	6.9	62	7.5	281	8.9
Other professional non-manual	260	22.4	185	22.5	776	24.5
Skilled non-manual	390	33.6	265	32.2	974	30.7
Skilled manual	187	16.1	137	16.6	452	14.2
Semi-skilled	170	14.7	118	14.3	406	12.8
Unskilled	29	2.5	20	2.4	79	2.5
Unemployed/not working	24	2.1	19	2.3	88	2.8
FSM (at Year 5 or earlier)	250	21.6	180	21.9	673	21.2
Salary of family (earned income)						
None	280	24.1	188	22.8	569	17.9
£ 2,500–17,499	235	20.3	172	20.9	485	15.3
£ 17,500–29,999	196	16.9	151	18.3	411	13.0
£ 30,000–37,499	107	9.2	73	8.9	271	8.5
£ 37,500–67,499	179	15.4	118	14.3	470	14.8
£ 67,500–132,000+	41	3.5	33	4.0	173	5.5
Missing salary data	122	10.5	88	10.7	792	25.0
Total multiple disadvantage index						
0 (low disadvantage)	235	20.3	156	19.0	644	20.3
1	282	24.3	192	23.3	781	24.6
2	236	20.3	172	20.9	613	19.3
3	145	12.5	110	13.4	391	12.3
4	102	8.8	76	9.2	257	8.1
5+ (high disadvantage)	85	7.3	59	7.2	213	6.7

It should be noted that all background variables were obtained from a parent interview at entry to the study, with the exception of maternal employment (not shown in Table 8.1) and family earned income. These measures were obtained during Key Stage 1. Measures of FSM eligibility and need of EAL support are collected yearly through a teacher-completed child profile. The measure obtained for a given year is that used in the models for that year's outcomes (for example, Year 5 FSM for Year 5 models, Year 1 FSM for

Year 1 models). The 'none' salary group may have income through benefits or other sources, such as a pension. This group is used as the reference group in comparisons.

Table 8.1 shows that for key characteristics the two samples were broadly consistent. For instance, looking at background, nearly three-quarters were of White UK heritage, and 12 per cent had EAL with nearly 5 per cent still needing EAL support. The majority of children (63.6 per cent) lived with one sibling, 18 per cent were singletons and 17 per cent were from larger families (with three-plus siblings). Just under half (44 per cent) had relatively high scores (25+) for the early years HLE and a substantial minority of children (31 per cent) had low scores for this measure (< 20).

About 13 per cent of both mothers' and fathers' qualifications were at degree level or higher, while the majority (75 per cent mothers, 56 per cent fathers[2]) were educated only to end-of-compulsory-schooling level (age 16 or GCSE) or below. Some 19 per cent had low family SES compared with half (49.7 per cent) with medium (skilled manual or skilled non-manual) SES, and 29 per cent were from the higher (professional) groups. Nearly a quarter of children in the sample (24 per cent) lived in households where parents reported no earned income and 22 per cent were eligible for FSM.

As Table 8.1 shows, overall, this subsample of children (1,160) is not significantly different from the total EPPSE sample as variations in the distribution of background characteristics are generally within 2 per cent (except for income). There is an overrepresentation of children whose reported family earned income is either 'none' or less than £15,000 (44.4 per cent in comparison with 33.2 per cent in the total sample) and of children whose mothers and fathers have a relatively lower '16-academic' level of qualification (39.7 per cent and 26.7 per cent respectively).

2. Global measures of teaching quality based on the COS-5 and IEO

The COS-5 and IEO instruments were explored in detail in Chapter 7, which showed that they had significant but relatively modest associations. This suggests that the two measured somewhat different aspects and seem to tap into somewhat different underlying dimensions of teacher/pupil behaviours.

Key dimensions in classroom processes

As noted in Chapter 7, a number of underlying dimensions (factors) were identified from IEO and the COS-5 (see Boxes 7.3 and 7.4). These factors are used in this chapter and are shown again here as a reminder (Boxes 8.1 and 8.2).

IEO DIMENSIONS

Literacy

Pedagogy
- classroom climate
- classroom routines
- social support for student learning
- student engagement
- instructional conversations.

Subject development
- higher-order thinking in writing
- purposeful development of writing skills.

Learning linkages
- cross-disciplinary connections
- linkage to life beyond the classroom.

Numeracy

Pedagogy
- classroom climate
- classroom routines
- social support for student learning
- student engagement.

Subject development
- use of maths analysis
- depth of knowledge and student understanding
- basic skills development in the context of problem-solving
- maths discourse and communication
- locus of maths authority.

Learning linkages
- cross-disciplinary connections
- linkage to life beyond the classroom.

Box 8.1: Underlying dimensions of IEO

COS-5 DIMENSIONS

Quality of pedagogy
- classroom code: richness of instructional methods
- classroom code: teacher detachment
- classroom code: positive classroom climate
- classroom code: productive use of instructional time
- classroom code: evaluative feedback
- classroom code: teacher sensitivity

Disorganization
- child code: disruptive
- classroom code: chaos
- classroom code: negative classroom climate

Child positivity
- child code: self-reliance
- child code: sociable/cooperative with peers
- child code: child–teacher relationship

Positive engagement
- child code: positive affect
- child code: activity level

Attention and control
- child code: attention
- classroom code: over-control

Box 8.2: Underlying dimensions of the COS-5

Each of the five dimensions of the COS-5 data was divided into four levels, as follows: low (below 1 SD of the mean), low-medium (within 1 SD below the mean), medium-high (within 1 SD above the mean) and high (above 1 SD of the mean).

The IEO dimensions (see Table 8.2) were divided into just three groups: low (bottom 20 per cent), medium (middle 60 per cent) and high (top 20 per cent). These groupings were then used to construct a global measure of teaching/classroom quality based on the sum of the combined classification of the individual dimensions. A global indicator of 'teaching quality' was created for both the overall COS-5 instrument and for the literacy and numeracy scales of IEO.

The global indicators were created in three stages. First, the individual dimensions were recoded such that scores below 1 SD of the mean received a value of (-1), scores within 1 SD of the mean received a value of (0) and scores above 1 SD of the mean received a value of (1). The recoded variables were then summed. The resulting distributions are shown in Table 8.2. Finally, as the extreme low and the extreme high categories consisted of very few numbers, the bottom two and top two categories were collapsed for all three global indicators to produce five categories representing varying levels of performance for the COS-5 global indicators of 'teaching quality' and three categories for each of the IEO global indicators.

Table 8.2: Distribution of children by overall 'teaching quality' dimension

COS-5 overall indicator of teaching quality (total n = 1,160)	Low	Low-medium	Medium	Medium-high	High
	n = 184	n = 269	n = 295	n = 311	n = 101
	15.9%	23.2%	25.4%	26.8%	8.7%
IEO overall indicator of teaching quality (total n = 757)	n = 208	n/a	n = 333	n/a	n = 216
	27.5%	n/a	44.0%	n/a	28.5%

n/a: not applicable.

Only 8.7 per cent of children attended schools where the Year 5 classes had high COS-5 scores for overall 'teaching quality', compared with nearly 16 per cent low quality. In terms of the IEO overall indicator, the proportions in the low and high categories were more similar at around 28 per cent.

Section 3 explores the relationships between the COS-5 and IEO (individual factors and global quality indicators) and children's academic progress.

3. The influence of classroom processes on children's academic progress between Years 1 and 5

The various IEO and COS-5 factors shown in Boxes 7.3 and 7.4 were entered individually into CVA multilevel models to predict children's progress (Sammons *et al.*, 2007a,b). Owing to the differences in numbers, the results for the COS-5 and IEO factors are reported separately.

It is important to note that the analyses cannot distinguish between the influence of individual teachers but reflects longer term both school and teacher influences across four school years. However, it is plausible that classroom practice may be generally better in schools where high quality in Year 5 was observed owing to a combination of school and teacher influences that create a stronger focus on teaching and learning, and supporting high-quality classroom practices throughout the school. This is why the in-depth study (see Chapters 3–6) used overall school measures as well as observation data to pick the purposive sample to study effective practice. It also means that it is likely to underestimate rather than overestimate the effects of overall teaching quality in Year 5 on children's progress.

Predicting progress using the COS-5

THE INFLUENCE OF OVERALL TEACHING QUALITY

It was hypothesized that children will make more progress in schools and classes where overall 'teaching quality' was observed to be higher. To investigate this, the categories in the overall quality indicator were tested in the multilevel models of children's academic progress.

'Teaching quality' was found to be a positive predictor of both reading and maths progress. This relationship held after control for the significant effects of child, family and early years HLE factors, as well as children's prior attainment in Year 1. Figure 8.1 shows the associations in terms of ESs. All teaching-quality groups are compared with the high category, which is the base category in the tables that follow. Because high is set as the reference category, it is shown at the base group, which is set to zero. Every other quality group is then compared with high quality to see if effects differ in comparison with the effects of the high-quality group.

Figure 8.1 shows that there is a clear stepped pattern for maths progress, distinguishing the different quality groups quite clearly. The largest differences are found between both the high and the medium-high group and other categories (ES = −0.35 between the highest and lowest categories).

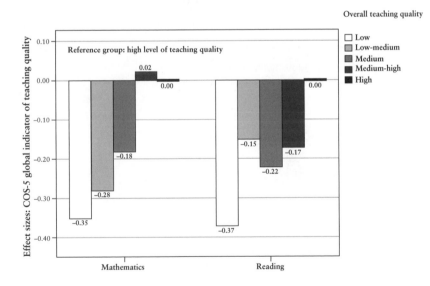

Figure 8.1: Effect of 'teaching quality' on children's academic progress

For children's reading progress there are also significant differences, although the pattern is less obviously stepped. The difference between the high and low categories is as large as that found for maths (ES = 0.37).

However, there is a less obvious gradation between the three remaining groups (low-medium, medium and medium-high), although they still show better effects for progress compared with the low group. This confirms the hypothesis that children made better academic progress in schools where the overall quality of teaching was high rather than low in Year 5.

Two important conclusions can be drawn from these results, as follows:

- It is possible to classify teachers in a meaningful way in terms of differences in overall 'teaching quality' across a range of different dimensions of classroom behaviour and practice based on the COS-5.
- Teaching quality is a significant predictor of better progress, and this is particularly evident at the extremes of high and low quality.

While the overall 'teaching quality' factor showed the strongest link with child outcomes, suggesting that it is a combination of quality factors that makes most difference to progress, the team nevertheless tested each of the COS-5 factors separately and collectively. Some interesting results were seen for the disorganization and the attention and control factors.

Disorganization
'Disorganization' was also associated with progress in both reading and maths.

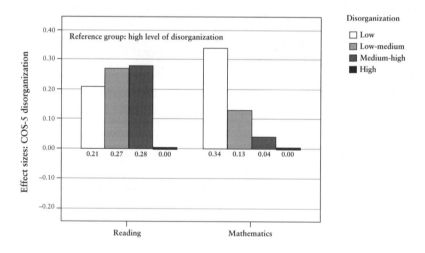

Figure 8.2: Net effects of 'disorganization' on children's academic progress

As Figure 8.2 shows, poorer progress was predicted by higher levels of 'disorganization' in class. For reading, the main contrast was between high levels of 'disorganization' and all other categories. High levels of 'disorganization' were linked to significantly poorer reading outcomes after control for other influences and prior attainment. For maths, the pattern was more clearly stepped and linear, with the difference in progress being predicted by attending a school where low levels of 'disorganization' had been observed compared with high levels of 'disorganization' (ES = –0.35).

Attention and control
'Attention' and 'control' were also found to be associated with academic progress in maths but not reading. In schools where classroom attention and control were high, children made more progress in maths. The main difference identified distinguished the high group from all others, as shown in Figure 8.3.

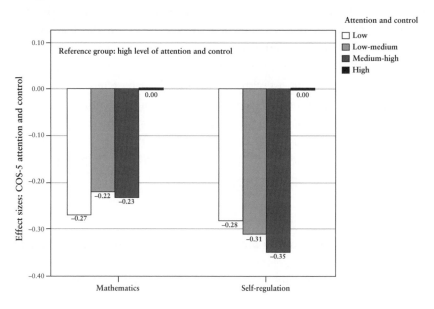

Figure 8.3: Effect of 'attention and control' on children's academic progress and self-regulation

This chapter has reported mainly on academic progress and not socio-behavioural development in this chapter, it is worth noting here the positive influence of 'attention and control' on children's self-regulation. (For details of other socio-behaviours, see Sammons *et al.*, 2007a.) The development of self-regulation is becoming a topic of increasing research interest globally because it is a learnt behaviour that appears to have some significant influences on academic attainment, particularly in reading and maths (Cadima *et al.*, 2015; Howse *et al.*, 2003; Ponitz *et al.*, 2009; Hammer *et al.*, 2018). In classrooms where the observed levels of classroom 'attention and control' were high, children not only made better progress in maths but also exercised better self-regulation. These results support the view that higher levels of teacher attention and a proactive approach to classroom management may help to promote more effective learning and assist children to become better at managing their own learning behaviour.

Taken together, the COS-5 results suggest that it is the overall combination of teacher behaviours, rather than particular isolated features, that can be used to identify differences in overall 'teaching quality' and provide the clearest distinctions in terms of predicting children's academic progress.

Predicting progress using IEO

Separate multilevel analyses of children's progress were conducted using the IEO data, given this instrument's specific focus on the teaching of literacy and numeracy (number of classes, 93). As previously stated, the IEO analyses identified three broad groups of practice across classes (high, medium and low). In contrast with the COS-5 indicator of 'teaching quality', there was no clear pattern between the three groups identified from the IEO overall 'teaching quality' in the progress analyses. This may reflect the reduced sample size , but it may also be that the COS-5 instrument is better at measuring features of overall quality of teaching that help to promote academic outcomes. Nonetheless, specific factors of the IEO instrument did predict outcomes.

PEDAGOGY IN LITERACY

Interestingly, the 'pedagogy in literacy' factor was found to be significantly associated with better academic progress in both reading and maths, but the pattern was clearer and showed a stronger stepped pattern for maths (see Figure 8.4).

The difference between the highest and lowest category was moderately strong (ES = −0.45) for maths but smaller (ES = −0.23) for reading. This suggests that elements of effective literacy teaching measured by the IEO instrument may be associated more broadly with better teaching overall.

PEDAGOGY IN NUMERACY

The 'pedagogy in numeracy' factor was also found to be significantly associated with children's progress in maths, as shown in Figure 8.5.

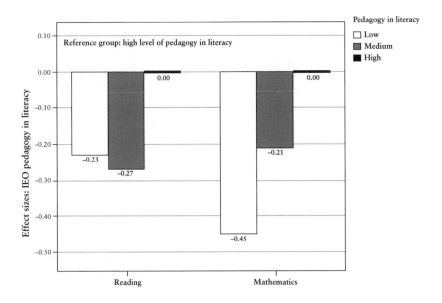

Figure 8.4: Effect of 'pedagogy in literacy' on academic progress

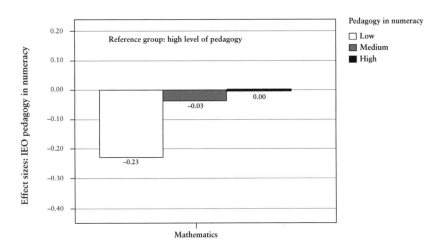

Figure 8.5: Effect of 'pedagogy in numeracy' on academic progress

The main distinction is between the low group of classes and the other groups (ES = –0.23 between the low group and the high group). The 'pedagogy in numeracy' factor was not associated with children's progress in reading.

SUBJECT DEVELOPMENT IN NUMERACY

The 'subject development in numeracy' factor was not found to be significantly related to children's progress in maths but was linked to better progress in reading. Again, this suggests that subject-specific measures may reveal general features of effective teaching, not just those specific to one subject.

Table 8.3 summarizes the main results from the multilevel models of children's academic progress for the two outcomes studied. It can be seen that the differences are consistent and moderately strong in the main. They are also generally in the directions predicted (higher scores for the various measures of quality being associated with better academic outcomes for EPPSE children, taking account of other background influences and prior attainment).

Table 8.3: Summary of relationships between classroom processes and children's progress

	Reading	Maths
COS-5	ES	ES
Global indicator	0.37*	0.35*
Quality of pedagogy		0.27*
Disorganization	0.21*	0.34*
Child positivity	0.39*	
Positive engagement		
Attention and control		0.27*
IEO		
Literacy		
Global indicator		
Pedagogy	0.23*	0.45*
Subject development		
Learning linkages		
Numeracy		
Global indicator		
Pedagogy		0.23*
Subject development	0.32*	
	Medium group	
Learning linkages		

Notes: Reference group: high. ES shows the net differences between the lowest- and highest-scoring groups.
* Unless otherwise stated, p < 0.05.

The results therefore broadly support the view that in primary schools where better practice was observed using the COS-5 and IEO, there appeared to be measurable benefits for children's outcomes.

Teacher survey results

To supplement the classroom observations, a teacher questionnaire explored teachers' views of different aspects of school and classroom processes and organization. A number of underlying dimensions were identified (Sammons *et al.*, 2006, 2008c). Schools were divided into a number of groups ranging from low to high, based on the teachers' responses for each dimension. These were then tested in the multilevel models to explore how they related to child outcomes. Two measures related to teachers' perceptions of overall 'school communication with parents', and the extent of overall 'parental support of their child's learning' were found to be significant predictors of better outcomes. Of the two, teachers' perceptions of 'school communication with parents' was the stronger predictor (see Figures 8.6 and 8.7). Again, the team reported effects on the academic outcomes and self-regulation.

TEACHERS' REPORTS ON PARENTAL INVOLVEMENT

For reading progress, the difference in outcomes between the high and low groups for 'school communication with parents' was moderately strong (ES = 0.38). The effect was similar for maths (ES = 0.34).

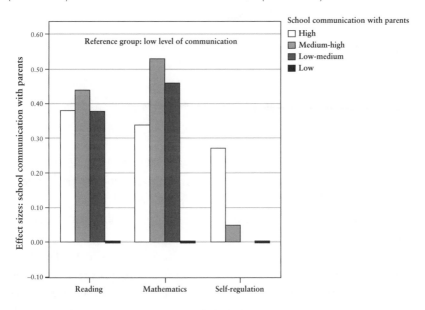

Figure 8.6: Effect of 'school communication with parents' on academic progress and self-regulation

This indicates that, after taking account of other influences, children made better academic progress in schools where teachers reported good communication with parents in aspects such as communicating expectations of pupils to parents, or regularly informing parents about their child's progress and achievements. The 'school communication with parents' factor also predicted better developmental progress for self-regulation (ES = 0.27) when the low and high groups were compared.

Teachers' reports of 'parental support of their child's learning' also showed a positive relationship with pupils' progress in reading (ES = 0.28, see Figure 8.7) but not maths.

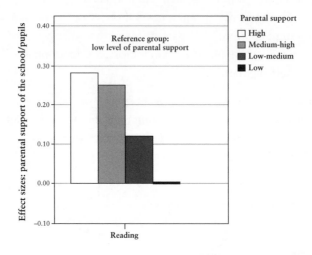

Figure 8.7: Effect of 'parental support of their child's learning' on reading progress

TEACHERS' REPORTS ON HOMEWORK

Teachers' reports on 'use of homework and school standards' also indicated a positive relationship with maths progress, although the strongest effects were for the medium group (ES = 0.27) followed by the high group (ES = 0.13). There was no significant effect for reading outcomes (see Figure 8.8).

Results for self-regulation have again been reported here. The items in this factor included whether most teachers set homework every week for their class, whether most teachers marked and returned homework promptly, and whether the overall standards set for pupils at the school were perceived to be high enough.

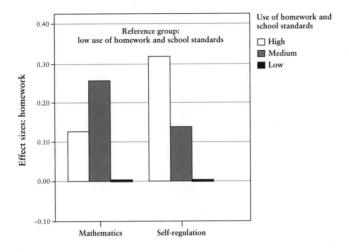

Figure 8.8: Effect of 'use of homework and school standards' on progress in maths and self-regulation

TEACHERS' REPORTS ON ANTI-ACADEMIC ETHOS

Teachers' reports of an 'anti-academic ethos' among pupils were also found to predict academic progress (see Figure 8.9).

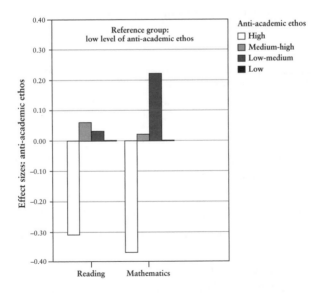

Figure 8.9: Effects of 'anti-academic ethos' on progress in reading and maths

Pupils in schools where an 'anti-academic ethos' was perceived by teachers to be high showed significantly poorer progress in reading (ES = −0.31) and maths (ES = −0.37). The differences were mainly between the high and low groups.

Table 8.4 summarizes teachers' perceptions and children's progress in relation to reading and maths.

Table 8.4: Summary: teachers' perceptions and children's progress

Criteria	Reading ES	Maths ES
School communication with parents	0.38*	0.34*
Parental support of child's learning	0.28*	
Use of homework and school standards		0.27* Medium group
Pupils' agency and voice	0.26~ Medium-high group	
Anti-academic ethos	0.31~	0.37~

Reference group: high
Effect sizes represent effect size differences between the lowest- and highest-scoring groups, unless otherwise stated.

*The probability of the effect occurring by chance is < 0.05.
~The probability of a significant effect does not reach but approaches statistical significance.

4. Summary and conclusions

This chapter provides results from the quantitative strand of the EPPSEM study, which focused on measuring the progress of 1,160 children from Years 1 to 5. The project was important because it explored the relationships between children's progress and various COS-5 and IEO measures of observed classroom practice, as detailed in Chapter 7. Given the four-year time period, it could not measure the effects of individual teachers directly but it could increase the chance of identifying overall school effects. It also included information regarding teachers' perceptions of various aspects of their school taken from a questionnaire.

It was hypothesized that higher-quality classroom experiences in Year 5 would predict better child progress, taking account of background factors. SER has drawn attention to the importance of the classroom level in accounting for variations in student outcomes in many studies, but such work has generally only tested limited measures of classroom processes

(Teddlie and Reynolds, 2000). Here the team studied a more detailed set of classroom indicators based on two international instruments when measuring children's academic outcomes and self-regulation.

What matters in the classroom?

The overall measure of the COS-5 'teaching quality' factor was a significant and moderately strong predictor of both reading (ES = 0.35) and maths progress (ES = 0.37). These differences refer to the contrast between the high and low categories in the overall measure of 'teaching quality'.

This suggests that it is possible to classify teachers in Year 5 classes in a meaningful way in terms of differences in overall 'teaching quality' across a range of different dimensions of classroom behaviour and practice, based on an internationally recognized observational instrument to provide evidence. The team found that 'teaching quality' is a significant predictor of better academic progress, and this is particularly evident at the extremes.

In other words, children in schools where Year 5 'teaching quality' was observed to be high overall did significantly better in both reading and maths than those attending schools where quality was observed to be low, controlling for other important predictors.

It is also interesting to note that the influence of overall 'teaching quality' on reading and maths was stronger than the net influence of some background factors, such as gender and family disadvantage (measured by eligibility for FSM), but weaker than the influence of early years HLE and mothers' qualifications.

Specific aspects of classroom processes were found to predict better academic progress. For example, classroom 'disorganization' was a significant predictor of poorer progress in reading and maths, higher levels of 'disorganization' being linked to significantly poorer outcomes. This factor is related to the behavioural climate of the classroom and supports the findings of earlier teacher and school effectiveness studies that point to the importance of a calm and orderly climate in facilitating learning and teaching. It may be harder for teachers to maintain good order in their classrooms if they teach in schools serving higher proportions of disadvantaged children. It may also be that poorer classroom practice is one contributory factor in explaining the poorer outcomes of children in more disadvantaged communities. Quite likely both explanations play a part. Multilevel analyses have tested and controlled for a range of child and family background measures (where significant), including parents' qualifications, occupations and income, and also the school context (level of disadvantage of school intake). The results show that, over and above such influences, features of classroom experience, such as 'disorganization', seem to play an important role in shaping academic outcomes.

Other research (Ross and Hutchings, 2003; Darling-Hammond, 2002; Wirt *et al.*, 2002, 2003) has suggested that schools in disadvantaged settings can find it harder to recruit and retain teachers. Given this, and in the light of the findings from this research, it is likely that a stronger emphasis on promoting overall 'teaching quality' and a more orderly classroom climate will be important features of programmes and initiatives to promote better educational outcomes for pupils in schools that serve above-average proportions of disadvantaged children.

While overall 'teaching quality' was important for promoting both better reading and maths progress, specific features of practice measured by the 'quality of pedagogy' factor showed stronger relationships with children's maths progress. Reviews of school and teacher effectiveness research have suggested that schools vary more in the effects on maths than on reading (Scheerens and Bosker, 1997; Muijs and Reynolds, 2003).

What matters in the school?

The teacher questionnaire explored teachers' reports on different aspects of their school. A number of underlying dimensions were identified. Two measures related to teachers' perceptions of overall 'school communication with parents' and the extent of overall 'parental support of their child's learning' were found to be significant predictors of better child outcomes, with 'school communication with parents' being the stronger of these predictors.

The dimension relating to teachers' reports on 'use of homework and school standards' also indicated a positive relationship with maths progress and self-regulation. Teachers' perceptions of an 'anti-academic ethos' among pupils also predicted academic progress. Schools in which an 'anti-academic ethos' was high showed significantly poorer progress in reading and maths. The differences were mainly between the high and low groups.

The percentage of pupils eligible for FSM was also associated with poorer progress in maths. Elsewhere it has been shown that only classroom measure was associated with the level of disadvantage (Sammons *et al.*, 2008c). Classroom 'disorganization' was weakly negatively associated with the FSM poverty measure.

Taken together, the findings in this chapter build on and extend those in Chapter 7, which revealed significant variations in the observed quality of teaching. This is important because quality of teaching is associated with better progress in reading and maths. Overall, these findings indicate that important educational influences (for example, organization) play a significant part in shaping children's outcomes, in addition to their own personal, family and HLE characteristics, and the level of social disadvantage of their schools. If all teachers practised as those observed in the classrooms with the highest ratings, children would benefit greatly. Given this, schools and teachers could use systematic classroom observations as a tool to reflect on their practice, as a way to identify priorities for CPD and as part of their strategies for school improvement to identify foci for raising, and reducing the variation in, the quality of children's day-to-day classroom experiences.

Endnotes

[1] In 2004, cohort 2 had 1,180 children in Year 5 in 483 schools. In 2005, cohort 3 had 1,435 children in 616 schools.

[2] Differences are accounted for by 21 per cent of children being in households with absent fathers.

Chapter 9

Using effective pedagogical practices: Overview and implications

As noted in the early chapters, a range of educationalists have written a great deal about pedagogy and effectiveness, and some of the work that links these has been inspiring and influential. The EPPSEM substudy (Siraj-Blatchford *et al.*, 2011), the processes and findings of which form the core of this book, sets out to examine this link between pedagogy and effectiveness in as much detail as possible. This volume has reported on findings that point to a bundle of teaching behaviours and approaches that, taken together, clearly influence children's development and progress, and, therefore, their later life chances.

The EPPSEM project was one of several substudies of the main EPPSE longitudinal mixed-methods research that was commissioned by the UK Government in 1997. It sought to identify any differences between poor, good and excellent teaching that it could find by analysing independent child outcome records, Ofsted judgements, and the COS-5 and IEO in a representative sample of English Year 5 classrooms. The project was a unique opportunity to link qualitative information (the observation notes and lesson plans) to quantitative data based on systematic observation instruments, and to children's progress and development. Furthermore, by using national measures of schools' academic effectiveness (based on national assessment and Ofsted inspection ratings), it was possible to examine pedagogical practices in the important context of a primary school's effectiveness status.

This book has attempted to provide the following:

1. a summary of the research team's strategy and methods
2. an explanation of the main differences and similarities found between three distinct groups of schools based on academic effectiveness and observed quality of pedagogy
3. a basic exploration of the key themes that the researchers drew from the many analyses

4. a series of brief excerpts from the researchers' field notes to illustrate the practice they observed
5. headline findings for policymakers and practitioners
6. an outline list of the pedagogical strategies that the researchers concluded distinguished the most effective primary-school teachers from their less effective colleagues.

While 5. and 6. have been seeded throughout this book, the strategies have been distilled in this last chapter to underline key messages.

Limitations and constraints

Every research project has limitations. None, therefore, can ever be deemed entirely conclusive. The observations were conducted only in Year 5 classrooms in England, so the results may not apply internationally or across all primary age groups.

Equally, the focus of the EPPSEM study, and this book, is on the teaching that was observed inside the classrooms of effective schools. Thus the team did not analyse the full array of other school and pupil-level factors outside the classroom, which may influence school effectiveness (for example, leadership, monitoring pupil progress, parental support, attendance and rates of exclusion). Some of these external factors are considered in the school effectiveness literature.

Although the team used the large amounts of quantitative data gained through the COS-5 and IEO research instruments, they drew attention in the EPPSEM study to the qualitative descriptions provided by their researchers collected along with the numerical ratings. They did this specifically to provide practitioners and policymakers with illuminating evidence on practice while at the same time reporting on the full quantitative data from the main EPPSE literature. This is an important feature of the mixed-methods research design and strengthens the team's inferences.

Finally, one small constraint of the research was that the observations focused on the pedagogical strategies described and measured by two research instruments. This meant that there was inevitably an inconsistent level of available data to support or refute the pedagogical strategies that they identified through the evidence-based literature search and professional focus-group discussions.

All good research raises questions and prompts further research. Following the findings about the nature of effective teaching in Year 5, it is immediately obvious that further similar, large-scale, mixed-methods research in whole-school contexts would be helpful (though probably expensive) to enable comparisons between high, medium and less effective groups of schools to investigate in more detail excellent, good and poor pedagogical practices across different age ranges and phases of schooling.

Despite these limitations, the findings point to a clear bundle of teaching behaviours and approaches that, taken together, influence children's development and progress, and therefore their later life chances. This is especially true for children from disadvantaged backgrounds, where other EPPSE research shows that what happens at the classroom level in pre-schools (Siraj-Blatchford *et al.*, 2011) and primary schools makes a vital difference to outcomes (Sylva *et al.*, 2010).

Some distinguishing markers of excellent teaching in academically highly effective schools with good-quality pedagogy

As described throughout this book, the researchers analysed the classroom observational data from a subsample of the 850 primary schools that were attended by the EPPSE's 3,000+ children.

They found the schools to be generally well-organized, happy places in which to learn. The teachers' objectives were usually clear. Children followed well-established class routines. Resources were well organized and appropriate for both children and learning objectives. The classroom climate was positive and supportive. Behaviour management was handled sensitively, and often through expectation. However, opportunities for collaborative work, dialogic learning and assessment for learning were rare.

At the end of their observations, analyses, discussions and reviews, the EPPSE team concluded that the differences that they had identified between the three groups of primary schools revealed 11 key distinguishing markers of teachers working in effective schools that appear, synergistically, to make a real difference to pupil's academic and socio-behavioural outcomes.

Strategy 1: Organization

The researchers established that the Year 5 teachers in academically highly effective schools with good-quality pedagogy (Group A) organized their lessons, materials and teaching time particularly well. They planned their lessons very carefully, used their learning and teaching time most productively, and produced especially well-organized and fit-for-purpose resources. The quickness of pace in their lessons left no time for pupils to slack off, and there was a sense of urgency about the learning taking place. There was also an atmosphere of liveliness and sometimes fun.

One interesting aspect of these teachers' effective organization was that the team found their pupils to be more self-reliant than their peers in Group B (medium-academic-effectiveness schools with medium-quality pedagogy) and Group C (low-academic-effectiveness schools with poor-quality pedagogy). It may be that better behaviour meant that teachers were more likely to encourage greater pupil independence, and poorer behaviour led to teachers limiting the degree to which pupils were allowed to be self-reliant. It is equally possible, however, that children in more effective schools were more self-reliant simply because their classrooms and resources were better organized. Because they always knew what to do and where to find their resources, they were able to function autonomously.

The EPPSE research is, of course, not alone in identifying pedagogical strategies that require special attention. Many scholars have written about the importance of good organizational skills, making productive use of instructional time, and developing whole-school policies on maximizing lesson times and whole-class interaction time (Evertson and Randolph, 1995; Muijs and Reynolds, 2003; Alexander, 2006). Other academics have also shown that children's learning experiences are enhanced when teachers maximize learning time with pace, variety and resources, and establish classroom routines with higher levels of pupil responsibility (Claxton and Carr, 2004; Gipps *et al.*, 2000; Watson *et al.*, 2007).

Strategy 2: Classroom climate

A positive climate appeared to be a key part of classroom life. The Group A classrooms observed were happy places where everyone (adults and children) demonstrated mutual respect and common purpose. The teachers excelled at creating warm, supportive environments where their pupils felt safe enough to take risks with their learning. They had excellent relationships with their pupils and were especially sensitive to the needs of individuals. Children in these classrooms demonstrated high levels of liking and respect for their fellow pupils.

Trust between teachers and children, and between the children themselves, may be an influential factor in the link between positive classroom climate and excellence. Children may be more willing to tackle new learning challenges when they do not need to worry about the reactions of their classmates and teachers to their mistakes.

Again, many scholars and researchers have emphasized the importance of a positive relationship between children, and between teachers and children. This is recognized as a major feature of excellent classroom teachers in both a comparative OECD study of 11 countries and a UK Department for Education and Employment review (DfEE, 2000a). Many other socio-cultural researchers have also stressed the importance of teacher sensitivity, good peer relations and creating communities of learners (Anderson *et al.*, 2004; Kutnick and Kington, 2005; Shulman, 2004).

A healthy classroom climate may also interact synergistically with collaborative work, dialogic learning and peer assessment, because group work and class discussions are more likely to be successful where pupils relate well. Children who learn in classrooms with a positive atmosphere will already have good models of cooperative behaviour, and more practice at working with and supporting each other, so they should be able to make better use of their opportunities to learn through collaboration and dialogue.

Strategy 3: Clear objectives, shared goals

The research team found that Year 5 teachers in Group A schools were particularly good at making certain that their lessons' learning intentions and activities were clear to all of their pupils. They ensured that all of their children understood the ideas and concepts associated with the activity, and they were much better at doing this than teachers in other schools. The plenary was an excellent opportunity to recap and consolidate the objectives, and how they had been met. This is not a new finding, because many academics have suggested that it is vital for teachers to share their objectives and make sure that their concepts and ideas are presented clearly (Borich, 2000; Gipps *et al.*, 2000). Rather, it is the depth and breadth of the evidence and analysis behind the EPPSE finding that is new.

Strategy 4: Behaviour management

The research team noted that the level of pupil disruption and classroom chaos was lower in Group A schools. The teachers managed their pupil behaviour with humour and sensitivity, by engaging them in their learning, and by dealing privately and informally with breaches of the rules.

Many studies demonstrate that effective discipline and sound behaviour management are part of excellent classroom practice (Rogers, 2007; Woodcock and Reupert, 2012). However, the EPPSE team showed that teachers in Group C schools commonly used over-control in seeking to manage their classrooms, and that this is not an effective approach.

Strategy 5: Collaborative learning

The team were surprised to discover that, overall, genuine collaborative learning was not common in most classrooms. However, children in excellent schools were likely to spend slightly more time working in groups, where their teachers encouraged them to provide feedback to each other, to work collaboratively on a complex problem, and to support each other's learning through peer-tutoring and response partners.

Teachers in the best schools did not group children of similar ability in literacy lessons. About half of them did group by ability in numeracy classes, and many of these teachers used this strategy to work discreetly with a specific cohort of children. Group A schools had the most positive classroom climate and fewest discipline issues. It makes sense that they also worked more than others in groups. Children in these classes become more self-reliant and so could work well together. They could also take responsibility for not only their learning but also that of their peers.

Many academics have studied collaborative and group learning for some time. They have associated small-group work with higher achievement and have presented group interaction as an integral part of learning (Veenam *et al.*, 2005; Gipps *et al.*, 2000; Fosnot, 1996; Barron, 2003; Tolmie *et al.*, 2010). Other studies have shown that effective teachers encourage children to work in groups to think through their ideas, to present their thinking, and to be involved in peer-tutoring (Whitebread *et al.*, 2007).

Strategy 6: Personalized learning

The EPPSE team noted that teachers in Group A schools provided the best teaching resources and were the most sensitive to their pupils' personal needs. They were the least detached, the most involved with their pupils and they best met their children's individual needs. They provided much more social support for their pupils' learning than their colleagues in other schools. Personalized learning was often accomplished by differentiated tasks/activities, and teaching was tailored to the individual interests, skills and abilities of pupils.

Once again, there is probably a healthy and productive interaction between positive classroom climate, good pupil behaviour, more group work and the higher ratings that teachers at excellent schools received for personalized learning. These were the teachers who made a point of getting to know their pupils and understanding their personal needs. This classroom backdrop of positive relationships meant that teachers in such schools were in a better position to adapt their teaching to their children's needs and interests.

Strategy 7: Dialogic teaching and learning

Although the research team were disappointed by how few instances of dialogic learning they observed, they concluded that some was better than none. When they found differences between schools, it was again the teachers in Group A schools who most used discussion and dialogue.

These were teachers with a desire and talent for engaging with their pupils at every level. They arranged their classrooms, routines and resources so that their children could be self-reliant. They were extremely sensitive to their pupils' needs, they modelled and encouraged (perhaps even insisted on) good relationships and, at least sometimes, they provided a collaborative working environment.

By laying these strong foundations, the teachers' classroom environments were perfect arenas for dialogic learning. Because the pupils knew that their opinions and contributions were respected and valued, they could engage confidently in dialogue with each other and the teacher. Because they learnt in a particularly positive and supportive environment, they were able to attempt new learning challenges more easily.

One of the EPPSEM study's more surprising findings was that teachers in excellent schools were much more likely to use dialogic learning in maths than in other subjects. This is particularly worth noting because numeracy is a subject where children need a real depth of understanding to make good progress.

Dialogic learning succeeds only in an environment where everyone feels safe enough to take risks. Teachers in excellent schools made sure that their classrooms were safe and supportive. Although direct teaching has an important place in the primary classroom, other strategies can stimulate children's thinking more, and these usually depend on the quality of interaction between teacher and pupil for their success.

The team's disappointment at the relative lack of dialogic learning was, at least partly, because it had been emphasized in so many important studies. Some scholars have argued for years that dialogic teaching is a key feature of effective classrooms and that this is characterized by the use of open-ended questions to develop deeper-level learning (Wells, 1999). Others have demonstrated its importance in the early years, where sustained, shared thinking has been found in effective practice (Siraj-Blatchford *et al.*, 2002). Still more have shown that a dialogic approach encourages analytical thought (because children reflect, explain and argue through their thinking and problem-solving) and enhances children's meta-cognitive skills (De Jager *et al.*, 2005). Although, like genuinely collaborative group work, dialogic learning was not evident in most classrooms, it was observed more in excellent settings, suggesting that it may be an important component in children making good progress.

Strategy 8: Assessment for learning

Since the turn of the century, much has been written about the importance of developing feedback strategies that are formative, delve into children's understanding and extend their learning. Evaluative feedback of this kind helps children to reflect on their learning by reviewing and assessing their work. It offers encouragement and promotes effort, especially when coupled with suggestions and strategies that guide pupils forward in their learning (Black and Wiliam, 1998a,b; Arter and Stiggins, 2005; Rittle-Johnson, 2006; Dweck, 2000).

Particularly influential in the UK were Black and Wiliam (1998a,b), whose work explored assessment practices and the role of formative feedback, as opposed to summative assessments, in order to raise standards. How teachers undertake formative assessment has been the subject of much study (Clarke, 1998; Stobart and Gipps, 1997; Tunstall and Gipps, 1996).

It seemed to the EPPSE team that assessment for learning (or assessment as learning) was a natural part of the ongoing dialogue between teachers and pupils in excellent schools. They saw that those teachers provided much more evaluative feedback and opportunities for their pupils to reflect on their learning than teachers in other schools.

Strategy 9: The plenary

Despite the unambiguously clear place of plenaries in the National Numeracy and Literacy Strategies (DfES, 2001a), the team found that these were used mainly in Group A schools, where teachers were twice as likely as those in Group C schools to include a session in their lessons.

The plenaries observed in the best schools were more than just a short session at the end of a lesson to check answers. Instead they offered pupils a real opportunity to reflect on, and consolidate, their learning, to deepen their understanding and to extend their thinking.

Strategy 10: Making clear links

The researchers observed disappointingly few teachers linking their immediate lesson with other areas of the curriculum and the world outside the classroom. This was perhaps not surprising for the teachers in Group C schools, who tended to be more detached from their pupils and less sensitive to their needs. They were likely to miss opportunities to link what their children were learning with their outside interests because they were unaware of the latter.

Although this is an area where teachers in the best schools had room for improvement, they were still better at making cross-disciplinary connections. With their better understanding of their pupils' lives and interests, it was easier for them to spot a lesson link when it occurred and therefore to make it clear to their pupils.

Overall, the general weakness of all teachers in making these links strengthens the case for an integrated approach to the curriculum (for example, topic work) rather than a subject-specific approach.

Strategy 11: Homework

While in-depth qualitative information about homework was not collected, the researchers' notes were peppered with references to it. Homework can take many forms, from work being set because of school requirements, to opportunities arising in lessons that lead to ad hoc arrangements. However, teachers in Group A and B schools appeared to set homework that was more meaningful and directly linked to what the children were learning than those in Group C. Teachers in better schools had a more flexible, informal and optional approach to assigning homework. Much has been written about homework (Trautwein, 2007; Hallam, 2004; DfEE 1998b; Hattie, 2012; Sharp *et al.*, 2001), but this finding should encourage teachers and head teachers to look again at their policies on homework and to better align their practices with direct classroom experiences to expand learning.

Teaching in effective primary schools

The picture is now as complete as it can be. There could always be more research, but the EPPSE reports testify that a great deal is now known about the sort of teaching that promotes good outcomes for children. The challenge now is to get on and do it.

To achieve excellence, teachers in effective schools do the following:

- **focus on developing excellent organizational skills** They share their clear learning objectives with the children in their classes, and ensure that they all understand these objectives and any associated concepts. Their resources are professional, fit for purpose and personalized for their children. Their classroom routines are well established, smooth and followed by all. They make sure that all their pupils know what they have to do and what they should do if they need help, and they give their children responsibility for managing their time and resources.

- **concentrate on establishing a positive feeling in their classrooms** They develop respectful, relationships between their children, between the adults, and between the adults and children, which are characterized by a true sense of liking and mutual goals. They turn their classrooms into happy and lively places filled with a buzz of productive learning activity. They manage their pupils' behaviour through expectation, and correct any misbehaviour quietly and with discretion. They are high in sensitivity and low in detachment.

- **personalize their teaching** They work hard to learn their pupils' needs and interests, and invest time in developing a variety of resources that suit the range of needs. They make clear links between learning, other subjects and the world outside the classroom. They have a light touch with homework and link it directly to what the children are learning in their lessons. They take advantage of opportunities that arise during lessons to suggest optional additional learning activities that can take place outside class time.

- **try hard to use dialogic learning, especially in numeracy** They encourage their children to work collaboratively in groups. They use instructional two-way conversations, are open to their pupils' suggestions and ideas, and then use them in their teaching. They provide the class with frequent opportunities to receive (and give) constructive evaluative feedback.

The best teachers want to keep improving as both scientist and artist. To do this they should be encouraged, and given the time and space, to read professional journals, follow national strategies (DfES, 2007), keep up to date with best practice and engage in CPD. They should continue to make use of plenary sessions where they facilitate further discussion, exploration and extension, make room for more feedback, and consolidate and deepen understanding at the end of their lessons.

These features of teaching in effective schools all work together synergistically. Good organizational skills, shared objectives, a positive classroom climate, gentle behaviour management, personalized learning, group work, dialogic teaching, evaluative feedback, the use of plenary sessions and so on all interact with, reinforce and strengthen each other. Just as Aristotle (340 BC) reminds us that 'the whole is greater than the sum of its parts', so effective teaching is more than just a bundle of different approaches. While the 11 strategies give insights into what makes for effective teaching, they should not be reduced this to a simple checklist of behaviours.

The challenge is to put this knowledge into practice and embed it in policies and classrooms. The EPPSE reports, and this book, have identified a number of strategies that, if given a higher profile in initial teacher training and in the CPD of teachers, would improve practice in all primary schools, and would therefore provide better educational experiences. This in turn would enhance children's learning and thereby improve their academic and socio-behavioural outcomes.

The findings are, of course, particularly relevant to policymakers at the national and local levels who have responsibility for investing in, and designing, programmes for the development of educational leaders and teachers. For these programmes to succeed, they must address pedagogy, because improving practice can significantly increase children's life chances by improving outcomes.

Ultimately, however, educational change depends not on the formal curricula, not on the agreed strategy, not on the official policy, not on the training programme and not even on the researchers' report. It depends on what individual teachers think and do. It is as simple and, at the same time, as complicated as that.

Appendix 1: Effective Pre-school, Primary- and Secondary-Education publications

Over the course of the 17-year project, the EPPSE team have published extensively, with more than 200 outputs including full technical reports, papers in academic journals, book chapters, and a range of other articles and commentaries.

Technical reports

There are far too many to list here but readers should be aware that all of the analyses of the EPPSE research are contained in a series of technical reports.

Each report has an associated research brief that summarizes the main report. The technical reports provide the analytical details of the influence of pre-school, the family and other characteristics for a range of ages 3–16+).

End-of-phase reports

The key end-of-phase reports are listed below.

Pre-school

Sylva, K., Melhuish, E.C., Sammons, P., Siraj, I. and Taggart, B. (2004) *The Effective Provision of Pre-School Education (EPPE) Project: The final report: Effective pre-school education* (Technical Paper 12). London: Institute of Education. Online. http://dera.ioe.ac.uk/18189/16/EPPE_ TechnicalPaper_12_2004.pdf (accessed 14 May 2019).

Primary school

Sylva, K., Melhuish, E.C., Sammons, P. Siraj, I. and Taggart, B. (2008) *Effective Pre-School and Primary Education 3–11 Project (EPPE 3–11): Final report from the primary phase: Pre-school, school and family influences on children's development during Key Stage 2 (age 7–11).* (Research Report DCSF-RR061). Nottingham: Department for Children School and Families. Online. http://dera.ioe.ac.uk/8543/1/Final%203-11%20report%20DfE-RR061%2027nov08.pdf (accessed 14 May 2019).

Early secondary school

Sylva, K., Melhuish, E., Sammons, P., Siraj-Blatchford, I., Taggart, B., Toth, K., Smees, R., Draghici, D., Mayo, A. and Welcomme, W. (2012) *Effective Pre-school, Primary and Secondary Education 3–14 Project (EPPSE 3–14): Final report from the Key Stage 3 phase: Influences on students' development from age 11–14* (Research Report DFE-RR202). London: Department for Education. Online. http://dera.ioe.ac.uk/14069/1/DFE-RR202.pdf (accessed 14 May 2019).

End of secondary school

Sylva, K., Melhuish, E.C., Sammons, P., Siraj, I. and Taggart, B. with Smees, R., Toth, K. and Welcomme W. (2014) *Effective Pre-school, Primary and Secondary Education 3–16 Project (EPPSE 3–16): Students' educational and developmental outcomes at age 16* (Report DFE-RR354). London: Department for Education. Online. https://dera.ioe.ac.uk/20873/1/RR354_-_Students__educational_and_developmental_outcomes_at_age_16.pdf (accessed 14 May 2019).

Post-16

Sammons. P., Toth, K., and Sylva., K with Melhuish, E., Siraj, I., and Taggart. B. (2015) *Effective Pre-school, Primary and Secondary Education Project (EPPSE): Pre-school and early home learning effects on A-Level outcomes* (Report DFE-RR472A). London: Department for Education. Online. https://assets.publishing.service.gov.uk/government/uploads/system/uploads/attachment_data/file/472867/RR472A_Pre-school_and_early_home_learning_effects_on_A_level_outcomes.pdf (accessed 14 May 2019).

The technical reports can be downloaded from the following sites:

University College London Institute of Education website: www.ucl.ac.uk/ioe/research/featured-research/effective-pre-school-primary-secondary-education-project.

University of Oxford website: www.education.ox.ac.uk/research/effective-pre-school-primary-secondary-education/.

UK Digital Education Resource Archive: (DERA) http://dera.ioe.ac.uk/view/organisations/EPPSE.html.

Other reports
Research brief summarizing the project

Taggart, B., Sylva, K., Melhuish, E., Sammons, P. and Siraj, I. (2015) *Effective Pre-School, Primary and Secondary Education Project (EPPSE 3–16+): How pre-school influences children and young people's attainment and developmental outcomes over time* (Research Brief DFE-RB455). London: Department for Education. Online. https://assets.publishing.service.gov.uk/ government/uploads/system/uploads/attachment_data/file/455670/RB455_ Effective_pre-school_primary_and_secondary_education_project.pdf.pdf (accessed 14 May 2019).

The Sutton Trust reports

Sammons, P., Toth, K. and Sylva, K. (2018) 'The drivers of academic success for "bright" but disadvantaged students: A longitudinal study of AS and A-level outcomes in England'. *Studies in Educational Evaluation*, 57, 31–41. Online. https://doi.org/10.1016/j.stueduc.2017.10.004 (accessed 14 May 2019).

Sammons, P., Toth, K. and Sylva, K. (2015a) *Subject to Background: What promotes better achievement for bright but disadvantaged students?* London: Sutton Trust. Online. http://tinyurl.com/ y65ra5o4. (accessed 14 May 2019). www.suttontrust.com/wp-content/ uploads/2015/03/SUBJECT-TO-BACKGROUND_FULL-REPORT.pdf.

Sammons, P., Toth, K. and Sylva, K. (2015b) *Background to Success: Differences in A-level entries by ethnicity, neighbourhood and gender.* London: Sutton Trust. Online. http://tinyurl.com/y52zzhyk (accessed 25 March 2019). www.suttontrust.com/wp-content/uploads/2015/11/ Background-to-Success-Final.pdf.

Sammons, P., Toth, K., Sylva, K., Melhuish, E., Siraj, I. and Taggart, B. (2015c) *Pre-School and Early Home Learning Effects on A-Level Outcomes: Effective Pre-school, Primary and Secondary Education Project (EPPSE)* (Research Report DFE-RR472A). London: Department for Education. Online. http://tinyurl.com/yy28heat (accessed 14 May 2019). https://www.gov.uk/government/uploads/system/uploads/attachment_data/ file/472867/RR472A_Pre-school_and_early_home_learning_effects_on_A_ level_outcomes.pdf.

The EPPSE team have published reports on subjects related to the influence of pre-school. Some of the subjects covered feature below.

Pedagogy in pre-schools and primary

Siraj, I. and Taggart, B. (2014) *Exploring Effective Pedagogy in Primary Schools: Evidence from research.* London: Pearson. Online. www.pearson. com/content/dam/one-dot-com/one-dot-com/global/Files/about-pearson/ innovation/open-ideas/ExploringEffectivePedagogy.pdf (accessed 14 May 2019).

Siraj, I., Sylva, K., Muttock, S., Gilden, R. and Bell, D. (2002) *Researching Effective Pedagogy in the Early Years (REPEY).* London:

Department for Education and Skills/Institute of Education. Online. http://dera.ioe.ac.uk/4650/1/RR356.pdf (accessed 14 May 2019).

Social equality

Siraj, I., Mayo, A., Melhuish, E.C., Taggart, B., Sammons, P. and Sylva, K. (2011) *Performing against the Odds: Developmental trajectories of children in the EPPSE 3-16 study*. London: Department for Education/Institute of Education. Online. https://assets.publishing.service.gov.uk/government/uploads/system/uploads/attachment_data/file/183318/DFE-RR128.pdf (accessed 14 May 2019).

Sylva, K., Melhuish, E., Sammons, P., Siraj-Blatchford, I. and Taggart, B. (2007) *Promoting equality in the early years: Report to the Equalities Review*. London: Department for Education and Skills/Institute of Education. Online. http://ro.uow.edu.au/cgi/viewcontent.cgi?article=2176&context=sspapers (accessed 14 May 2019).

Successful transitions from primary to secondary school

Evangelou, M., Taggart, B., Sylva, K., Melhuish, E.C. Sammons, P. and Siraj, I. (2008) *What Makes a Successful Transition from Primary to Secondary School?* London: Department for Children, School and Families/Institute of Education. Online. http://webarchive.nationalarchives. gov.uk/20130323004350/https://www.education.gov.uk/publications/eOrderingDownload/DCSF-RR019.pdf (accessed 14 May 2019).

Special educational needs

Sammons, P., Taggart, B., Smees, R., Sylva, K., Melhuish, E.C., Siraj, I. and Elliot, K. (2003) *The Early Years Transition and Special Educational Needs (EYTSEN) Project*. London: Department for Education and Skills/Institute of Education. Online. https://dera.ioe.ac.uk/18204/1/RR431.pdf (accessed 14 May 2019).

Miscellaneous publications

A list of more than 200 publications arising from the EPPE/EPPSE research programme is available to download: www.education.ox.ac.uk/wordpress/wp-content/uploads/2010/08/EPPE-EPPSE-publications-UPDATED-LATEST.pdf.

The research undertaken in universities across the UK is subject to regular review to assess its quality and impact on society. In 2014 the Research Excellence Framework listed the impact of the EPPSE research on the following websites: http://impact.ref.ac.uk/CaseStudies/CaseStudy.

aspx?Id=44317 (accessed 14 May 2019). http://impact.ref.ac.uk/CaseStudies/CaseStudy.aspx?Id=14571 (accessed 14 May 2019).

BERA recognized the EPPE project as a 'landmark study' that has had 'significant impact on educational policy, practice, research methodology and/or theory'. It was ranked in the top 40 pieces of outstanding research over a period of 40 years: www.bera.ac.uk/project/40at40 (accessed 14 May 2019).

Books

Sylva, K., Melhuish, E., Sammons, P., Siraj-Blatchford, I. and Taggart, B. (eds) (2010) *Early Childhood Matters: Evidence from the Effective Pre-school and Primary Education Project*. London: Routledge.

The learning trajectories of children aged 13–16 who were 'succeeding against the odds' because of their home and pre-school/school experiences is captured in another book, which was the first prize winner from the Society for Educational Studies):

Siraj, I. and Mayo, A. (2015) *Social Class and Educational Inequality: The impact of parents and schools*. Cambridge University Press.

Appendix 2: Chronology of the Department of Education

The government department responsible for education has undergone a number of name changes since its inception in 1856, as follows:

- Committee of the Privy Council on Education, 1839–1899
- Education Department (ED), 1856–1899
- Board of Education (BoE), 1899–1944
- Ministry of Education (MoE), 1944–1964
- Department of Education and Science (DES), 1964–1992
- Department for Education (DfE), 1992–1995
- Department for Education and Employment (DfEE), 1995–2001
- Department for Education and Skills (DfES), 2001–2007
- Department for Children, Schools and Families (DCSF), 2007–2010
- Department for Education (DfE), 2010+

References

Alexander, R. (2000) *Culture and Pedagogy: International comparisons in primary education*. Oxford: Blackwell.

Alexander, R.J. (2001) 'Border crossings: Towards a comparative pedagogy'. *Comparative Education*, 37 (4), 507–23.

Alexander, R. (2006) *Towards Dialogic Teaching: Rethinking classroom talk*. 3rd ed. Cambridge: Dialogos.

Alexander, R. (2008) 'Still no pedagogy? Principle, pragmatism and compliance in primary education'. In Norris, N. (ed.) *Curriculum and the Teacher: 35 years of the Cambridge Journal of Education*. London: Routledge, 331–57.

Alexander, R. (ed.) (2010) *Children, Their World, Their Education: Final report and recommendations of the Cambridge Primary Review*. London: Routledge.

Alexander, R., Willcocks, J. and Nelson, N. (1996) 'Discourse, pedagogy and the national curriculum: Change and continuity in primary schools'. *Research Papers in Education*, 11 (1), 81–120.

Anders, Y., Sammons, P., Taggart, B., Sylva, K., Melhuish, E. and Siraj-Blatchford, I. (2011) 'The influence of child, family, home factors and pre-school education on the identification of special educational needs at age 10'. *British Educational Research Journal*, 37 (3), 421–41.

Anderson, A., Hamilton, R.J. and Hattie, J. (2004) 'Classroom climate and motivated behaviour in secondary schools'. *Learning Environments Research*, 7 (3), 211–25.

Andrews, J. (2011) 'Book review: "Educational Dialogues: Understanding and promoting productive interaction"'. *International Journal of Lifelong Education*, 30 (6), 831–2.

Aristotle (340BCE) Metaphysics, Book 8.

Arnett, J. (1989) 'Caregivers in day-care centers: Does training matter?'. *Journal of Applied Developmental Psychology*, 10 (4), 541–52.

Arter, J. and Stiggins, R. (2005) 'Formative assessment as assessment for learning'. *National Council on Measurement in Education Newsletter*, 13 (3), 4–5.

Askew, M., Brown, M., Rhodes, V., Johnson, D. and Wiliam, D. (1997) *Effective Teachers of Numeracy: Final report: Report of a study carried out for the Teacher Training Agency 1995–96 by the School of Education, King's College London*. London: King's College London.

Barber, M. (1996) *The Learning Game: Arguments for an education revolution*. London: Gollancz.

Barber, M. (2007) *Instruction to Deliver: Tony Blair, public services and the challenge of achieving targets*. London: Politico's.

Barron, B. (2003) 'When smart groups fail'. *Journal of the Learning Sciences*, 12 (3), 307–59.

BERA (British Educational Research Association) (2008) *The 2008 BERA Charter for Research Staff: Promoting quality conditions for conducting quality research*. Online. https://www.bera.ac.uk/wp-content/uploads/2014/02/bera-charter.pdf?noredirect=1 (accessed April 2019).

BERA (British Educational Research Association) (2004) *Revised Ethical Guidelines for Educational Research*. London: British Educational Research Association. Online. https://tinyurl.com/yyuno5ux (accessed 24 March 2019).

Black, P., Harrison, C., Lee, C., Marshall, B. and Wiliam, D. (2003) *Assessment for Learning: Putting it into practice*. Maidenhead: Open University Press.

Black, P. and Wiliam, D. (1998a) 'Inside the black box: Raising standards through classroom assessment'. *Phi Delta Kappan*, 80 (2), 139–48.

Black, P. and Wiliam, D. (1998b) 'Assessment and classroom learning'. *Assessment in Education: Principles, Policy and Practice*, 5 (1), 7–74.

Bloom, H.S., Hill C.J., Rebeck Black, A. and Lipsey, M.W. (2008) 'Performance trajectories and performance gaps as achievement effect-size benchmarks for educational interventions'. *Journal of Research on Educational Effectiveness*, 1 (4), 289–328.

Borich, G.D. (2000) *Effective Teaching Methods*. 4th ed. Upper Saddle River, NJ: Merrill.

Brighouse, T. and Tomlinson, J. (1991) *Successful Schools* (Education and Training Paper 4). London: Institute of Public Policy Research.

Bruner, J.S. (2006) *In Search of Pedagogy: The selected works of Jerome S. Bruner*. London: Routledge.

Bryson, C. and Hand, L. (2007) 'The role of engagement in inspiring teaching and learning'. *Innovations in Education and Teaching International*, 44 (4), 349–62.

Cadima, J., Gamelas, A.M., McClelland, M. and Peixoto, C. (2015) 'Associations between early family risk, children's behavioral regulation, and academic achievement in Portugal'. *Early Education and Development*, 26 (5–6), 708–28.

Carran, D.T., Scott, K.G., Shaw, K. and Beydouin, S. (1989) 'The relative risk of educational handicaps in two birth cohorts of normal and low birthweight disadvantaged children'. Topics in Early Childhood Special Education 9 (1), 14–31. Online. https://doi.org/10.1177/027112148900900103 (accessed April 2019).

Chapman, C., Muijs, D., Reynolds, D., Sammons, P. and Teddlie, C. (eds) (2016) *The Routledge International Handbook of Educational Effectiveness and Improvement: Research, policy, and practice*. London: Routledge.

Charalambous, C.Y. and Litke, E. (2018) 'Studying instructional quality by using a content-specific lens: The case of the Mathematical Quality of Instruction framework'. *ZDM Mathematics Education*, 50 (3), 445–60.

Clarke, S. (1998) *Targeting Assessment in the Primary Classroom: Strategies for planning, assessment, pupil feedback and target setting*. London: Hodder and Stoughton.

Clarke, S. (2001) *Unlocking Formative Assessment: Practical strategies for enhancing pupils' learning in the primary classroom*. London: Hodder and Stoughton.

Clarke, S. (2014) *Outstanding Formative Assessment: Culture and practice*. London: Hodder Education.

Clarke-Stewart, A., (1998) The NICHD Study of Early Child Care. *Psychiatric Times*, 15 (3), 71–2. Online. www.psychiatrictimes.com/child-adolescent-psychiatry/nichd-study-early-child-care (accessed April 2019).

Claxton, G. and Carr, M. (2004) 'A framework for teaching learning: The dynamics of disposition'. *Early Years*, 24 (1), 87–97.

Coe, R., Aloisi, C., Higgins, S. and Elliot Major, L. (2014) *What Makes Great Teaching? Review of the underpinning research*. London: Sutton Trust.

Coleman, J.S., Campbell, E.Q., Hobson, C.J., McPartland, J., Mood, A.M., Weinfeld, F.D. and York, R.L. (1966) *Equality of Educational Opportunity*. Washington, DC: US Government Printing Office.

Cooper, H. (2006) *The Battle over Homework: Common ground for administrators, teachers, and parents*. 3rd ed. Thousand Oaks, CA: Corwin Press.

Cowan, R., Donlan, C., Newton, E.J. and Lloyd, D. (2005) 'Number skills and knowledge in children with specific language impairment'. *Journal of Educational Psychology*, 97 (4), 732–44.

Creemers, B.P.M. (1994) *The Effective Classroom*. London: Cassell.

Creemers, B.P.M. and Kyriakides, L. (2008) *The Dynamics of Educational Effectiveness: A contribution to policy, practice and theory in contemporary schools*. London: Routledge.

Creemers, B.P.M. and Kyriakides, L. (2010) 'Using the dynamic model to develop an evidence-based and theory-driven approach to school improvement'. *Irish Educational Studies*, 29 (1), 5–23.

Creemers, B.P.M. and Kyriakides, L. (2012) *Improving Quality in Education: Dynamic approaches to school improvement*. London: Routledge.

Creemers, B.P.M., Kyriakides, L. and Sammons, P. (eds) (2010) *Methodological Advances in Educational Effectiveness Research*. London: Routledge.

Creemers, B.P.M. and Reezigt, G.J. (1999) 'The role of school and classroom climate in elementary school learning environments'. In Freiberg, H.J. (ed.) *School Climate: Measuring, improving and sustaining healthy learning environments*. London: Falmer Press, 30–47.

Danielson, C. (2013) *The Framework for Teaching: Evaluation instrument*. Princeton: Danielson Group.

Darling-Hammond, L. (2002) 'Access to quality teaching: An analysis of inequality in California's public schools'. *Santa Clara Law Review*, 43 (4), 1045–184.

Day, C. (2004) *A Passion for Teaching*. London: RoutledgeFalmer.

Day, C., Sammons, P. and Kington, A. (2008) *Effective Classroom Practice: A mixed-method study of influences and outcomes*. Swindon: Economic and Social Research Council.

Day, C., Sammons, P., Kington, A., Regan, E., Gunraj, J. and Towle, J. (2007) *Effective Classroom Practice: A mixed methods study of influences and outcomes: Interim report submitted to the ESRC*. Swindon: Economic and Social Research Council.

DCSF (Department for Children, Schools and Families) (2008) *Statutory Framework for the Early Years Foundation Stage: Setting the standards for learning, development and care for children from birth to five*. Rev. ed. Nottingham: Department for Children, Schools and Families. Online. https://tinyurl.com/yy4767k4 (accessed 24 March 2019).

De Jager, B., Jansen, M. and Reezigt, G. (2005) 'The development of metacognition in primary school learning environments'. *School Effectiveness and School Improvement*, 16 (2), 179–96.

Devine, D., Fahie, D. and McGillicuddy, D. (2013) 'What is "good" teaching? Teacher beliefs and practices about their teaching'. *Irish Educational Studies*, 32 (1), 83–108.

Devine, D., Fahie, D., McGillicuddy, D., MacRuairc, G. and Harford, J. (2010) *Report on the Use of the ISTOF (International System of Teacher Observation and Feedback) Protocol in Irish Schools: Challenges, issues and teacher effect.* Dublin: University College Dublin.

DfEE (Department for Education and Employment) (1998a) *The Implementation of the National Numeracy Strategy: The final report of the Numeracy Task Force* (PP98/D14/34555/798/64). Sudbury: Department for Education and Employment.

DFEE (Department for Education and Employment) (1998b) *Homework: Guidelines for primary and secondary schools.* http://homepages.shu. ac.uk/~edsjlc/ict/dfes/homework/guidance_nov98/summary.pdf accessed 23 June 2019.

DfEE (Department for Education and Employment) (1998c) *Homework: Guidelines for primary and secondary schools.* London: Department for Education and Employment.

DfEE (Department for Education and Employment) (1999) *The National Numeracy Strategy: Framework for teaching mathematics from Reception to Year 6.* London: Department for Education and Employment.

DfEE (Department for Education and Employment) (2000a) *The National Literacy Strategy: Grammar for writing* (DfEE 0107/2000). London: Department for Education and Employment. Online. http://goo.gl/aPXCCP (accessed 24 March 2019).

DfEE (Department for Education and Employment) (2000b) *Unique Pupil Numbers (UPNs) – Policy and Practice: DfEE guidance for LEAs and schools.* London: Department for Education and Employment.

DfES (Department for Education and Skills) (2001a) *The National Literacy Strategy: Framework for teaching* (DfES 0500/2001). 3rd ed. London: Department for Education and Skills. Online. http://goo.gl/7rme3P (accessed 24 March 2019).

DfES (Department for Education and Skills) (2001b) *The National Literacy Strategy: Teaching writing: Support material for text level objectives.* London: Department for Education and Skills.

DfES (Department for Education and Skills) (2007) *Primary National Strategy: Leading improvement using the Primary Framework: Guidance for headteachers and senior leaders* (00484-2007BKT-EN). London: Department for Education and Skills. Online. http://goo.gl/r0j19H (accessed 24 March 2019).

Döbert, H., Klieme, E. and Sroka, W. (eds) (2004) *Conditions of School Performance in Seven Countries: A quest for understanding the international variation of PISA results.* Münster: Waxman.

Donlan, C., Cowan, R., Newton, E.J. and Lloyd, D. (2007) 'The role of language in mathematical development: Evidence from children with specific language impairments'. *Cognition*, 103 (1), 23–33.

Durden, T. (2008) 'Do your homework! Investigating the role of culturally relevant pedagogy in comprehensive school reform models serving diverse student populations'. *Urban Review*, 40 (4), 403–19.

Dweck, C.S. (2000) *Self-Theories: Their role in motivation, personality, and development.* Philadelphia: Psychology Press.

EEF (Education Endowment Foundation) and Sutton Trust (2011) *Teaching and Learning Toolkit.* Online. https://educationendowmentfoundation.org.uk/news/the-teaching-and-learning-toolkit-a-complex-summary (accessed 24 March 2019).

EIU (Economist Intelligence Unit) (2012) *The Learning Curve: Lessons in country performance in education.* London: Pearson. Online. https://tinyurl.com/y256px29 (accessed 24 March 2019).

EIU (Economist Intelligence Unit) (2014) *The Learning Curve: Education and skills for life.* London: Pearson. Online. https://tinyurl.com/y6yso7pm (accessed 24 March 2019).

Elliott, C.D., Smith, P. and McCulloch, K. (1996) *British Ability Scales (BAS-II).* 2nd ed. Windsor: NFER-Nelson.

Evertson, C.M. and Randolph, C.H. (1995) 'Classroom management in the learning-centered classroom'. In Ornstein, A.C. (ed.) *Teaching: Theory into practice.* Boston: Allyn and Bacon, 118–31.

Fosnot, C.T. (ed.) (1996) *Constructivism: Theory, perspectives and practice.* New York: Teachers College Press.

Gage, N.L. (1985) *Hard Gains in the Soft Sciences: The case of pedagogy.* Bloomington, IN: Phi Delta Kappa.

Galton, M. (1997) 'Primary culture and classroom teaching: The learning relationship in context'. In Kitson, N. and Merry, R. (eds) *Teaching in the Primary School: A learning relationship.* London: Routledge, 102–17.

Galton, M., Bernbaum, G., Patrick, K. and Appleyard, R. (1987) *Educational Provision in Small Primary Schools: Final report to the Department of Education and Science (DES).* Leicester: University of Leicester.

Galton, M., Hargreaves, L., Comber, C., Wall, D. and Pell, A. (1999) *Inside the Primary Classroom: 20 years on.* London: Routledge.

Galton, M. and Simon, B. (eds) (1980) *Progress and Performance in the Primary Classroom.* London: Routledge and Kegan Paul.

Galton, M., Simon, B. and Croll, P. (1980) *Inside the Primary Classroom.* London: Routledge and Kegan Paul.

Gipps, C., McCallum, B. and Hargreaves, E. (2000) *What Makes a Good Primary School Teacher? Expert classroom strategies.* London: RoutledgeFalmer.

Goldstein, H. (1987) *Multilevel Models in Educational and Social Research.* London: Griffin.

Goldstein, H. (1995) *Multilevel Statistical Models.* 2nd ed. London: Edward Arnold.

Goldstein, H. (1997) 'Methods in school effectiveness research'. *School Effectiveness and School Improvement,* 8 (4), 369–95.

Goldstein, H. (2003) *Multilevel Statistical Models.* 3rd ed. London: Edward Arnold.

Gonzalez, E.J. and Smith, T.A. (eds) (1997) *User Guide for the TIMSS International Database: Primary and middle school years.* Amsterdam: International Association for the Evaluation of Educational Achievement. Online. http://tinyurl.com/yytbb8lx (accessed 25 March 2019).

Goodman, R. (1997) 'The Strengths and Difficulties Questionnaire: A research note'. *Journal of Child Psychology and Psychiatry*, 38 (5), 581–6.

Hallam, S. (2004) *Homework: The evidence*. London: Institute of Education.

Hallam, S. and Rogers, L. (2018) *Homework: The evidence*. Rev. ed. London: UCL Institute of Education Press.

Halpin, P.F. and Kieffer, M.J. (2015) 'Describing profiles of instructional practice: A new approach to analyzing classroom observation data'. *Educational Researcher*, 44 (5), 263–77.

Hammer, D., Melhuish, E. and Howard, S.J. (2018) 'Antecedents and consequences of social-emotional development: A longitudinal study of academic achievement'. *Archives of Scientific Psychology*, 6 (1), 105–16.

Harms, T., Clifford, R.M. and Cryer, D. (1998) *Early Childhood Environment Rating Scale*. Rev. ed. New York: Teachers College Press.

Harris, R. and Ratcliffe, M. (2005) 'Socio-scientific issues and the quality of exploratory talk – what can be learned from schools involved in a "collapsed day" project?'. *Curriculum Journal*, 16 (4), 439–53.

Hattie, J. (2008) *Visible Learning*. London: Routledge.

Hattie, J. (2012) *Visible Learning for Teachers: Maximizing impact on learning*. London: Routledge.

Hay McBer (2000) *Research into Teacher Effectiveness: A model of teacher effectiveness* (Research Report 216). London: Department for Education and Employment. Online. http://goo.gl/RSEy1D (accessed 24 March 2019).

Henchey, N. (2001) *Schools That Make a Difference: Final report: Twelve Canadian secondary schools in low-income settings*. Kelowna, BC: Society for the Advancement of Excellence in Education.

Hill, P.W. and Rowe, K.J. (1996) 'Multilevel modelling in school effectiveness research'. *School Effectiveness and School Improvement*, 7 (1), 1–34.

Hill, P.W. and Rowe, K.J. (1998) 'Modelling student progress in studies of educational effectiveness'. *School Effectiveness and School Improvement*, 9 (3), 310–33.

Hopkins, D. (2001) *Meeting the Challenge: An improvement guide for schools facing challenging circumstances*. London: Department for Education and Skills.

Howse, R.B., Lange, G., Farran, D.C. and Boyles, C.D. (2003) 'Motivation and self-regulation as predictors of achievement in economically disadvantaged young children'. *Journal of Experimental Education*, 71 (2), 151–74.

James, C., Connolly, M., Dunning, G. and Elliott, T. (2006) *How Very Effective Primary Schools Work*. London: Paul Chapman Publishing.

Jencks, C., Smith, M., Acland, H., Bane, M.J., Cohen, D., Gintis, H., Heyns, B. and Michelson, S. (1972) *Inequality: A reassessment of the effect of family and schooling in America*. New York: Basic Books.

Kane, T.J., Kerr, K.A. and Pianta, R.C. (eds) (2014) *Designing Teacher Evaluation Systems: New guidance from the Measures of Effective Teaching Project*. San Francisco: Jossey-Bass.

Keiser, K.A. and Schulte, L.E. (2009) 'Seeking the sense of community: A comparison of two elementary schools' ethical climates'. *School Community Journal*, 19 (2), 45–58.

Kesner, J.E. (2005) 'Gifted children's relationships with teachers'. *International Education Journal*, 6 (2), 218–23.

Kington, A., Sammons, P., Regan, E., Brown, E., Ko, J. and Buckler, S. (2014) *Effective Classroom Practice*. Maidenhead: Open University Press.

Ko, J. and Sammons, P. (2008) *Variations in Effective Classroom Practices: Confirmatory factor analysis: Results from analysis of measures from the International System for Teacher Observation and Feedback (ISTOF) Scale and Quality and Teaching Lesson Observation Indicator (GRIFT) Scale*. Nottingham: University of Nottingham.

Ko, J., Sammons, P. and Bakkum, L. (2013) *Effective Teaching: A review of research and evidence*. Reading: CfBT Education Trust.

Kutnick, P. and Kington, A. (2005) 'Children's friendships and learning in school: Cognitive enhancement through social interaction?'. *British Journal of Educational Psychology*, 75 (4), 521–38.

Leach, J. and Moon, B. (2008) *The Power of Pedagogy*. London: SAGE Publications.

Leithwood, K., Day, C., Sammons, P., Harris, A. and Hopkins, D. (2006) *Seven Strong Claims about Successful School Leadership*. Nottingham: National College for School Leadership. Online. http://tinyurl.com/hapkomv (accessed 25 March 2019).

Lindorff, A. and Sammons, P. (2018) 'Going beyond structured observations: Looking at classroom practice through a mixed method lens'. *ZDM Mathematics Education*, 50 (3), 521–34.

Machin, S. and McNally, S. (2004a) 'Large benefits, low cost'. *CentrePiece*, 9 (1), 2–7. Online. http://goo.gl/xRvGcY (accessed 21 March 2019).

Machin, S. and McNally, S. (2004b) *The Literacy Hour*. London: Centre for the Economics of Education. Online. http://goo.gl/hnYKZD (accessed 25 March 2019).

McGuey, G. and Moore, L. (2007) *The Inspirational Teacher*. Larchmont, NY: Eye On Education.

Matthews, P. and Sammons, P. (2004) *Improvement through Inspection: An evaluation of the impact of Ofsted's work*. London: Ofsted. Online. https://dera.ioe.ac.uk/4969/3/3696.pdf (accessed April 2019).

Melhuish, E.C., Phan, M.B., Sylva, K., Sammons, P., Siraj-Blatchford, I. and Taggart, B. (2008) 'Effects of the home learning environment and preschool center experience upon literacy and numeracy development in early primary school'. *Journal of Social Issues*, 64 (1), 95–114.

Melhuish, E., Romaniuk, H., Sammons, P., Sylva, K., Siraj-Blatchford, I. and Taggart, B. (2006) *Effective Pre-School and Primary Education 3–11 Project (EPPE 3-11): The effectiveness of primary schools in England in Key Stage 2 for 2002, 2003 and 2004*. London: Institute of Education.

Melhuish, E., Sylva, K., Sammons, P., Siraj-Blatchford, I. and Taggart, B. (2001) *The Effective Provision of Pre-School Education (EPPE) Project: Social/ behavioural and cognitive development at 3–4 years in relation to family background* (Technical Paper 7). London: Institute of Education.

Mortimore, P., Sammons, P., Stoll, L., Lewis, D. and Ecob, R. (1988) *School Matters: The junior years*. Wells: Open Books.

Muijs, D., Harris, A., Chapman, C., Stoll, L. and Russ, J. (2004) 'Improving schools in socioeconomically disadvantaged areas: A review of research evidence'. *School Effectiveness and School Improvement*, 15 (2), 149–75.

Muijs, D., Kyriakides, L., Van der Werf, G., Creemers, B., Timperley, H. and Earl, L. (2014) 'State of the art – teacher effectiveness and professional learning'. *School Effectiveness and School Improvement,* 25 (2), 231–56.

Muijs, D. and Reynolds, D. (2000) 'School effectiveness and teacher effectiveness in mathematics: Some preliminary findings from the evaluation of the mathematics enhancement programme (primary)'. *School Effectiveness and School Improvement,* 11 (3), 273–303.

Muijs, D. and Reynolds, D. (2003) 'Student background and teacher effects on achievement and attainment in mathematics: A longitudinal study'. *Educational Research and Evaluation,* 9 (3), 289–314.

Muijs, D. and Reynolds, D. (2011) *Effective Teaching: Evidence and Practice.* 3rd ed. London: SAGE Publications.

Muijs, D., Reynolds, D., Sammons, P., Kyriakides, L., Creemers, B.P.M. and Teddlie, C. (2018) 'Assessing individual lessons using a generic teacher observation instrument: How useful is the International System for Teacher Observation and Feedback (ISTOF)?'. *ZDM Mathematics Education,* 50 (3), 395–406.

Mullis, I.V.S., Martin, M.O., Gonzalez, E.J. and Kennedy, A.M. (2001) *PIRLS 2001 International Report: IEA's study of reading literacy achievement in primary school in 35 countries.* Amsterdam: International Association for the Evaluation of Educational Achievement. Online. http://tinyurl.com/yyojlmj7 (accessed 25 March 2019).

Murphy, C.E. and Milner, J. (2009) Always Working an Angle: Exploration of the teacher–student relationship and engagement. Studies in Teaching.

NICHD (National Institute of Child Health and Human Development) (2001) *Fifth Grade School Observation Procedures Manual* (NICHD Study of Early Child Care and Youth Development). Rockville, MD: National Institute of Child Health and Human Development.

OECD (Organisation for Economic Co-operation and Development) (1994) *Teacher Quality: Synthesis of country studies.* Paris: Organisation for Economic Co-operation and Development.

OECD (Organisation for Economic Co-operation and Development) (2000) *Measuring Student Knowledge and Skills: The PISA 2000 assessment of reading, mathematical and scientific literacy.* Paris: Organisation for Economic Co-operation and Development.

OECD (Organisation for Economic Co-operation and Development) (2005) *Teachers Matter: Attracting, developing and retaining effective teachers.* Paris: Organisation for Economic Co-operation and Development.

Ofsted (Office for Standards in Education) (1995) *Homework in Primary and Secondary Schools: A report from the Office of Her Majesty's Chief Inspector of Schools.* London: HMSO.

Ofsted (Office for Standards in Education) (2000) *The Annual Report of Her Majesty's Chief Inspector of Schools: Standards and quality in education 1998/99.* London: The Stationery Office.

Pianta, R.C. (2000) *Enhancing Relationships between Children and Teachers.* Washington, DC: American Psychological Association.

Pianta, R.C. (2003) *Standardized Classroom Observations from Pre-K to 3rd Grade: A mechanism for improving classroom quality and practices, consistency of P-3 experiences, and child outcomes.* New York: Foundation for Child Development.

Pianta, R.C. (2005) 'Classroom observation, professional development, and teacher quality'. *Harvard Evaluation Exchange*, 11 (4), 8.

Pianta, R.C., Belsky, J., Vandergrift, N., Houts, R. and Morrison, F.J. (2008a) 'Classroom effects on children's achievement trajectories in elementary school'. *American Educational Research Journal*, 45 (2), 365–97.

Pianta, R.C., LaParo, K.M. and Hamre, B.K. (2008b) *Classroom Assessment Scoring System (CLASS) Manual: K-3.* Baltimore: Brookes Publishing.

Ponitz, C.C., McClelland, M.M., Matthews, J.S. and Morrison, F.J. (2009) 'A structured observation of behavioral self-regulation and its contribution to kindergarten outcomes'. *Developmental Psychology*, 45 (3), 605–19.

Praetorius, A.-K., Klieme, E., Herbert, B. and Pinger, P. (2018) 'Generic dimensions of teaching quality: The German framework of Three Basic Dimensions'. *ZDM Mathematics Education*, 50 (3), 407–26.

QCA (Qualifications and Curriculum Authority) (2000) *Curriculum Guidance for the Foundation Stage* (QCA/00/587). London: Qualifications and Curriculum Authority.

Raham, H. (2002) 'Looking inside high-achieving low-income schools'. *Education Analyst – Society for the Advancement of Excellence in Education*, Winter 2000, 8–9.

Reynolds, D. (2004) *The High Reliability Schools Project: Some preliminary results and analyses* (NSIN Research Matters 22). London: Institute of Education.

Reynolds, D. (2006) 'World class schools: Some methodological and substantive findings and implications of the International School Effectiveness Research Project (ISERP)'. *Educational Research and Evaluation*, 12 (6), 535–60.

Reynolds, D., Creemers, B., Stringfield, S., Teddlie, C. and Schaffer, G. (eds) (2002) *World Class Schools: International perspectives on school effectiveness.* London: RoutledgeFalmer.

Reynolds, D. and Farrell, S. (1996) *Worlds Apart? A review of international surveys of educational achievement involving England.* London: HMSO.

Reynolds, D. and Muijs, D. (1999) 'The effective teaching of mathematics: A review of research'. *School Leadership and Management*, 19 (3), 273–88.

Reynolds, D., Sammons, P., De Fraine, B., Van Damme, J., Townsend, T., Teddlie, C. and Stringfield, S. (2014) 'Educational effectiveness research (EER): A state-of-the-art review'. *School Effectiveness and School Improvement*, 25 (2), 197–230.

Rittle-Johnson, B. (2006) 'Promoting transfer: Effects of self-explanation and direct instruction'. *Child Development*, 77 (1), 1–15.

Rogers, B. (2007) *Behaviour Management: A whole-school approach.* 2nd ed. London: Paul Chapman Publishing.

Rojas-Drummond, S. and Mercer, N. (2003) 'Scaffolding the development of effective collaboration and learning'. *International Journal of Educational Research*, 39 (1–2), 99–111.

Rose, J. (2006) *Independent Review of the Teaching of Early Reading*. Nottingham: Department for Education and Skills.

Ross, A. and Hutchings, M. (2003) *Attracting, Developing and Retaining Effective Teachers in the United Kingdom of Great Britain and Northern Ireland* (OECD Country Background Report). Paris: Organisation for Economic Co-operation and Development.

Rutter, M., Maughan, B., Mortimore, P., Ouston, J. and Smith, A. (1979) *Fifteen Thousand Hours: Secondary schools and their effects on children*. London: Open Books.

Sammons, P. (1996) 'Complexities in the judgement of school effectiveness'. *Educational Research and Evaluation*, 2 (2), 113–49.

Sammons, P. (1999) *School Effectiveness: Coming of age in the twenty-first century*. Lisse: Swets & Zeitlinger.

Sammons, P. (2007) *School Effectiveness and Equity: Making connections*. Reading: CfBT Education Trust.

Sammons, P. (2008) 'Zero tolerance of failure and New Labour approaches to school improvement in England'. *Oxford Review of Education*, 34 (6), 651–64.

Sammons, P. and Davis, S. (2017) 'Mixed methods approaches and their application in educational research'. In Wyse, D., Selwyn, N., Smith, E. and Suter, L.E. (eds) *The BERA/SAGE Handbook of Educational Research*. London: SAGE Publications, 477–504.

Sammons, P., Kington, A., Lindorff-Vijayendran, A. and Ortega, L. (2014a) *Inspiring Teachers: Perspectives and practices*. Reading: CfBT Education Trust.

Sammons, P., Kington, A., Lindorff-Vijayendran, A. and Ortega, L. (2014b) *Inspiring Teaching: What we can learn from exemplary practitioners*. Reading: CfBT Education Trust.

Sammons, P., Lindorff, A.M., Ortega, L. and Kington, A. (2016) 'Inspiring teaching: Learning from exemplary practitioners'. *Journal of Professional Capital and Community*, 1 (2), 124–44.

Sammons, P., Siraj-Blatchford, I., Sylva, K., Melhuish, E., Taggart, B. and Elliot, K. (2005) 'Investigating the effects of pre-school provision: Using mixed methods in the EPPE research'. *International Journal of Social Research Methodology*, 8 (3), 207–24.

Sammons, P., Sylva, K., Melhuish, E., Siraj-Blatchford, I., Taggart, B., Barreau, S. and Grabbe, Y. (2007a) *Effective Pre-School and Primary Education 3–11 Project (EPPE 3–11): Influences on children's development and progress in Key Stage 2: Social/behavioural outcomes in Year 5* (Research Report DCSF-RR007). Nottingham: Department for Children, Schools and Families.

Sammons, P., Sylva, K., Melhuish, E., Siraj-Blatchford, I., Taggart, B., Barreau, S. and Grabbe, Y. (2008c) *Effective Pre-School and Primary Education 3–11 Project (EPPE 3–11): The influence of school and teaching quality on children's progress in primary school* (Research Report DCSF-RR028). Nottingham: Department for Children, Schools and Families.

Sammons, P., Sylva, K., Melhuish, E., Siraj-Blatchford, I., Taggart, B. and Elliot, K. (2002) *The Effective Provision of Pre-School Education (EPPE) Project: Measuring the impact of pre-school on children's cognitive progress over the pre-school period* (Technical Paper 8a). London: Institute of Education.

Sammons, P., Sylva, K., Melhuish, E., Siraj-Blatchford, I., Taggart, B. and Elliot, K. (2003) *The Effective Provision of Pre-School Education (EPPE) Project: Measuring the impact of pre-school on children's social/behavioural development over the pre-school period* (Technical Paper 8b). London: Institute of Education.

Sammons, P., Sylva, K., Melhuish, E., Siraj-Blatchford, I., Taggart, B., Elliot, K. and Marsh, A. (2004) *The Effective Provision of Pre-School Education (EPPE) Project: Report on age 6 assessments* (Technical Paper 9). London: Institute of Education.

Sammons, P., Sylva, K., Melhuish, E., Siraj-Blatchford, I., Taggart, B., Grabbe, Y. and Barreau, S. (2007b) *Effective Pre-School and Primary Education 3–11 Project (EPPE 3–11): Influences on children's attainment and progress in Key Stage 2: Cognitive outcomes in Year 5.* Nottingham: Department for Education and Skills.

Sammons, P., Sylva, K., Melhuish, E., Siraj-Blatchford, I., Taggart, B. and Hunt, S. (2008a) *Effective Pre-School and Primary Education 3–11 Project (EPPE 3–11): Influences on children's attainment and progress in Key Stage 2: Cognitive outcomes in Year 6* (Research Report DCSF-RR048). Nottingham: Department for Children, Schools and Families.

Sammons, P., Sylva, K., Melhuish, E., Siraj-Blatchford, I., Taggart, B. and Jelicic, H. (2008b) *Effective Pre-School and Primary Education 3–11 Project (EPPE 3–11): Influences on children's development and progress in Key Stage 2: Social/ behavioural outcomes in Year 6* (Research Report DCSF-RR049). Nottingham: Department for Children, Schools and Families.

Sammons, P., Sylva, K., Melhuish, E., Siraj-Blatchford, I., Taggart, B., Toth, K., Draghici, D. and Smees, R. (2011) *Effective Pre-School, Primary and Secondary Education Project (EPPSE 3–14): Influences on students' attainment and progress in Key Stage 3: Academic outcomes in English, maths and science in Year 9.* London: Institute of Education/Department for Education.

Sammons, P., Taggart, B., Siraj-Blatchford, I., Sylva, K., Melhuish, E., Barreau, S. and Manni, L. (2006) *Effective Pre-School and Primary Education 3–11 Project (EPPE 3–11): Summary report: Variations in teacher and pupil behaviours in Year 5 classes* (Research Report RR817). Nottingham: Department for Education and Skills.

Sammons, P., Thomas, S. and Mortimore, P. (1997) *Forging Links: Effective schools and effective departments.* London: Paul Chapman Publishing.

Sammons, P., Toth, K. and Sylva, K. (2015a) *Subject to Background: What promotes better achievement for bright but disadvantaged students?* London: Sutton Trust. Online. http://tinyurl.com/y65ra5o4 (accessed 25 March 2019).

Sammons, P., Toth, K. and Sylva, K. (2015b) *Background to Success: Differences in A-level entries by ethnicity, neighbourhood and gender.* London: Sutton Trust. Online. http://tinyurl.com/y52zzhyk (accessed 25 March 2019).

Sammons, P., Toth, K. and Sylva, K. (2018) 'The drivers of academic success for "bright" but disadvantaged students: A longitudinal study of AS and A-level outcomes in England'. *Studies in Educational Evaluation*, 57, 31–41.

Sammons, P., Toth, K., Sylva, K., Melhuish, E., Siraj, I. and Taggart, B. (2015c) *Pre-School and Early Home Learning Effects on A-Level Outcomes: Effective Pre-school, Primary and Secondary Education Project (EPPSE)* (Research Report DFE-RR472A). London: Department for Education. Online. http://tinyurl.com/yy28heat (accessed 25 March 2019).

Sargent, C., Foot, E., Houghton, E. and O'Donnell, S. (2013) International Review of Curriculum and Assessment Frameworks Internet Archive (INCA) Comparative Tables. Slough: National Foundation for Educational Research.

Schagen, I. and Elliot, K. (2004) What Does It Mean? The use of effect sizes in educational research. Slough: National Foundation for Educational Research. Online. https://www.nfer.ac.uk/but-what-does-it-mean-the-use-of-effect-sizes-in-educational-research (accessed 14 May 2019).

Schaffer, E.C., Nesselrodt, P.S. and Stringfield, S. (1994) 'The contributions of classroom observation to school effectiveness research'. In Reynolds, D., Creemers, B.P.M., Nesselrodt, P.S., Schaffer, E.C., Stringfield, S. and Teddlie, C. *Advances in School Effectiveness Research and Practice*. Oxford: Pergamon, 133–50.

Schagen, I. and Elliot, K. (eds) (2004) *But What Does It Mean? The use of effect sizes in educational research*. Slough: National Foundation for Educational Research.

Scheerens, J. (1992) *Effective Schooling: Research, theory and practice*. London: Cassell.

Scheerens, J. and Bosker, R.J. (1997) *The Foundations of Educational Effectiveness*. Oxford: Pergamon.

Sharp, C., Keys, W. and Benefield, P. (2001) *Homework: A review of recent research*. Slough: National Foundation for Educational Research.

Sharples, J., Slavin, R., Chambers, B. and Sharp, C. (2011) *Effective Classroom Strategies for Closing the Gap in Educational Achievement for Children and Young People Living in Poverty, including White Working-Class Boys* (Schools and Communities Research Review 4). London: Centre for Excellence and Outcomes in Children and Young People's Services. Online. http://tinyurl.com/yxh2qt43 (accessed 25 March 2019).

Shulman, L.S. (2004) *The Wisdom of Practice: Essays on teaching, learning, and learning to teach*. San Francisco: Jossey-Bass.

Simon, B. (1999) 'Why no pedagogy in England?'. In Leach, J. and Moon, B. (eds) *Learners and Pedagogy*. London: Paul Chapman Publishing, 34–45.

Siraj, I. and Taggart, B. (2014) *Exploring Effective Pedagogy in Primary Schools: Evidence from research*. London: Pearson.

Siraj-Blatchford, I., Sammons, P., Taggart, B., Sylva, K. and Melhuish, E. (2006) 'Educational research and evidence-based policy: The mixed-method approach of the EPPE Project'. *Evaluation and Research in Education*, 19 (2), 63–82.

Siraj-Blatchford, I., Shepherd, D.-L., Melhuish, E., Taggart, B., Sammons, P. and Sylva, K. (2011) *Effective Primary Pedagogical Strategies in English and Mathematics in Key Stage 2: A study of Year 5 classroom practice from the EPPSE 3–16 longitudinal study* (Research Report DFE-RR129). London: Department for Education.

Siraj-Blatchford, I., Sylva, K., Muttock, S., Gilden, R. and Bell, D. (2002) *Researching Effective Pedagogy in the Early Years* (Research Report RR356). London: Department for Education and Skills.

Siraj-Blatchford, I., Sylva, K., Taggart, B., Sammons, P., Melhuish, E. and Elliot, K. (2003) *The Effective Provision of Pre-School Education (EPPE) Project: Intensive case studies of practice across the Foundation Stage* (Technical Paper 10). London: Institute of Education.

Siraj-Blatchford, I., Taggart, B., Sylva, K., Sammons, P. and Melhuish, E. (2008) 'Towards the transformation of practice in early childhood education: The Effective Provision of Pre-school Education (EPPE) Project'. *Cambridge Journal of Education*, 38 (1), 23–36.

Stipek, D. (1999) *Instructional Environment Observation Scale* (MacArthur Pathways through Middle Childhood Network). Los Angeles: University of California.

Stobart, G. and Gipps, C. (1997) *Assessment: A teacher's guide to the issues.* 3rd ed. London: Hodder and Stoughton.

Stoll, L. and Fink, D. (1996) *Changing Our Schools: Linking school effectiveness and school improvement.* Buckingham: Open University Press.

Sylva, K., Melhuish, E., Sammons, P., Siraj-Blatchford, I. and Taggart, B. (2004) *The Effective Provision of Pre-School Education (EPPE) Project: The final report: Effective pre-school education* (Technical Paper 12). London: Institute of Education.

Sylva, K., Melhuish, E., Sammons, P., Siraj-Blatchford, I. and Taggart, B. (2008) *Effective Pre-School and Primary Education 3–11 Project (EPPE 3–11): Final report from the primary phase: Pre-school, school and family influences on children's development during Key Stage 2 (age 7–11)* (Research Report DCSF-RR061). Nottingham: Department for Children, Schools and Families.

Sylva, K., Melhuish, E., Sammons, P., Siraj-Blatchford, I. and Taggart, B. (eds) (2010) *Early Childhood Matters: Evidence from the Effective Pre-school and Primary Education Project.* London: Routledge.

Sylva, K., Melhuish, E., Sammons, P., Siraj-Blatchford, I., Taggart, B., Toth, K., Smees, R., Draghici, D., Mayo, A. and Welcomme, W. (2012) *Effective Pre-School, Primary and Secondary Education 3–14 Project (EPPSE 3–14): Final report from the Key Stage 3 phase: Influences on students' development from age 11–14* (Research Report DFE-RR202). London: Department for Education.

Sylva, K., Siraj-Blatchford, I., Melhuish, E., Sammons, P., Taggart, B., Evans, E., Dobson, A., Jeavons, M., Lewis, K., Morahan, M. and Sadler, S. (1999a) *The Effective Provision of Pre-School Education* (EPPE) *Project: Characteristics of pre-school environments* (Technical Paper 6a). London: Institute of Education.

Sylva, K., Siraj-Blatchford, I., Melhuish, E., Sammons, P., Taggart, B., Evans, E., Dobson, A., Jeavons, M., Lewis, K., Morahan, M. and Sadler, S. (1999b) *The Effective Provision of Pre-School Education* (EPPE) *Project: Characteristics of the centres in the EPPE sample: Observational profiles* (Technical Paper 6). London: Institute of Education.

Sylva, K., Siraj-Blatchford, I. and Taggart, B. (2003) *The Early Childhood Environment Rating Scales: 4 curricular subscales.* Stoke-on-Trent: Trentham Books.

Sylva, K., Siraj-Blatchford, I. and Taggart, B. (2011) *ECERS-E: The four curricular subscales extension to the Early Childhood Environment Rating Scale (ECERS-R).* 4th ed. New York: Teachers College Press.

Sylva, K., Siraj-Blatchford, I., Taggart, B., Sammons, P., Melhuish, E., Elliot, K. and Totsika, V. (2006) 'Capturing quality in early childhood through environmental rating scales'. *Early Childhood Research Quarterly*, 21 (1), 76–92.

Taggart, B., Siraj-Blatchford, I., Sylva, K., Melhuish, E. and Sammons, P. (2008) 'Influencing policy and practice through research on early childhood education'. *International Journal of Early Childhood Education*, 14 (2), 7–21.

Taggart, B., Sylva, K., Melhuish, E., Sammons, P. and Siraj, I. (2015) *Effective Pre-School, Primary and Secondary Education Project (EPPSE 3–16+): How pre-school influences children and young people's attainment and developmental outcomes over time* (Research Brief DFE-RB455). London: Department for Education.

Teddlie, C., Creemers, B., Kyriakides, L., Muijs, D. and Yu, F. (2006) 'The International System for Teacher Observation and Feedback: Evolution of an international study of teacher effectiveness constructs'. *Educational Research and Evaluation*, 12 (6), 561–82.

Teddlie, C., Kirby, P.C. and Stringfield, S. (1989) 'Effective versus ineffective schools: Observable differences in the classroom'. *American Journal of Education*, 97 (3), 221–36.

Teddlie, C. and Reynolds, D. (2000) *The International Handbook of School Effectiveness Research*. London: Falmer Press.

Teddlie., C. and Sammons, P. (2010) 'Applications of mixed methods to the field of educational effectiveness research'. In Creemers, B.P.M., Kyriakides, L. and Sammons, P. (eds) *Methodological Advances in Educational Effectiveness Research*. London: Routledge, 115–52.

Tolmie, A.K., Topping, K.J., Christie, D., Donaldson, C., Howe, C., Jessiman, E., Livingston, K. and Thurston, A. (2010) 'Social effects of collaborative learning in primary schools'. *Learning and Instruction*, 20 (3), 177–91.

Townsend, T. (ed.) (2007) *International Handbook of School Effectiveness and Improvement*. Dordrecht: Springer.

Trautwein, U. (2007) 'The homework–achievement relation reconsidered: Differentiating homework time, homework frequency, and homework effort'. *Learning and Instruction*, 17 (3), 372–88.

Tunstall, P. and Gipps, C. (1996) '"How does your teacher help you to make your work better?": Children's understanding of formative assessment'. *Curriculum Journal*, 7 (2), 185–203.

Van de Grift, W. (2007) 'Quality of teaching in four European countries: A review of the literature and application of an assessment instrument'. *Educational Research*, 49 (2), 127–52.

Van de Grift, W.J.C.M. (2014) 'Measuring teaching quality in several European countries'. *School Effectiveness and School Improvement*, 25 (3), 295–311.

Van de Grift, W., Matthews, P., Tabak, L., and De Rijcke, F. (2004) *Preliminary Lesson Observation Form for Evaluating the Quality of Teaching*. Utrecht: Inspectie van het Onderwijs/Office for Standards in Education.

Van der Lans, R.M., Van de Grift, W.J.C.M., Van Veen, K. and Fokkens-Bruinsma, M. (2016) 'Once is not enough: Establishing reliability criteria for feedback and evaluation decisions based on classroom observations'. *Studies in Educational Evaluation*, 50, 88–95.

Veenam, S., Denessen, E., Van den Akker, A. and Van der Rijt, J. (2005) 'Effects of a cooperative learning program on the elaborations of students during help seeking and help giving'. *American Educational Research Journal,* 42 (1), 115–51.

Vygotsky, L.S. (1963) 'Learning and mental development at school age'. In Simon, B. and Simon, J. (eds) *Educational Psychology in the USSR.* London: Routledge and Kegan Paul, 21–34.

Watkins, C. and Mortimore, P. (1999) 'Pedagogy: What do we know?'. In Mortimore, P. (ed.) *Understanding Pedagogy and Its Impact on Learning.* London: Paul Chapman Publishing, 1–19.

Watson, S., Goodwin, M., Ackerman, B.E. and Parker, K.L. (2007) 'Improving instruction for teacher candidates in classroom management and discipline issues'. Paper presented at the American Association of Colleges for Teacher Education (AACTE) Annual Meeting, New York, 24–27 February 2007.

Wells, G. (1999) *Dialogic Inquiry: Towards a sociocultural practice and theory of education.* Cambridge: Cambridge University Press.

West, A. and Pennell, H. (2002) 'How new is New Labour? The quasi-market and English schools 1997 to 2001'. *British Journal of Educational Studies,* 50 (2), 206–24.

West, M. and Muijs, D. (2009) 'Personalized learning'. In Chapman, C. and Gunter, H.M. (eds) *Radical Reforms: Perspectives on an era of educational change.* London: Routledge, 128–40.

Whitebook, M., Gomby, D., Bellm, D., Sakai, L. and Kipnis, F. (2009) *Preparing Teachers of Young Children: The current state of knowledge, and a blueprint for the future: Part I: Teacher preparation and professional development in Grades K-12 and in early care and education: Differences and similarities, and implications for research* (Policy Report). Berkeley: Center for the Study of Child Care Employment.

Whitebread, D., Bingham, S., Grau, V., Pino Pasternak, D. and Sangster, C. (2007) 'Development of metacognition and self-regulated learning in young children: Role of collaborative and peer-assisted learning'. *Journal of Cognitive Education and Psychology,* 6 (3), 433–55.

Williams, P. (2008) *Independent Review of Mathematics Teaching in Early Years Settings and Primary Schools: Final report.* Nottingham: Department for Children, Schools and Families.

Wirt, J., Choy, S., Gerald, D., Provasnik, S., Rooney, P., Watanabe, S. and Tobin, R. (2002) *The Condition of Education 2002.* Washington, DC: National Center for Education Statistics.

Wirt, J., Choy, S., Provasnik, S., Rooney, P., Sen, A. and Tobin, R. (2003) *The Condition of Education 2003.* Washington, DC: National Center for Education Statistics.

Woodcock, S. and Reupert, A. (2012) 'A cross-sectional study of student teachers' behaviour management strategies throughout their training years'. *Australian Educational Researcher,* 39 (2), 159–72.

Index